INTEGRATING STUDENTS
WITH SPECIAL NEEDS
INTO
MAINSTREAM SCHOOLS

KT-165-296

CHICHESTER INSTITUTE OF
HIGHER EDUCATION LIBRARY

WS 2096095 6

AUTHOR
—

TITLE
INTEGRATING

CLASS No.
371.9

ORGANISATION FOR ECONOMIC CO-OPERATION AND DEVELOPMENT

JUN95

ORGANISATION FOR ECONOMIC CO-OPERATION AND DEVELOPMENT

Pursuant to Article 1 of the Convention signed in Paris on 14th December 1960, and which came into force on 30th September 1961, the Organisation for Economic Co-operation and Development (OECD) shall promote policies designed:

— to achieve the highest sustainable economic growth and employment and a rising standard of living in Member countries, while maintaining financial stability, and thus to contribute to the development of the world economy;
— to contribute to sound economic expansion in Member as well as non-member countries in the process of economic development; and
— to contribute to the expansion of world trade on a multilateral, non-discriminatory basis in accordance with international obligations.

The original Member countries of the OECD are Austria, Belgium, Canada, Denmark, France, Germany, Greece, Iceland, Ireland, Italy, Luxembourg, the Netherlands, Norway, Portugal, Spain, Sweden, Switzerland, Turkey, the United Kingdom and the United States. The following countries became Members subsequently through accession at the dates indicated hereafter: Japan (28th April 1964), Finland (28th January 1969), Australia (7th June 1971), New Zealand (29th May 1973) and Mexico (18th May 1994). The Commission of the European Communities takes part in the work of the OECD (Article 13 of the OECD Convention).

The Centre for Educational Research and Innovation was created in June 1968 by the Council of the Organisation for Economic Co-operation and Development and all Member countries of the OECD are participants.

The main objectives of the Centre are as follows:

— *to promote and support the development of research activities in education and undertake such research activities where appropriate;*
— *to promote and support pilot experiments with a view to introducing and testing innovations in the educational system;*
— *to promote the development of co-operation between Member countries in the field of educational research and innovation.*

The Centre functions within the Organisation for Economic Co-operation and Development in accordance with the decisions of the Council of the Organisation, under the authority of the Secretary-General. It is supervised by a Governing Board composed of one national expert in its field of competence from each of the countries participating in its programme of work.

Publié en français sous le titre :
L'INTÉGRATION SCOLAIRE DES ÉLÈVES A BESOINS PARTICULIERS

i

© OECD 1995
Applications for permission to reproduce or translate all or part
of this publication should be made to:
Head of Publications Service, OECD
2, rue André-Pascal, 75775 PARIS CEDEX 16, France.

Foreword

The integration of children with special needs into mainstream schools has been a concern for educational systems for many years, and developments in policy and practice have been followed by the Centre for Educational Research and Innovation (CERI) since 1978. This publication explores the theme of integration, the principles, practices and prospects for special education and integration, based on information provided by OECD countries, and describes successful case studies carried out by the countries.

The work described in the *first part* is based on a large number of meetings of country representatives and researchers, held over the period 1990 to 1993, during which the design of the study was determined, a definition of integration agreed and the structure and texts of the reports constructed. The chapter concerning the statistics is of especial note since its preparation required much discussion and iteration to establish the accuracy of the figures given. A special vote of thanks must be given to all those involved in its preparation.

The *second part* is based on 64 case studies carried out in 19 Member countries according to an agreed common outline. They were completed in 1993. The examples of good practice themselves were selected by the countries concerned and the observations and accounts written were also completed by them. The schools selected were neither in receipt of any particular special support nor were they part of an experimental programme. In addition the researchers were asked to think of schools in their administrative contexts, since educating disabled pupils in regular provision involves considerable support from services external to the school.

The report has been prepared by the CERI secretariat in collaboration with Dr Don Labon and contributions of many experts. It is published under the responsibility of the Secretary-General of the OECD.

CHICHESTER INSTITUTE

OF

HIGHER EDUCATION

LIBRARY

Table of Contents

Part I

POLICIES AND PRACTICES

Chapter 1

Principles and Practice

Chapter 2

Organisation

Chapter 3

Statistics

Chapter 4

Curriculum

Chapter 5

Teacher Training

Chapter 6

Parental Involvement

Chapter 7

Resources

Chapter 8

Prospects

Appendix: Case studies

Part II
CASE STUDIES

Chapter 1
Orientation

Chapter 2
Learning Programmes

Chapter 3
Relationships

Chapter 4
Whole School Approaches

Chapter 5
Parental and Community Involvement

Chapter 6
Roles of Special Schools

Chapter 7
External Support Services

Chapter 8
Training

Chapter 9
Problems and Solutions

Chapter 10
Good Practice

Part I

POLICIES AND PRACTICES

Summary

The account given in this part is based on data provided by 21 participating OECD countries. Integration is defined as "that process which maximises the interaction between disabled and non-disabled pupils". The information requested has been organised into chapters covering areas of interest agreed with country representatives. They focus on the principles and practices of integration; the implications of the organisation of education; statistics, definitions and terminology relating to handicap, disability and special educational needs and the placement of the children concerned; the curriculum; teacher training; the role of parents; resources; and prospects for the future. An extensive appendix is provided in the form of "thumbnail" sketches of legal frameworks, policies and statistics pertaining to the Member countries involved. It is clear that government policies across OECD countries now favour integration. To achieve it, developments are needed in the identification of disabled children and the formulation of a realistic action plan which takes account of a country's current position as well as the wide range of relevant issues identified below, within a framework which stresses evaluation and resource allocation.

Effective integration requires the development of a number of key features. In the first place children must have access to the school curriculum which means that consideration must be given not only to modifications to buildings and equipment but also to pedagogy. In addition the organisation of the school is significant with streaming and the repetition of years being seen as obstacles to full integration. Thus the flexible organisation of classes and deployment of teachers is essential. In order to achieve these changes, there is a need to provide courses on special education at all levels of teacher training, including in-service and post-graduate levels, to develop the necessary skills and attitudes at the appropriate depth. Such courses must also include the acquisition of the attitudes, skills and competencies necessary to involve parents as fully as possible in the education of their children. A condition which is seen as essential in attaining the best outcome.

As part of the work extensive statistical data was gathered. Their comparison points to the great variation that exists between countries not only in terms of definition but also in the extent of integration. To make accurate international comparisons and develop more sophisticated evaluations, for instance of resource implications, these differences will need to be taken into account. The data that was supplied on financing special educators, although meagre, consistently suggests that interpreted placements are less costly than segregated ones.

Chapter 1

Principles and Practice

by

Peter Evans, Don Labon and Mary Ann McGovern

Introduction

In this OECD/CERI study the agreed definition of integration is: "that process which maximises the interaction between disabled and non-disabled pupils". While defining the concept is straightforward, achieving integration is highly complex. It requires changes in laws, policies, organisational structures, definitions, curriculum, pedagogy, teacher training, attitudes and financial arrangements. From educationalists it also requires cooperation with parents, with members of voluntary agencies and with professionals from health and social services.

Despite the obvious difficulties in stimulating change across such a wide range of issues, Member countries of the OECD have embarked on this process of social and educational reform, which in 1987 also became the official policy of the European Community. Inevitably OECD Member countries are at different stages in the process.

Subsequent chapters of this report consider the stages reached across OECD countries with respect to the main areas in which change is required: educational organisation, definitions of disability, curriculum, teacher training, parental involvement, resources. This first chapter provides a background, outlining ways in which current principles and practice have developed. The final chapter considers prospects for further development. In doing so it draws together findings of the study that may be relevant to the planning of a country's, region's* or district's integration programme.

---

* "Region" is used in the body of this report as a generalised reference to major division within a country, thus avoiding the use of a variety of terms ("canton", "*Länder*", "state", etc.) particular to individual countries. Similarly, "district" is used as a generalised reference to a recognised area, town, locality, etc., within a region.

Concepts

From the 1950s onwards, within economically developed countries there has been a steady shift away from the concept of the disabled as a relatively unchanging group, requiring fixed provision different from that of the majority. Instead, it is realised increasingly:

- that they can respond flexibly if their learning opportunities are appropriate;
- that there are many ways in which they can lead normal lives;
- that living relatively normally requires some adjustment both from them and from people without disabilities;
- that their needs can best be met through a continuity of special provision.

Flexibility

The present-day integration policies of countries such as Denmark, Italy, Sweden and the United Kingdom grew out of and gained momentum through their changes in the 1950s and 1960s away from selective secondary education. The development of comprehensive schools marked two fundamental changes in thinking: firstly towards the idea that the intelligence of all children could be made increasingly effective through education; secondly towards the idea that individual schools could provide effectively for children of a very wide range of ability.

The first change involved abandoning the idea of *the constancy of the IQ*: the belief that intelligent action was determined through the relatively straightforward application of biological principles of genetic inheritance. Within this context, diagnosis of handicap had been a medical rather than an educational matter, the scientific term for children with learning difficulties had been "subnormal", differences in their educational needs were not fully understood and they tended to be "treated" as though they were "suffering" from some "condition" . The second change emphasised the importance that had to be attached to modifying school organisation and the curriculum to meet this wider range of ability. New attitudes, methods and resources were developed, and they appeared to be successful.

Normalisation

The early 1970s   sh concept of normalisation (Wolfensberger, 1972;   t emphasised the belief that disabled people should   d opportunities as everyone else. In addition, concern was expressed at   _gative aspects of labelling. This continues to be a dilemma in the field of special education; while identifying children as disabled is administratively necessary if the resources they need are to be directed their way, this labelling process implies low expectations and can lead to lower achievement.

Thus at the beginning of the 1970s the scene was being set. It had been realised that, by changing the ways in which schools taught, more children could be successfully educated within the same framework – so why should the educational needs of the disabled be excluded? However, it was also recognised that some additional special support would be necessary, and the concept of special educational needs (SEN), as defined in the Warnock Committee Report (Department of Education and Science, 1978), emerged.

During the late 60s and early 70s it was generally accepted in economically developed countries that only a small proportion of children of school age were disabled enough to require education in special institutions. Surveys such as that of Rutter *et al.* (1970), however, demonstrated that they were by no means the only ones to be experiencing educational difficulties. Two distinct and largely complementary approaches emerged.

One approach was to extend the scope of the legal definition of disability. In the United States this was implemented for children of school age in 1975 through Public Law 94-142, which was amended in 1986 (P.L. 99-457) to include children from birth and in 1990 (P.L. 101-476) to require transition services from 16.

The other approach, as advocated in the United Kingdom in the 1978 Warnock report, and as adopted also in countries such as Canada (New Brunswick) and Italy, was to abolish categories of disability for educational purposes and to replace them with the much broader term ''special educational needs''. In discussions concerning the education of the disabled, special educational needs has now become the preferred term in many countries. It was considered by the Warnock Committee to apply to some one sixth of the population at any one time. Terminology used in relation to disabilities, however, continues to vary considerably from one country to another, making comparisons extremely difficult. This issue is discussed further in Chapter 3 (Part I).

In more recent years the pressure towards integration has increased as a result of worldwide concern about human and civil rights. This has been reflected, for instance, in the United Nations Year of the Disabled, 1981, and in the Children's Charter of 1989. A number of other influences have also played their part in encouraging new thinking about the possibilities of integration. These include parental and professional groups, progress in other countries and the reduction in school numbers.

Research evidence, too, strongly favours integration. Across many countries, recent reviews of the research literature have demonstrated that disabled children can achieve higher academic standards in integrated settings, although there is also some suggestion that their self-concept may suffer. Other research findings suggest that segregated schooling does not provide the clear advantages that might have been expected. The research literature has been reviewed as part of this study (see Evans, 1993).

Recent developments in the concept of integration have been considered in detail in a previous OECD report (1994). With the principle of integration generally accepted, the focus of interest is now on the processes through which successful integration works in practice.

Assimilation, accommodation and adaptation

One purpose of integration is to create mutual understanding and acceptance between the disabled and non-disabled, in the context of equality of opportunity. Clearly, this involves give and take on both sides; three relevant processes of adjustment have been identified.

Assimilation emphasises that the disabled should take on the ways of the majority. *Accommodation* recognises the rights of the disabled to be themselves and puts the pressure to adjust onto the majority. In Sweden, for example, hearing impaired groups have objected to assimilation because it does not necessarily involve the environment accommodating to their differences. *Adaptation* requires both the disabled and the non-disabled to adjust. According to Canevaro *et al.* (1985), this is the goal of integration in Italy.

Continuity

Since the 1950s, concepts about the disabled have shifted away from the idea that they can be placed in readily definable separate categories. We now recognise a considerable overlap from one disability to another and regard the distribution of abilities as largely continuous. Consequently, with respect to any ability, those whom we classify as disabled simply occupy positions towards one end of the relevant continuum.

By the same token, it can be argued that special educational provision should also form a continuum, ranging from full integration to full segregation. Models of provision reflecting this continuity include Deno's "cascade" and the Warnock Committee's distinction between locational, social and functional integration. Similarly, the Public Law 94-142 concept of "least restrictive environment" maintains every child's position on the educational continuum at a point as close to full integration as is practicable.

However, while such organisational models imply that the curriculum on offer should provide appropriate continuity, they do not guarantee that each individual will have access to the curriculum required. Access is such an important condition for successful integration that it is dealt with separately in the next section.

Curriculum access

Even when children with special needs have physical access to all the classrooms, laboratories, gymnasia, etc., in their schools, curriculum access involves a number of additional considerations. Broadly speaking curriculum content can be thought of as having two dimensions. The first describes the range of curriculum content. The second describes progression over time through the content areas. The teachers' job is to manage children's interactions with the curriculum so that progression is made in content areas.

For those with special educational needs, special adjustments must be introduced to enable them to interact effectively with the curriculum. Some children require a change in the medium of instruction: for example, sign language for the deaf, Braille for the blind.

Some need changes in the step size, whereby the issues to be learned and the rules to be abstracted are made more precise – an approach especially relevant to meeting the needs of those with cognitive difficulties. Some need help in overcoming problems in coming to terms with the social experience of schooling.

These adjustments are required not only of the teacher in the ordinary school but also of the organisational framework of the school as a whole and of its interactions with support services based outside the school. People within the system need to develop not only the new teaching and support skills but also the skills involved in persuading others to adjust as well. In order to move this process along, policies need to press for active inclusion of children with special needs in ordinary school curricula, not simply for their non-exclusion from ordinary schools. At the same time, due consideration must be given to the roles of special schools and other special education support services.

Legislation

The existence of segregated special school provision continues to be the norm across OECD Member countries and, as the review by Gaylord-Ross (1987) and the statistics reported in Chapter 3 (Part I) demonstrate, there are longstanding differences from one country to another in prevalence of special schooling. All OECD countries have policies favouring increased integration. They vary substantially, though, in the extent to which these policies are implemented through legislation. Given the changes that have taken place in education over the past 30 years, this is not surprising. Some countries have segregated special education, little legislation favouring integration and, at government level, only mild apparent interest in promoting it. On the other hand, integration is a major component of educational reform in other countries such as Germany, the Netherlands and Spain.

The fact that pro-integration policy is supported by legislation does not necessarily make integration a less controversial issue. In the Nordic countries, for example, legislation and resulting practice are such that the proportion of children with special needs educated outside ordinary schools is relatively low. Moreover, these countries provide many examples of successful integration. Nevertheless, reports from Finland, Iceland and Norway refer to the continuing existence of scepticism, with some administrators, teachers and parents expressing the belief that integrating children with special needs can impede the progress of the majority.

Some common elements can be identified. Many countries have abandoned categories of disability (although developments in Italy illustrate the fact that maintaining categories does not necessarily prevent integrative policies). Furthermore, many countries now recognise curriculum accessibility as *the* key issue which drives policy in areas such as resource provision and teacher training. In the New Brunswick Province of Canada, for example, the legal onus is now on the system to show that a child must be segregated. That is to say, the school must show that it cannot meet the needs of the child, not that the child cannot adjust to the demands of the school.

Provision

Countries differ considerably in their provision of preschool, primary, secondary and special education. Furthermore, particularly in countries such as Australia, Switzerland, the United Kingdom and the United States, where decentralised systems are operating, there are many within-country variations. Despite these differences, countries implementing their integration policies tend to have two main approaches in common. One is that they develop a continuum of provision. The other is that they reconsider the role of their special schools.

A continuum of provision

The goal of a continuum of provision can readily be seen in the practices of many countries, including Australia, Austria, Belgium, Denmark, France, Germany, Greece, Ireland, the Netherlands, Sweden, Switzerland, the United Kingdom and the United States. In some regions of Germany, for example, an increasing number of integration classes are being established in ordinary schools, usually in the primary phase, for the joint teaching of disabled and non-disabled children.

Several countries have set up pilot projects in integration with a view to evaluating them before deciding whether to implement them more generally. In Greece, experimental programmes integrating deaf children and blind children into ordinary schools have had positive results. In Austria, four models are being evaluated experimentally: integrated classes; cooperating classes, where ordinary and special classes come together for part of the time; small classes taught by special teachers in ordinary schools; support from peripatetic teachers. In addition, the Viennese School Board has set up an experimental school project in integration with specific objectives over a defined time span.

The role of special schools

In countries such as Canada, Finland, Iceland, Italy, Norway and Spain, where a continuum of provision is already established, a change of role for special schools is under active consideration. In Iceland the aim is to transfer as many children as possible to ordinary schools and for the special schools to provide the ordinary schools with specialist support services. In Norway, similarly, the majority of the 40 boarding special schools are being emptied and transformed into national public competence centres staffed by highly qualified personnel and offering different specialist services, either nationally or regionally. It is intended that these centres will carry out research and development work and act as resource centres.

In Spain, ordinary schools have been invited to volunteer to become integration schools which receive additional resources and support from a system of specialist resource centres. In the New Brunswick Province of Canada, separate special schools no longer exist and children are therefore being returned to their neighbourhood schools. Legislation there requires that children with special needs be educated in ordinary classes unless a case made out for their removal is successful.

Many countries are moving towards the provision of peripatetic teachers and resource room facilities to support ordinary teachers in integrating children with special needs into ordinary schools. In Finland the aim is to provide education within the least restrictive environment with modifications as needed and appropriate.

Overview

During the second half of this century perceptions concerning the prospects for disabled children in economically developed countries have become increasingly, and justifiably, optimistic. Former emphasis on medical classification of disabled children has given way to the now dominant belief that, if their special educational needs are met appropriately, their development can accelerate and many of them can lead productive and relatively normal lives.

There is substantial support for the view that many of the children traditionally educated in separate special schools could and should benefit, along with the broader group of children with special needs, by attending ordinary schools. Government policies across OECD countries now favour increased integration and, with the principle agreed, the emphasis has shifted to determining the most effective means of achieving this in practice. There are considerable differences across countries, and in some cases within countries, in the stages reached.

There is a general recognition that the key to successful integration lies in designing the ordinary school curriculum to ensure that children with special needs have access to it. Several countries have already reached the intermediate stage of establishing a continuum of provision, thus bridging ordinary school and special school education. The extent to which current educational organisation within different OECD countries helps or hinders integration is the topic of the next chapter.

Chapter 2

Organisation

by

Cor Meijer

Introduction

Many aspects of the organisation of any country's education can influence the extent to which children with special needs are integrated into ordinary schools. Among these are ways in which the government might delegate the running of education, the organisation of the schools themselves and the nature of the outside-school support services available. In particular, some kinds of school organisation can enhance full integration, whereas others can inhibit or even prevent it.

This chapter demonstrates the considerable diversity of practice across Member countries of the OECD and in doing so provides a context for subsequent consideration of integration issues. It also serves to highlight those aspects of educational organisation that appear to have a direct bearing on opportunities for integration in individual cases.

Administration

The vast majority of children across OECD countries are educated in publicly run schools. Even in countries where schools are managed by religious organisations, in Ireland and in the Netherlands for example, the government retains responsibility for the financing of education. In some countries, though, a significant proportion of children attend private schools run independently of the government. Statistics collected in England (Department For Education, 1992), for instance, indicate that some 8 per cent of all schools there, are independent. Such schools fall outside the scope of this CERI study and it should be borne in mind that their practices are not necessarily reflected in this report.

In countries where education is administered centrally, for example in France and in Greece, the government can in principle exert a strong influence on the extent to which children with special needs are integrated within ordinary schools. In practice, however, they often delegate much of the supervision of schools to regional authorities or to district boards, with the government taking direct responsibility only for aspects such as the setting of overall attainment targets and the monitoring of examination results.

In some countries, notably in Belgium and in Germany, regions function autonomously, carry their own legislative responsibilities and can vary considerably in their practices. In other countries, including Australia, Canada and Switzerland, education is largely decentralised to district level, though co-operation and co-ordination remain with respect to certain aspects of policy.

Decentralisation does not necessarily reduce a government's influence on local practice with respect to integration. For example the Australian government, with its education extensively decentralised, recently introduced a "Disability Reform Package" which has set the pattern for all the country's federal services for the disabled.

Compulsory schooling

Whatever the administration and funding arrangements, across OECD countries there is an age range within which school attendance is compulsory. In most countries compulsory schooling starts at six years. In a few, such as the Netherlands and the United Kingdom, it starts at five and in Nordic countries at seven except in Iceland at six.

In most countries compulsory schooling ends at the age of 16. In a few, in Greece and in Japan for instance, it ends at 15. In some, in Belgium and in the Netherlands for example, it continues on a part-time basis to 18. Regulations for the disabled can differ from those for the majority; in Finland, compulsory schooling for the disabled runs from 6 to 17.

While the period of full-time compulsory schooling generally covers some nine to eleven years of children's lives, it is the practice in almost every country for at least some children to start school before the compulsory period and for some to receive education well beyond it. In the United States the intention is to provide early intervention and special education and related services to those with disabilities from birth to age 21. It is general practice across OECD countries to divide compulsory schooling into at least two phases, primary and secondary, and the point at which this division occurs invariably carries implications for integration practice.

Elementary schools

OECD countries vary appreciably with respect to number of years devoted to the primary phase of compulsory schooling, length of school day, size of elementary school, size of class, grouping of children in terms of age and ability, and transition to the secondary phase. Some of these variations have clear effects on decisions as to whether children with special needs will be educated on an integrated basis within ordinary schools.

Duration

In most countries the primary phase lasts for six years, with children entering elementary schools at the age of five or six and leaving at eleven or twelve. Exceptions include Austria and most regions of Germany, where this phase is for four years only, from age six to age ten. At the other extreme, in countries such as the Netherlands and Northern Ireland, the primary phase lasts for more than seven years. In some countries, such as Belgium, France and Spain, the primary phase is sub-divided. In Finland the division is into a lower six-year stage and an upper three-year stage.

It is general for time in school to increase from between 15 and 18 hours a week for the youngest primary phase children to between 25 and 30 hours for the oldest. In some forms of school organisation it is difficult to estimate the time spent there by individual children. Under the new reformation law for primary education in Italy, for instance, there is a modular arrangement whereby three regular teachers and sometimes an additional support teacher are together responsible for two classes, running a flexible timetable ranging from 24 to 32 hours a week.

In any one elementary school year, duration of schooling can vary within countries as well as across them. In countries such as Switzerland and the United Kingdom there is considerable variation in timetabling from one region to another. In some countries there are six four-hour days a week and in others the school week consists of five six-hour days. Number of school days per year ranges from 180 in some countries to 220 in others.

Size

As with time spent in school, the variations in size of elementary school and size of class are considerable, both within countries and across them. Some countries, notably Finland, France, Greece and Ireland, have a high proportion of very small schools. In France, for example, many of these schools have only one class. Smallness of school is only partially accounted for by low density of population; the Netherlands, a densely populated country, also has very small schools.

The smaller the school, the greater the likelihood that children of different year groups will be educated in the same classes; consequently, the greater the spread of skills and interests in each class. It can be argued that, where the teacher has already had to adapt to such a diverse class, the introduction of a child with special needs is less likely to require a drastic review of class management style than it would have, had the existing range been relatively narrow.

The average class size in France and in Greece is about 25, and this is fairly typical. Average class sizes as low as 16 are achieved in some regions of Switzerland, where the national average is 18, and in Italy the maximum size of an ordinary class including a disabled child is 20. By contrast, classes may consist of more than 30 children in Canada (New Brunswick), Ireland, the Netherlands, Spain and the United Kingdom. It is self-evident that smaller classes provide greater opportunities for teachers to take account of the children's individual differences.

Grouping

Although the countries studied differ with respect to the ways in which children in elementary schools are grouped in their classes, these countries are remarkably similar in their declared policies. All seek to make primary education as comprehensive as possible and all seek to avoid situations in which some children have to repeat a year in order to achieve a certain standard before they can move up to the next class. Selection across the ability range, therefore, is regarded as a preparation for the secondary phase rather than a means of allocating children to elementary school classes.

In practice the countries differ significantly with respect to two distinct kinds of grouping within classes: *mixed-ability* grouping and *homogeneous* grouping. It is possible for the two to co-exist; in a single school, for example, the younger children may follow the former pattern and the older children the latter. In fact, though, the tendency throughout each country is for either one kind or the other to predominate.

In countries where mixed ability grouping is usual, children are grouped according to age and they generally move up from one class to the next regardless of ability. Strategies used by teachers to take account of varying abilities within a class include setting different work for different children and allowing them to do the same work at different rates. Clearly these arrangements can be conducive to the integration of those with learning difficulties. In some of these countries, in Finland and in Italy, for example, mixed ability grouping in elementary schools is reinforced by legislation to the extent that streaming children of the same age group into classes consisting of different bands of ability is explicitly prohibited.

In countries where homogeneous grouping is the common practice, for example in Austria, Belgium, Germany, the Netherlands and Switzerland, all the children in a class are expected to complete the set syllabus and those not doing so may well have to repeat a year. It can be argued that streaming into classes of differing ability bands may help authorities to place children with learning difficulties in ordinary schools as opposed to special schools. It is, however, self-evident that this kind of grouping also precludes their full integration.

Transition

While transition from primary to secondary education invariably carries some implications for integration practice, countries differ in the extent to which this transition involves change. In Iceland, for instance, the change is likely to be relatively slight. The Icelandic Basic School covers both the primary and secondary stage from age 6 to 16. In countries such as France, Greece and Italy, where transition is also from comprehensive elementary schools to comprehensive secondary schools, there are likely to be fewer changes than in countries where the transition is from comprehensive elementary schools to selective secondary schools.

In countries where selective secondary schools are the norm, the final year of elementary schooling is characterised by assessment in the form of tests and examinations. The various processes of assessment are considered in Chapter 4 (Part I).

Secondary schools

Secondary education systems vary greatly across OECD countries and to some extent within them. However, they have in common the fact that they all pose far greater problems for integration than do primary education systems. This is partly because of their tendency to be selective, usually in their later stages, in order to meet students' and societies' needs for specialisation. It may also result from a tendency for secondary school teachers to see themselves as people concerned with the knowledge inherent to their own individual subject specialisms rather than as people concerned with children's overall approaches to learning.

Most secondary schools are comprehensive at entry stage and remain so for two or three years. Then, when students opt for specialisms and may be chosen for them, they may well be able to follow them without having to change school. In schools carrying multiple specialisms, the existence of modules, whereby one module can service different specialisms, can help students take combinations of modules particularly suited to their individual interests.

A key variable for integration in secondary schools is the age at which students specialise. France, Greece, Iceland, Italy, Norway and Spain are all countries in which specialisation is delayed. In Greece, participation in the initial three-year phase of secondary schooling (the *gymnasium*) is compulsory for all. In France, similarly, specialisation is preceded by attendance from age 11 to 14 at the *collège*. In countries such as Belgium, Germany and the United Kingdom there are mixed modes, whereby some schools have three-year pre-specialisation stages and others stream earlier, sometimes from the moment of secondary school entry. In other countries there is a one-year or two-year orientation' stage, following which the students move on to general education, vocational education or pre-university education.

Special education

Special education in OECD countries occurs across a widely recognised continuum of placements, ranging from full integration in an ordinary day school to complete segregation in a residential special school. This can be illustrated by the use in the United Kingdom of eight points along this continuum, including special help in the ordinary classroom, periodic withdrawal from the ordinary class for individual or small-group help in specific subjects, division of time between ordinary and special class, full-time special class attendance and part-time or full-time attendance at a special school. The United States has a similar array of basic setting options, ranging from the least restrictive to the most restrictive environment.

Similarly, special education in ordinary schools can be provided through an ordinary class cascade system, as described for example in the report on practice in the New Brunswick Province of Canada. The cascade system is so called because it involves various levels of modification to a child's curriculum within the ordinary class. These may include, should they become necessary, increasingly specialised learning programmes and increasing advice and support from specialist teachers. This kind of gradation of provision occurs in other countries too, in Australia for example, which also has support teachers in the ordinary classroom, school support centres, and material resources are designed specifically to support integration.

For present purposes it is convenient to consider special education in three discrete settings: in ordinary classes in ordinary schools, in special classes in ordinary schools, and in special schools. In adopting this terminology, however, the reader should bear in mind the fact that in some OECD countries the term "special education" is thought of as being synonymous with special schooling. Australia, Switzerland and the United Kingdom are notable in that they run highly diverse systems, with all three elements represented and with considerable variation from one region to another; in Switzerland, though, this is within an overall emphasis on a system of segregated special education.

 ### In ordinary classes in ordinary schools

Among countries with a strong emphasis on the integration of children with special educational needs into ordinary classes are Canada (New Brunswick), Iceland, Italy and Norway. Each of these countries has a relatively low incidence of special classes and special schools. Norwegian policy, being implemented through a current project, is to change the last few remaining special schools into resource centres, developing a multiplicity of resources designed to stimulate and maintain integration. The question arises as to the proportion of time a child with special needs should spend in an ordinary class to be considered to be locationally integrated. In the United States, for example, this is fixed at 79 per cent.

 ### In special classes in ordinary schools

Special classes within or attached to ordinary schools exist in almost all countries and within countries their occurrence often varies considerably from one region to another. Gathering statistics concerning their existence is often difficult, as their organisation tends to be flexible and admission procedures informal. They are, however, particularly prevalent in France, Greece and Switzerland.

Size of school can influence decisions concerning the establishment of special classes. In Finland, for example, small rural schools have the services of a peripatetic special education teacher, travelling from school to school within a defined catchment area, whereas the larger school tends to have its own special education teacher working from a resource base or, if there are enough children with special needs in the school, running a special class.

The distinction between part-time and full-time special classes is an important one, as the former can facilitate periods of full integration. In the United States, for example, children based in the "resource room" (as opposed to those in the "self-contained special class") follow parts of the regular curriculum with their non-disabled peers. Even full-time special classes can provide a focus for moves towards integration. In France, for example, they have been re-titled as integration classes, to express this goal.

In special schools

Countries relying extensively on systems of separate special schools include Austria, Belgium, Germany and the Netherlands. Their systems tend to be highly differentiated, sometimes with eight or more different types of special school; in the Netherlands there are as many as fifteen.

Allocation

Methods of allocation of children to one or other form of special education vary from one country to another in their degrees of informality, flexibility and delegation to local level. Within any one country, these characteristics are likely to be the most evident in allocation to ordinary classes and least evident in allocation to special schools, though this is not invariably the case. Across OECD countries the general trend is towards increased informality, flexibility and delegation.

Allocation of extra help for children with special needs in ordinary schools does not necessarily require formal assessment. In the New Brunswick Province of Canada, for example, special education is an integrated part of ordinary school education and funding is delegated to the individual school district. Here, the ordinary school's managing body can allocate and if necessary change the resources informally without reference to any outside group and parents can be involved in choosing from a range of in-school services. Similar informalities exist in Australia, Norway and to some extent in Greece. In Iceland, short-term help can be provided informally but long-term support is conditional on recommendations arising from formal assessment procedures.

In some countries the provision of extra teaching help or equipment to support special education even in ordinary classes can be conditional on formal multi-disciplinary assessment (as described in the next section) and on decisions at regional or even national level. The English ''statement'' system and the Italian ''certificate'' arrangements provide examples of these degrees of formality and centralisation.

Allocation to special schools is in most countries dependent on recommendations arising from formal assessment, usually undertaken by a multi-disciplinary team. Within Belgium, France, Germany, Ireland, the Netherlands, Spain, the United Kingdom and the United States, for example, such procedures are compulsory.

In a few countries, in the Netherlands for instance, there is an admission committee attached to each special school. In other countries, allocation is organised by regional authorities, each able to choose from a range of special school placements. In some countries, for instance in Germany and in the Netherlands, there are nationally recommended procedures for allocation of children to special education provision, but in practice regional variations can be distinguished.

Support services

Whether children with special educational needs are educated in ordinary classes, special classes or special schools, most of the day-to-day help available to them comes from their families and from their class teachers. In addition, there is across OECD countries a variety of other means of support, mostly available on an occasional or periodic basis. The nature of this support varies considerably from one country to another and support service staff with similar job titles in different countries may fulfil different roles. In many countries the range of support services is highly complex, with significant regional variation and with different groups of professionals working for different organisations that may be largely independent of one another.

Special education support service staff may work with the child, with parents, with teachers, with other support service staff or with administrators. They may teach, consult, advise, assess, evaluate, monitor, inspect or report. Support services may be based within the child's school or outside it. For present purposes it makes sense to start with those services closest to the classroom and then move outwards. As before, while individual countries are referred to by way of example, it should not be assumed that these are the only ones engaging in the activities described.

Within schools

Within ordinary classes, particularly in those countries placing strong emphasis on integration, class teachers may have extra adult help, usually on a part-time basis, to enable children with special needs in these classes to follow either the normal class curriculum or some modification of it. A helper without special expertise may work under the direction of the class teacher. A helper with the necessary expertise, in consultation with the class teacher, may well modify the child's learning programme. The arrangement may be informal and even voluntary, or it may be an outcome of formal assessment. In England, for example, the provision of in-class special support assistance is a common outcome of statement procedures prescribed through an Education Act.

Co-operation between class teacher and support teacher is an important feature of successful work. One valuable mode of co-operation, as found in Spain, for instance, is for the two to exchange roles, so that the class teacher can personally get a better idea of the nature of the child's special needs. In Germany and in Norway, co-operation is cemented through an established two-teacher system. Co-operation between class teacher and support teacher is also intrinsic to the Canadian (New Brunswick) cascade system referred to near the beginning of the previous section.

Also intrinsic to the cascade system is the existence of special education resource centres in the ordinary schools. As well as housing special materials the resource centre can provide a base for support service staff and a place to which a child can be withdrawn temporarily for a specific learning programme or to cope with a crisis. Resource centres also feature in special education provision in several other countries; in Australia and in Finland, for example.

Across schools

The employment of peripatetic teachers to provide specialist in-class support across a range of ordinary schools is a regular feature of special education in many countries, including Austria, Belgium, Finland, Germany, Ireland, the Netherlands, Norway, Spain and the United Kingdom. It tends to occur in rural areas with small scattered schools, and here may sometimes be a response to the problems of wide dispersal of children with special needs rather than a conscious attempt to support full integration. It can also be found in some urban areas, however, where it is clearly integrationist in intent and where it also enables one person's special education expertise to influence several schools.

Support services for staff of ordinary schools helping children with special needs can on occasion be provided by staff of special schools or classes, and staff of ordinary schools may be able to reciprocate, say on the basis of their knowledge of the normal curriculum. Organised co-operation of this kind exists in many countries, including Austria, France, Germany, Greece, Iceland, the Netherlands and the United Kingdom.

Across OECD countries there are support services based outside schools, and often organised on a regional basis. Many countries have child guidance and counselling services, though their functions vary from one country to another. In Germany their work includes helping families and teachers tackle learning difficulties and solve problems concerning careers, whereas in Greece the school counsellor appointed to each district also offers advice on the curriculum and on teaching methods more generally.

The work of district or regional special education advisers and inspectors, as seen in the United Kingdom for example, includes providing professional advice, monitoring provision and organising in-service training. Some of this work overlaps with that of educational psychologists, who assess children's learning difficulties, offer counselling and contribute to placement decisions. Psychological services in Finland, France, Iceland, Italy, Norway and Switzerland follow a similar pattern. Not all regional support to schools is organised on the basis of educational services; in Ireland, for example, health services are very active in this field.

Nationally

Some special education support services operate at national level. In the Netherlands, for example, there are national as well as regional educational advisory centres. Whereas the regional services support elementary and some special schools, the three national advisory centres are mainly concerned with secondary school counselling and with implementing educational innovation across the system. In Norway, some of the special schools are being transformed into national resource centres which will provide information and offer counselling. In Spain, a national resource centre for special education provides information, offers teacher training and conducts research. In Japan, the national institute for special education carries similar functions, in association with an adjacent special school and 27 regional centres. In Finland the national centre undertakes curriculum development.

Overview

Opportunities for integration can be enhanced through strategic allocation of teachers to ordinary school classes, through flexible organisation of those classes, through the use of small groups, through the deployment of within-class support teachers and through recourse to within-school and externally-based support services. Full integration is precluded if classes are streamed according to ability or if a proportion failing to reach a designated standard by the end of a school year have to repeat the same work by remaining in the same class for a further year.

The academic and pre-vocational requirements of secondary schools present problems for full integration, notably from the point at which students of differing abilities are assigned to different courses, though such arrangements may increase opportunities for attendance at an ordinary school rather than a special school.

It is hardly surprising that the organisation of special education across OECD countries contributing to the CERI study of integration varies considerably, to the extent that no two countries are alike. Also, within most countries there is marked variation from one region to another. There are, however, striking similarities, both in terms of countries' aspirations and in terms of current practice.

Common aspirations are reflected by the fact that among OECD countries there is a decided trend towards further integration in the education of children with special needs. The nature of the trend varies, depending on the extent to which countries have travelled along the road already. In some cases the shift is from a special school to a special class in the ordinary school; in others it involves spending more time in an ordinary class as opposed to a special class. Furthermore, there is a remarkable consistency in that integration issues are under active consideration in all countries, including those furthest along the road. Educators are continuously seeking flexible solutions to complex problems, and questioning the effectiveness of the solutions found.

Flexibility appears to be a key to successful development. Whereas national laws and regulations are necessary to implement government policies concerning integration, they need to be expressed in such a way as to enable integration models to be adapted to suit differing regional and local conditions.

While overall current practice in each country is unique, each facet of that practice to some extent mirrors a facet of practice elsewhere. Because whatever one country is trying out is probably being attempted in several other countries, special educators in different countries have much to learn from one another. Promising features of several countries' developments include resource centres in ordinary schools, peripatetic teachers, and co-operation across schools. The barriers that selective education presents for integration are well recognised. Countries are beginning to focus on the curriculum as an important consideration in implementing integration. Ways in which they are doing this are considered in Chapter 4 (Part I). However, before these issues are discussed, basic statistical information is given in the next chapter.

Chapter 3

Statistics

by

Jennifer Evans, Peter Evans and Mary Ann McGovern

Introduction

This chapter outlines issues relating to the gathering of comparative statistical data concerning disability and integration, presents summary tables, draws some conclusions and proposes future projects. Further statistical information relating to individual countries is included in the appendices.

Difficulties encountered in gathering statistics

The data in this chapter were gathered from the country reports of the OECD countries participating in this project. The data are concerned with the educational provision made for children identified as either disabled or with special educational needs (SEN). The data are drawn from the period 1987-91. At the outset, however, it is necessary to acknowledge the difficulty of constructing comparative statistical tables across the OECD countries because of the extreme variability amongst countries in terms of classification, terminology, the methodology employed during the data collection and the concept of integration. These matters are discussed further below.

Issues of classification

Broadly speaking there are two classification systems which are currently in use. The first involves a description of disabled children according to a set of categories of handicap or disability that have their origin in a ''medical'' treatment model which emphasises the impairment or disability. This model, which has been extended in various ways, is widely used, but the conceptual framework of the World Health Organisation's International Classification of Impairments, Disabilities, and Handicaps (WHO, 1980) is commonly employed. This schema was developed to assist in the identification and measurement of the bodily, functional and social consequences of disease and trauma.

The second system which is becoming used more and more extensively has been developed following the recognition that medically based categories are not adequate in determining the educational placement of disabled children. Many disabled children have educational requirements which are not necessarily best met in special provision made for their principal medical condition. For this reason, and following recommendations made in the influential Warnock Report (DES, 1978), many countries have abandoned categories in favour of the term "special educational needs". This description has the advantage of allowing for an analysis of the child's educational needs and subsequent placement in provision best able to meet that child's needs.

These two descriptive systems have wide ramifications both in theory and practice. Because of its derivation from a medical approach that emphasises "treatment", the categorical model implies that the learning problems lie within the individual child. On the other hand, the description of SEN recognises that educational outcome is dependent on the interaction between the child, the education provided in school, and the influences of the home and the community more generally. Thus the teaching and education offered in any particular school may have a crucial impact on whether a child is identified as being in need of special provision. The same child might be a candidate for special education in one school but not in another. In summary, it may be said that the first approach emphasises absolute characteristics while the second privileges the relative aspects.

Terminology

Whichever method of description is used by a country there is still, even to the initiated, a bewildering array of terminology in use as Table 3.1 reveals. To further complicate the matter, different operational definitions appear to be in use even within particular disability categories, such as visual, hearing and motor impairment. This point is elaborated later.

As noted above, the countries taking part in this study use a wide range of descriptive categories. Some countries use one (for example, Italy and the United Kingdom). Other countries use ten or more (Germany, Netherlands, Spain, and Switzerland). Canada (New Brunswick) classifies all (both gifted and disabled) as "exceptional". Clearly, there are differences in the ways in which countries assess children's needs.

Some countries (such as Norway and Spain) have a large "other" category, which includes children in ordinary and special schools whose difficulties are not statistically differentiated. The notes from Spain indicate that, in an ordinary school, this "other" category includes a "fuzzy" grouping of children with learning disabilities and those with poorly diagnosed problems as well as children from ethnic and socially disadvantaged families. Conversely, in a special school this "other" term refers to children who have syndromes that are difficult to classify. Table 3.1 provides a summary of the terms in use.

There are differences between countries, not only in the terms that are used, but in the groupings into which they place children with various difficulties. For this reason, comparison of one country's special needs population with another is rather complicated.

Table 3.1. **Terms used to describe children with special educational needs in participating countries**

	1	2	3	4	5	6	7	8	9	10	11	12	13	14	15	16
Australia			*		*	→	*	→	*	*						*
Austria		*	*	*	*	*	*	*	*	*		*			*	
Belgium	*	*	*	*	*	→	*	→	*	*		*				
Canada (New Brunswick)					*	→	*	→								*
Denmark	*	*	*	*	*	→		*	*	*	*					
Finland	*	*	*	*	*	→	*	→	*	*		*			*	*
France	*	*	*		*	*	*	*	*	*					*	
Germany	*	*	*	*	*	*	*	*	*	*		*				
Greece	*	*	*	*	*	→	*	→	*	*						
Iceland	*	*	*	*		*		*	*	*	*				*	
Ireland	*	*	*	*	*	→	*	→	*	*			*		*	
Italy																*
Japan		*	*	*	*	*	*	*	*	*		*			*	
Netherlands	*	*	*	*	*	*	*	*	*	*		*			*	
Norway	*	*		*	*	→	*	*	*	*						*
Spain	*	*	*		*	→	*	→	*	*	*					*
Sweden		*			*	→	*	→		*						
Switzerland	*	*	*	*	*	*	*	*	*	*	*	*		*	*	
Turkey		*	*	*	*	→	*	→	*	*		*				*
United Kingdom																*
United States	*	*	*	*	*	→	*	→	*	*		*			*	

1. Mild learning difficulties, learning disabilities, specific learning disabilities, subject-related disabilities.
2. Moderate learning difficulties, educable mentally retarded, educable mental handicap, general learning disabilities, moderate mental retardation.
3. Severe learning difficulties, severe mental retardation, severe mental handicap, trainable mental handicap, profound mental handicap.
4. Speech difficulties, language and communication disabilities, specific language impairment, speech and communication difficulty, speech handicap.
5. Hearing impairment, hard of hearing.
6. Deaf.
7. Visual impairment, visual handicap, partially sighted.
8. Blind.
9. Emotional/behavioural difficulties, psycho-social disabilities, psychiatric difficulties, personality difficulties, deviant behavior, serious emotional disturbance.
10. Physically handicapped, motor impairment, sensori-motor disabilities, orthopaedically handicapped, orthopaedic impairment.
11. Autistic.
12. Chronic conditions requiring prolonged hospitalisation, paediological institutes, other health impairments.
13. Children of the travelling community.
14. Pupils whose first language is foreign.
15. Multiply-handicapped, severe sensory/mentally retarded, multiple disabilities.
16. Exceptional children, children with special educational needs, handicapped children, gifted, deaf-blindness, others.
→ These countries use one term to describe blind/partially sighted and deaf/partially hearing children.

35

For example, only two countries, Iceland and Spain, recognise the term "autistic" in their statistics. Presumably other countries have children with similar difficulties, but classify them under another term, such as severe learning difficulties. France uses two classifications for physical impairment: "motor deficiency" and "physical handicap", whereas most of the other countries use one term. There are some countries which make a distinction between "blindness" and "visual impairment" and "deafness" and "hearing impairment" and others which do not. Some countries distinguish between "emotional/behavioral" difficulties, "social" difficulties and "psychiatric" difficulties, whereas other countries collect statistics on such disabilities under one heading. Ireland includes children of "travellers". In Switzerland children whose first language is foreign are also included but clearly these children, who do have special needs, would not in the most part be disabled or have an impairment in the way these terms are defined by the WHO. Presumably they are included because an administrative procedure is needed to identify and obtain additional resources for this group.

Methodology and data collection

Wide differences exist between countries in the range and the detail of the statistics they collect on children with special educational needs. This partly depends on the level at which the responsibility for the organisation of special education is located. For example, in Australia and Canada (New Brunswick), education is the responsibility of each region, and national figures are difficult to aggregate since the data are collected using different criteria for categorisation in each administrative authority. In Australia for instance, each region can choose its own classification system, but when the data are gathered at the federal level, the classification system used is the International Classification of Impairments, Disabilities, and Handicaps – a schema not widely used by the regions.

The level of detail provided also varies from country to country. For example, France analyses placement according to age, sex and type of disability. The United Kingdom provides only an overall percentage figure of children placed in state or private special schools although detailed statistics are gathered at the local level for the purposes of planning and monitoring placement and provision. However, these are not aggregated at the national level. Furthermore, in some countries data are collected as part of the national census and thus there may be discrepancies in the accuracy and detail of what is reported. Some disabled people, for instance, may not want to specify their problems.

A further problem with the statistics is that they are, in a few cases, incomplete. For example, the statistics for Spain used in this report refer only to the MEC area (the area directly managed by the Ministry of Education and Science, i.e. those autonomous communities which have not as yet assumed full powers in educational matters) which covers some 45 per cent of the total school-age population of Spain. Likewise the statistics for Canada only report on the Province of New Brunswick as other provinces are not participating in this study.

The recording of children with multiple disabilities is also problematic since less than half the countries participating in this project include this category in their data format. Statistics for Germany record the numbers of children in schools for different types of handicap. This suggests a one-to-one correspondence between school placement and individual handicap, which may not be the case since diagnostic criteria are not necessarily mutually exclusive. In addition, children can be sent to a particular special school on the pragmatic criterion that there is available space.

Integration as a process

Definitional and terminological issues notwithstanding, the problems are further exacerbated when considering the issue of integration. This is because the concept of integration, stimulated particularly by the concept of educating disabled children in the least restrictive environment (LRE) provided for by United States Public Law 94-142, is not a static one but is viewed as a process extending from segregation, at one extreme, through various forms of part time integration to full time integration. Cutting across this continuum is a dimension of locational, social and functional integration. Locational integration refers to disabled children being on the same site as non-disabled children. Social integration implies some mixing of children during non-academic activities, while functional integration implies common teaching and curriculum. For these reasons terms used in this chapter such as "special unit" or "special class" cannot be assumed to refer to the same actual provision. The terms conceal many potentially large differences in the degree of integration involved. For instance, a special class that is situated within an ordinary school may isolate disabled and non-disabled children more completely than a special school which has a close link with an ordinary school and operates part time functional integration.

Reasons for gathering data

Apart from meeting OECD goals of improving the educational data base and putting aside the inherent difficulties with gathering statistics, there are many good reasons for gathering such data. All the countries represented in this study have policies and a majority have legislation concerning integration. The implementation of these policies with regard, for instance, to resource planning and carrying out cost-effectiveness analyses, the implications for teacher training and the employment of the disabled would be difficult to monitor in those countries which are not collecting detailed statistics. For example, how would a country know whether children with different types of disability (sensori-motor, intellectual, behavioral, etc.) are being successfully integrated and whether integration is more common for children with particular types of disability, if detailed statistics on the placement of children with those SENs are not kept? It may be felt, by countries that have moved away from categorising children, that it would be a backward step to begin collecting statistics based on a medical model. Canada (New Brunswick), Denmark and others state that they have no need to gather statistics about each particular type of disability. Canada (New Brunswick) for example stated that they "have legislation that recognises the individual, funding that does not require categorization, and instruction that is moving towards including all children as individuals".

Clearly more information is needed to understand exactly how this approach works and might operate elsewhere. But in the meantime, as far as other countries are concerned, to be unwilling to use descriptive labels to monitor integration, because they may not reflect the complexity of children's special educational needs, may lead to a loss of valuable data which could aid the process of evaluating integration.

It is worth repeating the caveat already made. In interpreting the tables given in this report due consideration must be given to variation between countries in assumptions and methods of calculating percentages as well as the different definitions used by countries to determine classes of disabilities.

Placement

Placement outside ordinary classes

In order to provide some basic comparative data, Table 3.2 shows children with SEN as a percentage of the total school population. Additional columns reveal the percentage of children with SEN who are outside education, *i.e.* those being educated in facilities not apparently under the direct control of the education authorities, and the percentages in special schools (or units) and in special classes in ordinary schools. The final column shows the approximate sum total of those children who are outside of the mainstream of education.

Table 3.2 shows the large differences between countries in the percentages of children considered to have SEN. The different descriptive frameworks that can lead to this situation have already been discussed. Following the Warnock report, which was itself influenced by a number of epidemiological studies, it has become widely accepted that up to 20 per cent of children, on average, will need special education at some point during their schooling. This contrasts to the approximately 2 per cent who are included under the categorical model. It may be noted, however, that many countries now include a category of "learning disabilities" in this system *e.g.* dyslexic children, which increases the proportion to 4 per cent and above; a figure that remains, nonetheless, substantially less than 20 per cent. These differences are reflected in the first column of Table 3.2 which shows estimates of the proportion of children that have SEN, and for whom provision is made, varying from 0.74 per cent (Turkey) to 17.08 percent (Finland).

The next point to note is that, in a few countries, the responsibility for some children with special educational needs lies with agencies other than the education department; usually health and/or social services department(s). This occurs in Finland, France, Greece, Ireland and the Netherlands. In France, some disabled children (1.38 per cent of all children) are boarded in establishments run by other ministries, although a proportion of these children may be educated in ordinary schools. There may be such children outside the education system in the other countries as well, but statistics have not been obtainable. There is also probably another group of older, disaffected children who have learning problems or behaviour problems and who do not attend school, but on whom no statistics are collected. In Ireland, 11 per cent of the Travelling Community do not attend school.

Table 3.2. **Proportion of children with SEN for whom provision is made: in special schools and units, special classes, and outside the education system**

	% of pupils with SEN for whom provision is made	Outside education	In special school and unit	In special class	Total outside mainstream
Australia	5.22	nil	0.63	0.92	1.55
Austria	2.55	< 0.1	2.55	< 0.1	2.55
Belgium	3.08	< 0.1	3.08	n.a.	3.08
Canada (New Brunswick)	10.79[1]	nil	n.a.	n.a.	n.a.
Denmark	13.03	nil	0.65	0.98	1.63
Finland	17.08	0.14	1.85	0.83	2.82
France	3.54	1.38[2]	1.26	0.64	3.28
Germany[3]	7.00	nil	3.69	n.a.	3.69
Greece	0.86	0.18	0.20	0.48[4]	0.38
Iceland	15.71	nil	0.58	0.71[4]	1.29
Ireland	1.45	0.22	1.04	0.41	1.67
Italy	1.27	n.a.	n.a.	n.a.	n.a.
Japan[5]	0.89	nil	0.37	0.52	0.89
Netherlands	3.63	< 0.1	3.63	nil	3.63
Norway[6]	6.00	< 0.1	0.6 (schools and classes)		< 0.7
Spain	2.03	n.a.	0.80	0.23	1.03
Sweden	1.60	nil	1.03	→	1.03
Switzerland	4.90	nil	4.90 (schools and classes)		4.90
Turkey[7]	0.74	n.a.	0.28	0.33	0.61
United Kingdom[8]	1.85	nil	1.3	n.a.	1.3
United States	7.00	nil	n.a.	n.a.	2.90[9]

n.a. = not available.
1. This figure includes gifted students.
2. Children in establishments provided by the Ministry of Social Security. A proportion of these are educated in ordinary schools.
3. Former Federal Republic of Germany only (1989). The 7% figure is an estimate.
4. Part-time only; otherwise, in ordinary class.
5. Column one covers those children of compulsory school age.
6. Many more than the 6% quoted have individualized help for minor disabilities.
7. An estimated 14% of children between 0 and 18 years are handicapped.
8. England and Wales only.
9. This figure was derived by adding together children who were receiving a good to fair proportion of their education outside the mainstream as described in the detailed notes on the United States.

The table further reveals that the percentage of children who are educated in separate special schools varies considerably across the countries participating in the study. In Australia, Denmark, Greece, Iceland, Norway and Spain, less than 1 per cent of children are educated in special schools. In Finland, France, Ireland, and the United Kingdom between 1 and 2 per cent are educated in special schools and in Austria between 2 and 3 per cent. In Belgium, Germany, the Netherlands and Switzerland, more than 3 per cent of children are educated in special schools.

The percentage of children educated in segregated settings in each of these countries is difficult to determine, since, in some countries, large proportions of children with special needs are educated in special classes, which may or may not mean that they are segregated for a large part of their lesson time. In some countries (for example the United Kingdom and the United States), there has been a shift away from separate special schooling towards classes and support units situated in ordinary schools. However, it is difficult to estimate the degree of integration of children with special educational needs brought about by such changes. France, also, has increased the proportion of children educated in special classes, both at primary and secondary levels.

In countries with a dispersed rural population, for example Greece and Ireland, where there would not be enough children in any one area to justify maintaining a special school, special classes are an alternative to placing children in residential special schools.

The final column of the table estimates the percentage of the school aged population who are educated outside the mainstream. This has been done by summing the relevant column entries where the exact figures are known. The table also shows large differences between countries in the number of children who are outside the mainstream, varying between 4.90 per cent in Switzerland to 0.61 per cent in Turkey. These figures must be interpreted with caution. For example although the figure for Turkey reveals that a very small proportion are outside the mainstream, this does not mean that those in the mainstream are receiving special education services. The report from Turkey would indicate that this is the case. There, 14 per cent of pupils aged 0-18 are estimated to have disabilities. The proportion in Italy, given that country's policy towards integration, would also be small but the figures are not available. Thus the reasons that lie behind these variations are complex but differences in policy and school practices in OECD countries play a big part.

Placement of children by level of schooling

In addition the degree of integration varies between the primary and secondary periods of schooling and this factor, in a complete analysis, should be taken into account. Table 3.3 exemplifies these differences in percentages for the countries which have supplied their statistics in a format that differentiated the levels.

A primary/secondary breakdown is insufficient to reveal various differences from one age group to the next, and the reasons for variation in percentages across age groups differ from country to country. In the Flemish community in Belgium, numbers in special schools rise from 2.5 per cent at age 7 to a peak of 4.8 per cent at age 11 and decline to 3.4 per cent at age 15. In France, numbers rise from 3 per cent at age 11 to 4.9 per cent at ages 13 and 14, as the demands of the secondary curriculum become more intense. In Greece, secondary education is compulsory only up to the age of 15, and many of those with learning difficulties after elementary schooling, continue to secondary school, together with the ordinary students and without any special programme. Consequently, the proportion of students with SEN and with special help at this level is relatively small.

In Ireland, the proportion is relatively constant at both stages. This may be due to the fact that a small proportion of children are classified as having special educational needs,

Table 3.3. **Percentage of children in special school by level of schooling**

	Preschool	Primary	Secondary
Belgium	0.55	3.90	3.40
Finland	n.a.	6.21	3.70
France	0.30	2.00	3.70
Greece	0.10	1.40	0.12
Ireland	n.a.	1.00	0.90
Japan	n.a.	0.33	0.44
Netherlands	0.71	5.64	2.48
Norway	n.a.	0.21	0.38
Spain	0.50	0.90	0.20

n.a. = not available.

and these will be the children who have more severe needs, and who will be identified at an early stage in their schooling. In Norway, where the percentage consistently rises from one age group to the next, with only 0.17 per cent at age 7 and 0.52 per cent at age 15, this probably reflects a year by year reduction in intake to special schools, as integration policy is progressively implemented.

There can be noteworthy differences between sets of figures gathered in different years. For Greece, statistics gathered more recently than those presented in Table 3.3 show that by 1992 the proportion at secondary level had halved, down to 0.06 per cent, whereas that at primary level had increased to 1.56 percent. In the Netherlands, the proportion in special schools at the secondary stage continued to be smaller than that at primary, but the percentages rose sharply between 1989 and 1991. Nevertheless the government is taking steps to try to promote more integration both at primary and secondary levels.

Prevalence of different types of disability

Differences in proportions of children deemed to have SEN are reflected in the balance of the SEN population within the different types of disability groups defined by each country. The first column of Table 3.4 shows the proportion of the whole school population identified as having SEN. The subsequent columns indicate the proportion of children classified according to the description given as a percentage of the total population with SEN.

The categories used to produce this table represent the collection of terminology which has been used by the participating countries to describe their population of children with special educational needs. If each column is examined it is evident that countries identify very different proportions of their special needs populations within the different categories. This may of course represent the true position but it seems likely that

Table 3.4. **Percentage of total school population classified as handicapped and classification of various handicaps as percentage of the SEN population in 21 OECD countries**

	% SEN	1	2	3	4	5	6	7	8	9	10	11	12	13	14	15	16 Others
Australia[1]	5.22					10.89	→	2.92	→								
Austria	2.55	40.95	66.30	16.70	3.20	0.80	2.10	0.70	0.30	2.80	2.50		4.60			2.41	0.81
Belgium[2]	3.08		28.42	6.28	4.15	2.40	→	1.20	→	9.30	5.00					5.21	
Canada (New Brunswick)	10.79					0.27	→	0.18	→								
Denmark	13.02																
Finland	17.08	43.49	8.36	2.43	26.39	0.89	→	0.19	→	12.34	1.21						4.68
France	3.54	32.03	11.57	3.60		4.02	→	1.39	0.43	36.18	7.56						0.81
Germany[3,4]	7.00	55.00	15.30		8.01	1.94	1.10	0.81	0.51	3.54	5.48		3.00				
Greece	0.86	55.62	15.31	10.84		4.60	0.23	0.69	→		2.74						10.20
Iceland[4]	15.71		1.65	1.00						0.49	0.23	0.12					96.29
Ireland	1.45	46.40	18.82	1.64	0.16	5.97	→	1.23	→	6.14	4.09			13.91		0.39	
Italy	1.27																
Japan	0.89	41.19	41.72	23.57	4.64	1.13	3.19	0.15	1.30	8.58	10.58		5.13				
Netherlands	3.63	56.00	31.69	6.98	0.32	3.80	0.81	0.28	0.21	5.23	3.20		4.72			1.58	
Norway[5]	6.00	56.00	→	→	5.00	3.00	→	2.00	→	24.00	5.00	1.28					5.00
Spain[6]	2.03	35.80	12.00	8.10		5.71	→	1.43	→	7.49	7.44						20.70
Sweden	1.60		68.56	→		9.34	3.11	6.22	0.31		12.45						
Switzerland	4.90	52.30	20.20	→	2.40	2.10	→	0.60	→	14.20	1.90		0.30		5.10		0.89
Turkey[7]	0.74		54.78	3.12		37.65	→	5.60	→		1.25						
United Kingdom	1.85																
United States	7.00	49.11	12.66	→	22.68	1.36	→	0.54	→	8.99	1.13		1.27			2.24	0.0

42

Table 3.4. Notes from Table 3.4 on previous page

Columns:

1. Mild learning difficulties, learning disabilities, specific learning disabilities, subject-related disabilities.
2. Moderate learning difficulties, educable mentally retarded, educable mental handicap, general learning disabilities, moderate mental retardation.
3. Severe learning difficulties, severe mental retardation, severe mental handicap, trainable mental handicap, profound mental handicap.
4. Speech difficulties, language and communication disabilities, specific language impairment, speech and communication difficulty, speech handicap.
5. Hearing impairment, hard of hearing.
6. Deaf.
7. Visual impairment, visual handicap, partially sighted.
8. Blind.
9. Emotional/behavioral difficulties, psycho-social disabilities, psychiatric difficulties, personality difficulties, deviant behavior, serious emotional disturbance.
10. Physically handicapped, motor impairment, sensori-motor disabilities, orthopaedically handicapped, orthopaedic impairment.
11. Autistic.
12. Chronic conditions requiring prolonged hospitalisation, paediological institutes, other health impairments.
13. Children of the travelling community.
14. Pupils whose first language is foreign.
15. Multiply-handicapped, severe sensory/mentally retarded, multiple disabilities.
16. Exceptional children, children with special educational needs, handicapped children, gifted, deaf-blindness, others.

Notes:

1. See section on Australia in appendices for further explanation.
2. Some column entries are derived from several figures provided by Belgium. See the section on Belgium in appendices.
3. Former Federal Republic of Germany only (1989).
4. Figures for individual disabilities are only for children in segregated special education.
5. Many more than the 6% quoted have individualised help for minor disabilities.
6. Breakdown of columns 1, 2 and 3 given by countries' representatives since only one category is used in Spain to cover the three utilised here.
7. Special schools only.
→ These countries use one term to describe mentally retarded, blind/partially sighted and deaf/partially hearing children.

43

Table 3.5. **Pupils with identified special educational needs as percentages of the total school population in 21 OECD countries**

	% SEN	1	2	3	4	5	6	7	8	9	10	11	12	13	14	15	16 Others
Australia[1]	5.22					0.57	→	0.15	→								
Austria	2.55		1.66	0.42	0.08	0.02	0.05	0.02	0.01	0.07	0.06		0.16				
Belgium[2]	3.08	1.26	0.88	0.19	0.13	0.08	→	0.04	→	0.29	0.16		0.07				
Canada (New Brunswick)	10.79					0.27	→	0.18	→								
Denmark	13.03																
Finland	17.08	1.43	1.43	0.42	4.51	0.15		0.03		2.11	0.21						0.79
France	3.54	1.13	0.41	0.13		0.14	→	0.05	0.01	1.29	0.27					0.08	0.03
Germany[3,4]	7.00	2.04	0.56	→	0.30	0.07	0.04	0.03	0.02	0.13	0.20		0.11			0.19	
Greece	0.86	0.48	0.13	0.09		0.04	→	0.01	→		0.02						0.09
Iceland[4]	15.71	0.67	0.26	0.16			0.04	n.a.	n.a.	0.08	0.04	0.02					15.13
Ireland	1.45		0.27	0.02	0.002	0.09	→	0.02	→	0.08	0.05			0.20			0.006
Italy	1.27																
Japan	0.89		0.37	0.21	0.04	0.01	0.03	0.001	0.01	0.08	0.09		0.05				
Netherlands	3.63	1.50	1.15	0.25	0.01	0.14	0.03	0.01	0.008	0.19	0.12		0.17			0.06	
Norway[5]	6.0								← NOT AVAILABLE →								
Spain[6]	2.03	0.73	0.24	0.16		0.12		0.03	0.005	0.15	0.15	0.03					0.42
Sweden	1.60		1.1.	→		0.15	0.05	0.10			0.20					0.001	
Switzerland	4.90	2.56	0.99	→	0.12	0.10	→	0.03	→	0.70	0.09		0.02		0.25		0.04
Turkey[7]	0.74		0.32	0.02		0.22	→	0.03	→		0.007						
United Kingdom	1.85																
United States	7.00	3.17	0.82		1.46	0.09	→	0.03	→	0.58	0.07		0.08			0.14	0.002

Notes from Table 3.5 on previous page

Columns:

1. Mild learning difficulties, learning disabilities, specific learning disabilities, subject-related disabilities.
2. Moderate learning difficulties, educable mentally retarded, educable mental handicap, general learning disabilities, moderate mental retardation.
3. Severe learning difficulties, severe mental retardation, severe mental handicap, trainable mental handicap, profound mental handicap.
4. Speech difficulties, language and communication disabilities, specific language impairment, speech and communication difficulty, speech handicap.
5. Hearing impairment, hard of hearing.
6. Deaf.
7. Visual impairment, visual handicap, partially sighted.
8. Blind.
9. Emotional/behavioral difficulties, psycho-social disabilities, psychiatric difficulties, personality difficulties, deviant behavior, serious emotional disturbance.
10. Physically handicapped, motor impairment, sensori-motor disabilities, orthopaedically handicapped, orthopaedic impairment.
11. Autistic.
12. Chronic conditions requiring prolonged hospitalisation, paediological institutes, other health impairments.
13. Children of the travelling community.
14. Pupils whose first language is foreign.
15. Multiply-handicapped, severe sensory/mentally retarded, multiple disabilities.
16. Exceptional children, children with special educational needs, handicapped children, gifted, deaf-blindness, others.

Notes:

n.a. = not available.

1. See section on Australia in appendices for further explanation.
2. Some column entries are derived from several figures provided by Belgium. See the section on Belgium in appendices.
3. Former Federal Republic of Germany only (1989).
4. Figures for individual disabilities are only for children in segregated special education.
5. Many more than the 6% quoted have individualised help for minor disabilities.
6. Breakdown of columns 1, 2 and 3 given by countries' representatives since only one category is used in Spain to cover the three utilised here.
7. Special schools only. See appendix on Turkey for further details.
→ These countries use one term to describe mentally retarded, blind/partially sighted and deaf/partially hearing children.

45

a substantial proportion of this variation is accounted for by different definitions being used to place children in categories. This point may be illustrated by looking in more detail at columns 1 (mild learning difficulties, etc.), 2 (moderate learning difficulties, etc.), 3 (severe learning difficulties, etc.) and 9 (behavioral difficulties etc). These four columns account for between 63.39 per cent (Spain) to 86.7 percent (Switzerland) of the proportion of children said to have SEN in the 11 countries whose data allow comparisons of this type. It is clear that countries vary substantially in the way these categories are used. In France for instance, 36.18 per cent fall into column 9 which contrasts with 3.54 per cent in Germany. Proportionally, however, more children in Germany (65.3 per cent) are said to have learning difficulties (summing columns 1, 2 and 3) than in France (47.2 per cent). It is impossible to tell at this stage what underlies these differences, but it seems that different systems of classification and definition as well as the various educational systems that exist will contribute significantly to a full explanation. It is most unlikely that differences of this size will be due entirely to "medical" conditions.

The column marked "others" is also of interest, given the size of the entries for some countries. The table shows, for instance, 96.29 per cent for Iceland. This presumably points to the inadequacy of the classification scheme that has been used to assemble this table, as it may not reflect appropriately the situation in all participating countries. This discussion again emphasises the difficulties of the task.

Table 3.5 shows the same data as Table 3.4 but expressed as percentages of the whole school population for any particular country. This table reveals the inherent difficulties very clearly. Again there are wide variations shown in all columns suggesting marked differences in the prevalence of the conditions indicated by the categories in participating countries. It must be born in mind, for instance, that the figure of 1.50 per cent in column 1 given by the Netherlands will reflect a very different population of children to the 7.43 per cent reported for Finland, given the large difference in the proportion of children identified as SEN. By referring to the individual country summaries provided in the appendix, it can be seen that these students in the Netherlands will nearly all be in special schools, while in Finland they will all be in mainstream schools.

Interpretational difficulties can be further exemplified by closer consideration of column 3 (severe learning difficulties, etc.). Epidemiological studies have revealed a prevalence of 0.3 to 0.4 per cent of school aged children with mental retardation (i.e. intelligence quotients less than 50). But the figures in column 3 do not reflect this finding, since they range from 0.02 per cent (Ireland and Turkey) to 0.42 percent (Austria and Finland). Some of the figures may be accounted for by including children with more severe handicaps in column 2 along with those with less severe learning difficulties. If columns 2 and 3 are summed for Iceland, Ireland and Spain the respective figures of 0.42 per cent. 0.29 per cent and 0.40 percent which emerge are in the expected range. However, this hypothesis will not account for all observed differences and it seems likely that in many countries those children with severe learning difficulties are divided into two groups and offered different provision. Thus it must be assumed that there are other influences leading to the observed variations in these figures.

It must also be added that these tables show average scores. In reality there are substantial variations within countries in the proportions identified. In Switzerland, for example, the proportions vary from 1 per cent to 10 per cent according to the canton.

Apart from these difficulties there are some interesting but expected consistencies. For instance in both Tables 3.4 and 3.5, the proportions of children in column 1 for each country is always greater than column 2 which is always greater than column 3, presumably reflecting the way in which ability is normally distributed. But in spite of this consistency there remain very substantial difficulties in deciding which group should be placed in which column. Column 1 is intended for those children with IQs in the normal range but who are having difficulties in coping with the normal school curriculum. Column 2 is for those with IQs between 70/75 and 50, *i.e.* with moderate learning difficulties, and column 3 for those with severe learning difficulties, *i.e.* IQs of less than 50. In practice it has proved extremely difficult to make the distinction, given the information that has been provided by the countries, and this will certainly account for some of the problems and inconsistencies that have emerged. In Belgium for instance special calculations had to be made in order to make the data fit the categorisation used here. This is explained more fully in the section on Belgium in the appendices. The problem is, however, not unexpected since many learning difficulties, especially those included in columns 1 and 2, have no clear aetiology and relate to difficulties that have emerged during schooling.

Other categories of disability such as the visual, hearing and motor impairment have a clearer aetiology and these groups are considered in more details in the next section.

Visual, hearing and motor impairment

In the light of the point noted above on the inconsistencies between epidemiological studies of children with severe learning difficulties and the data provided by participating countries it is instructive to consider in more detail data on the visually impaired, the hearing impaired and the motor impaired. These three groups have been chosen because there are usually clear biological reasons for the impairments and because it might be expected that in OECD countries, with relatively similar health care, the prevalences might be expected to be fairly similar.

Even accepting the assumptions made in the previous paragraph the tables below reveal again the complexity of comparing one country's statistics with those of another in the absence of agreed definitions and terminology. Tables 3.6, 3.7 and 3.8 refer to children with visual, hearing and motor impairment respectively. In addition they illustrate the placement of children by disability group for those countries which provided statistics in this form.

Table 3.6 illustrates some interesting differences between countries in the prevalence of visual handicap as identified in their statistics. Finland (0.03 per cent), Ireland (0.02 per cent), Spain (0.03 per cent) and Sweden (0.02 per cent) have identified similar percentages. Belgium (0.04 per cent), and France (0.06 per cent) identify around twice the rate. Canada (New Brunswick) identifies approximately three times the rate of

Table 3.6. **Placement of children with visual impairment**

	Number of children	% of total school population	Number in special school or class	% in special school or class	Number in mainstream	% in mainstream
Belgium	903	0.04	598	66	308	34
Canada (New Brunswick)	163	0.18	6	4	157	96
Finland	188	0.03	40	10	370	90
France						
Blind	1 517	0.01	1 230	81	287	19
Partially sighted	4 920	0.05	2 677	54	2 243	46
Ireland	500	0.02	150	30	350	70
Spain*						
Visually impaired	572	0.03	266	47	306	53
Sweden						
Blind	45	0.005	0	0	45	100
Partially sighted	900	0.1	0	0	900	100

* 6-14 year-olds in the MEC area only (area that is managed by the Ministry of Education and Science).

Belgium and France, six times the rate of Finland and Spain and nine times the rate for Ireland. If we accept that the epidemiological prevalence of visual impairment is unlikely to vary significantly between countries whose standards of living and health care provision are similar, then these differences must be ones of definition, identification and recording. It may be that, in those countries such as Canada (New Brunswick) and France, where the identification of visual handicap gives access to extra funding, or funding not paid for out of the education budget, there is an incentive to include less severely handicapped children within the visual impairment group. In France, for example, 1 005 children recorded as blind (66.24 per cent of the total population of blind students) and 1 600 recorded as partially-sighted (32.52 per cent of the total population of partially sighted students) are in establishments managed by the medical and social services.

These recorded differences in prevalence make comparisons in terms of integration more formidable. However, it should be noted that in Finland where a low proportion 0.03 per cent of children (arguably the more severely handicapped) are recorded as having visual impairment, 90 per cent of these are educated in mainstream schools. By contrast in France, where 0.05 per cent of children are recorded as partially sighted (less severely handicapped?), 46 per cent are educated in mainstream. In Sweden, 100 percent of children recorded as partially-sighted and 100 per cent of those recorded as blind are educated in mainstream schools.

Table 3.7 illustrates differences between countries in the percentages of children they identify with hearing impairment. Finland (0.15 per cent), France (0.14 per cent) and Spain (0.12 per cent) record similar percentages while Canada (0.27 per cent) (New Brunswick and Sweden (0.20 per cent) note approximately twice the percentage. The differences here may be in the level of severity of handicap which is being recorded.

Table 3.7. **Placement of children with hearing impairment**

	Number of children	% of total school population	Number in special school or class	% in special school or class	Number in mainstream	% in mainstream
Belgium	1 730	0.08	1 298	75	432	25
Canada (New Brunswick)	242	0.27	32	13	210	87
Finland	864	0.15	651	76	213	24
France	14 208	0.14	8 937	63	5 271	37
Ireland	2 200	0.09	700	32	1 500	68
Spain*	2 293	0.12	1 438	63	855	37
Sweden	1 800	0.20	810	45	990	55

* 6-14 year olds MEC area only.

Again, given the complexities of definition it is difficult to make comparisons between countries in terms of placement. There are also philosophical arguments about the best environment for the education of deaf children. In some countries (for example, Iceland and Sweden) the acquisition of sign language is seen as an important cultural as well as educational factor in the placement of children with hearing impairment. It is argued that it is important for deaf children to be with their peers to enable them to express themselves in their own language. However, there appears to be an increasing trend towards educating those with less severe hearing impairment in ordinary schools. In Canada (New Brunswick) 87 per cent are educated in mainstream schools in contrast *e.g.* to Finland (24 per cent), Belgium (23 per cent) and Sweden (55 per cent).

As Table 3.8 shows, there is again a wide variation in the percentage of children recorded as having physical handicap, from Spain (0.15 per cent) to France (0.27 per cent). There is also wide variation in placement, with 87 per cent of children recorded as having motor impairment in Belgium being educated in special schools and 80 per cent of children with motor impairment in Sweden being educated in mainstream schools.

Table 3.8. **Placement of children with motor impairment**

	Number of children	% of total school population	Number in special school or class	% in special school or class	Number in mainstream	% in mainstream
Belgium	3 279	0.16	2 853	87	426	13
Finland	1 168	0.21	921	79	247	21
France	26 686	0.27	20 695	78	5 991	22
Spain*	2 986	0.15	1 930	65	1 056	35
Sweden	1 800	0.20	360	20	1 440	80

* 6-14 year olds MEC area only.

In summary it may be concluded from these tables:

- either that the prevalence of these three disabilities genuinely varies between countries;
- or that the observed differences are due to methodological factors such as definitions and the way in which data is collected;
- or that they are due to variations in educational policies and practices.

Probably some combination of all three points is likely. But it does seem possible that some countries have policies and practices that lead to the unnecessary inclusion of relatively non-disabled children in a special needs category, perhaps assisted by the route through which additional funds become available.

The second main point to emerge from the data is that countries vary considerably in the extent to which children with these particular disabilities are integrated. These differences *must* be due to variations in policies and practices. A fuller understanding must await the collection of more data, when it may prove possible to reach further conclusions based on an analysis which takes into account the type of special education placement.

Conclusions

This chapter has gathered the most extensive set of statistics on the prevalence of children with SEN and the educational provision made for them in OECD countries to date. These data are as accurate as resources have permitted. It is clear that a substantial number of difficulties exist in terms of classification systems, terminology, operational definitions and methodology not only in regard to describing the special educational needs themselves but also of the integrated practices concerned. Underlying these points are the different models used to identify those with SEN, the vast differences in the numbers of children identified as SEN, the wide range or terminology employed and the very different ways in which the process of integration is being developed. This manifests itself quantitatively, in terms of the proportions of time spent in the different forms of integrated and segregated provision, and qualitatively in terms of the nature (locational, social or functional) of the integration practised.

The tables presented in the text show only too clearly the variations that exist between countries in terms of the extent of provision made as well as in the apparent prevalence of the disabilities. These are key issues. If these prevalence rates are real then serious epidemiological work would need to be undertaken to establish the causes. But such a search would be unlikely to come to any clear conclusions. It is much more likely that the differences are as much due to variations in policies and educational and medical practices in Member countries as they are to "medical conditions" or any other "objective" diagnosis. And it is for this reason that many countries have abandoned a categorical model which can give a false scientific status to what, in fact, is an administrative structure.

The features discussed above make the interpretation of statistics especially difficult. Clearly, however, there are differences between countries in the degree to which integration is taking place. These relate to policy issues not only in rather general terms, but also in the extent to which countries are prepared to reform their classification systems and the ensuing provision which is often closely tied to these schemata.

However, it should not be concluded from this discussion that monitoring the educational experiences of children with SENs should be abandoned. Quite the contrary – without the appropriate data how else are the necessary resources to be allocated and systematic planning achieved?

There are two other highly pertinent issues that should be given serious further consideration and which are important reasons for wishing to investigate further how integration can be developed and effectively evaluated. These are factors relating to educational standards and costs.

Standards

Such evidence that exists supports the argument that academic standards are little affected by integrative practices for either disabled or non-disabled children. This is a proposition worth pursuing but which, for its evaluation, in a comparative international context, would require the resolution of the problems identified above.

Costs

Again such evidence that exists (OECD, 1994) supports the view that integrated provision is less expensive than segregated provision. To pursue this proposition within a cost effectiveness framework, in a comparative international context, would also require the resolution of the problems identified above.

A way forward

It has been argued that gathering comparable data on disability and integration is of great importance. This may be seen as part of the process of achieving equity and equality of educational provision in OECD countries. It is worth reminding readers that disabled people have been segregated from society in many countries for many years and are discriminated against in most areas of life including employment.

In order to pursue this work it would be necessary to develop international agreement, on a classification system and the definitions contained within it, that would allow the integration process to be monitored. This requires a coordinated effort on the part not only of Member countries but also other organisations such as the United Nations Educational, Scientific and Cultural Organisation (UNESCO) and the World Bank, who have a particular interest in integration especially outside the OECD network of countries.

If agreement could be reached and appropriate data collected, it would be possible to develop a much stronger evaluation of integration practices in countries and to feed more accurate data into broader frameworks such as those being developed through educational indicators. What is required is a classification scheme that leads to the appropriate allotment and distribution of resources and which at the same time encourages effective education of those with special educational needs.

Chapter 4

Curriculum

by

Peter Evans, Don Labon and Cor Meijer

Introduction

It is important at the outset to note that in education the term "curriculum" can carry various meanings, ranging from a narrow focus on the subjects taught in class to a broad consideration of whatever impinges directly on children's school lives. This latter definition includes not only lesson content but also teaching methods, teachers' and children's attitudes, their relationships, the ways in which the staff are managed, involvement of parents, contributions of support services and so on. As integration issues involve a great deal more than just the subjects taught, the broad definition is the one used in this chapter.

Participating countries provided rather less information on processes of teaching and learning than they did either on the classification of special needs or on the organisation of special education. No doubt this reflects the fact that questions as to how to teach children with special needs are harder to answer than are questions as to how to identify them and where to place them.

Across different countries the history of special education has started with the recognition of those children unable to cope with the ordinary school curriculum and the provision of segregated special schooling for them. As expertise in special education develops, it becomes more apparent that some children in special schools could be taught just as effectively in ordinary schools, perhaps using methods and materials developed in special schools and found to be successful there. In OECD countries, as elsewhere, consideration of ways in which the ordinary school curriculum can be adapted to meet special needs is relatively recent, and in some countries it is just beginning.

Even in countries with a strong record of integrating children with special needs into ordinary schools, the initial "natural" response to a newly identified condition may be to segregate. The danger here is that attention may be paid to the child's physical or medical condition but not to the child's special educational needs: hence the use of the term "medical model" to refer to the basis for this kind of response. In the United States for instance in recent years special schools have been set up for children of mothers who

53

have taken cocaine during pregnancy, despite the fact that their educational problems (lack of concentration, emotional difficulties, motor impairment) are the same as those of many other children with special needs.

The main issues considered in this chapter are ways of ensuring that children with special needs have access to the curriculum on offer, ways in which the curriculum can be differentiated to meet individual needs, and ways in which children's progress can be assessed.

Access

It is generally recognised across OECD countries that children's easy access to whatever curricula

are thought suitable for them cannot simply be assumed, and that special steps may be needed to ensure access. Information from Australia, for example, goes so far as to identify such steps as being essential for successful integration.

When it comes to deciding which curricula are suitable for children with special needs, however, there are marked differences between countries, reflecting their differing underlying beliefs as to the basic aims of education. In some OECD countries there is a dominant belief that all children have the right to experience the same broad curriculum content and should do so.

At the other extreme there are countries where children with special needs, notably from the early secondary phase, are taken along curriculum routes differing in kind from those of the majority, with these "special" routes anticipating, and to a large extent predetermining, a restricted range of employment options after school.

Some countries occupy the middle ground. In the United States, for example, the individualized education plan determines the extent to which children with special needs will participate in the general educational curriculum. Those with severe disabilities may receive an alternative curriculum focusing on the particular skills, in some ways different from those of the majority, that they will require as they reach adulthood. In Japanese special schools, while much of the curriculum follows that of ordinary schools, there are additional "educational therapeutic activities", such as tactile exercises for the blind and mobility work for the physically disabled.

Country reports identify three aspects of access to the curriculum, all highly relevant to integration: physical access, access to learning, and access through funding.

The need to ensure physical access to school buildings is at its most self-evident where children have physical disabilities and may require ramps, lifts, adapted toilets and so on if they are to be able to participate in the life of the school. Once in the classroom they may also require special seating arrangements and modifications to equipment such as taps, switches, laboratory apparatus and computers. Similarly, children with sensory disabilities require devices to aid their hearing and vision. Some of these devices, radio microphones for example, need to be used by the teachers and by non-disabled children.

Once problems of physical access are solved, children with special needs can be integrated locationally, in the sense that they can be educated in the company of ordinary children. It is likely that they can also be integrated socially, as they are then in a position to communicate with their non-disabled peers.

The conditions for access to learning, however, are more demanding. For children with sensory disabilities, amplification of sounds and magnification of images may not in themselves be sufficient to ensure their access to learning. They, their teachers and perhaps their peers may have to learn and use elements of a specialised communication system such as a sign language or Braille writing. Children who are limited intellectually may need to have spoken and written information simplified, may need to be allowed more time to complete the same amount of work and may need to leave out certain more complex aspects of the syllabus.

The third aspect of access to the curriculum, access through funding, can in some cases facilitate integration and in other cases set up barriers against it. In the United Kingdom, for example, the official system of compiling "statements" about selected children's special needs can ensure that they are provided with special equipment and/or help necessary to their being integrated into ordinary schools. On the other hand, the very process of tying funding specifically to disabilities can, in some countries, serve to "label" the children concerned and steer them in the direction of segregated special schooling.

Other elements of national policy, while not directly concerned with either curriculum access or integration, may nevertheless have some impact on both. Again in the United Kingdom, recent legislation has introduced funding for schools based largely on numbers of children on roll, so that schools have to compete for children. Parents are also encouraged to choose among schools on the basis of published levels of children's academic achievement. As a result, heads may feel pressured to pass their less able children on to special schools.

As full access for children with special needs to the curriculum of the ordinary school requires careful planning, it is clear that it can only succeed if those able to influence it have the will to make it work. Key figures must include politicians at national level, regional administrators, school heads and class teachers. The fact that scepticism concerning integration continues to exist even in countries where it has been shown to work, for example in Scandinavian countries, indicates that the need to influence the beliefs and attitudes of doubters will continue even after integration is largely achieved.

Within the ordinary school, the positive approach of the staff can be enhanced if it is formalised through an explicit whole school policy promoting integration. Descriptions of good practice, in Australia, Canada and the United States for example, illustrate the value of also having a graduated system of within-school and outside-school support, enabling class teachers to draw on the different levels of help, expertise and specialist materials they may require. Whatever encouragement and support are available, though, full access to the curriculum on a day-to-day basis depends directly on the classroom teacher's skill in ensuring that all the children in the class have appropriate learning opportunities.

Differentiation

As children's attainments vary considerably, even if all the children in the class have been selected as being in the same age group and ability band, it is incumbent on the teacher to differentiate the curriculum on offer in order to cater for these variations. While there are contrasts from one country to another in the extent to which teachers differentiate the curriculum, the strategies used by those teachers who do achieve curriculum differentiation appear to be broadly the same.

Across OECD countries, teachers differentiating the curriculum are able to depart from teaching the whole class the same content at the same time. In doing so they set separate tasks for different groups within the class and occasionally, particularly where children have special needs, for individuals. Each group is likely to consist of children of similar levels of attainment, though it is possible to have a mixed ability group in which children contribute to a common task on the basis of their differing capabilities: for example, one may search for relevant information, another may summarise it, another may supply illustrations and so on. Whatever the grouping, the teacher can foster co-operative learning, whereby those children who can manage tasks help those who cannot.

Although tasks vary, all the children in the class are likely to be working to a common objective within the progression of the curriculum. For example, in a mathematics lesson concerned with handling data, a class of eight-year-olds might share the tasks of measuring the height of each Member of the class and distributing the measures across five colour-coded categories: very short, short, medium etc. The majority, helped as necessary, would be able to graph the results. Those who could not would probably be able to predict which children fell into which category and perhaps group the results using coloured blocks. The most able could be asked to work out the average and possibly construct pie charts.

Effective curriculum differentiation invariably places heavy demands on teachers' time, knowledge and organising skills. In elementary schools, teachers taking the same class of children for all subjects must be familiar with the content of all these subjects at many levels of difficulty. In the secondary phase, a teacher offering one subject throughout the school must get to know the attainment levels and interests of a great many students.

Both in the primary and in the secondary phase, various arrangements are used to ensure that the teaching work is manageable. One is the allowance of non-teaching time, so that teachers can consult, plan and evaluate. Another is the provision of support teaching, particularly in helping children with special needs, or of non-teaching assistants. Another is the availability of materials, possibly in computerised and interactive form, for individual learning. The report on practice in Germany, for example, stressed the need for the development of such teaching materials on an organised basis across schools.

Another arrangement helping teachers achieve curriculum differentiation is the framework of a common curriculum with well-defined levels. In the United Kingdom, for example, a start has been made on a national curriculum in which each of ten subjects has ten levels of difficulty, each with broadly defined programmes of study and attainment targets.

Contrastingly, there are in some OECD countries prevalent arrangements that make curriculum differentiation more difficult. Where the content of each school subject is prescribed in detail, there is little opportunity for teachers to interpret it flexibly and adapt it to make it relevant to the differing needs and interests of children varying in age, ability and cultural background.

Such difficulties can be compounded if standard textbooks are prescribed and if at each age level all children are expected to reach the same goals. At the extreme, on any particular day a teacher may feel a greater obligation to teach to the "correct" page of the textbook than to make sure that all the children in the class are learning. Increasingly, countries are moving away from such standardisation. In France, for example, the new reforms to the elementary school system recognise the need for flexibility.

Assessment

In order to differentiate the curriculum successfully, teachers must be able to assess children's achievements formatively, in the sense that the results of their assessments form a basis for their decisions as to what the children should learn next and how they might best be taught. This level of precision is not always achieved. It may be, for example, that teachers assess children only once or twice a year, when they provide written reports for parents on children's progress in different subjects.

From the point of view of curriculum differentiation it is unfortunate that in many countries formative assessment by individual teachers is overshadowed by an emphasis on summative assessment, whereby end-of-year tests and examinations are devised on a national or regional basis, their results summated and expressed in the form of grades or percentages. This emphasis is particularly strong in countries where higher achievers move on to separate secondary schools.

The results of summative assessment are generally used to provide an indication of the overall achievements of the school and to aid decisions concerning placement of individuals for the following year. Low scorers may be placed in special classes or special schools, or may have to repeat a year.

A child repeating a year may literally be exposed to a repetition of the curriculum offered in the previous year, without any modification to match that child's particular learning needs or changing interests. In Japan, many children are sent for private coaching, in the hope that this will enable them to avoid repetition. In some countries there is an almost automatic procedure whereby children who have been required to follow the same curriculum for two or three years in succession are transferred to special schools.

Overview

As with the organisation of education, the way in which the curriculum is offered in schools varies considerably across OECD countries but the issues being dealt with are essentially the same. The fundamental problem is that of making a broadly common body of knowledge and skills accessible to children who, at any one age level, display considerable diversity in their abilities and interests. Countries' responses to this problem can be clustered into three types. They are not mutually exclusive; in fact, all three can be found to co-exist within a single school.

A relatively unsophisticated type of response is that of extreme standardisation, whereby at a given age level the expectation is that all the children will learn the same subject content to a prescribed level of achievement. Inevitably some fail; they may then be selected out into a special class or special school, or they may have to repeat a year. Either way, their and their teachers' time has been wasted. While extreme standardisation is not the singular characteristic of the curriculum of any OECD country, elements of it are still fairly widespread; the phenomenon of repeating a year, for example, is not uncommon.

Another mode of response is to provide different curricula, in different classes, for children thought likely to achieve at different levels and eventually to develop different adult lifestyles. Across OECD countries this is fairly prevalent in the secondary phase, less so in elementary schools. Country reports at this stage of the study were not sufficiently detailed to identify the nature or appropriateness of these curriculum variations. It should be pointed out here, though, that such prophesies can be self-fulfilling. Students placed on "non-academic" courses, for example, even if they develop academic aptitude later, can have difficulty in transferring to academic courses.

The third mode of response is to make some physical adaptations to ordinary schools to ensure that children with disabilities have access to whatever curriculum is on offer there, and to provide a curriculum that is differentiated sufficiently to enable children of different abilities to work individually or in groups on similar tasks at their own levels in the same classroom.

Within-class curriculum differentiation, while common in only a few OECD countries, is gaining ground generally and is the only approach seen to sustain any significant degree of integration. To be effective it requires endorsement at national, regional and local policy levels, flexible support services, formative assessment linked with teaching, and high levels of skill among class teachers. The fact that it is professionally demanding carries strong implications for teacher training, the theme of Chapter 5.

Chapter 5

Teacher Training

by

Seamus Hegarty

Introduction

As indicated in Chapter 3, in many of the OECD countries' children with special educational needs are already being educated in ordinary schools, either in ordinary or in special classes. The prevalence of children with special educational needs is such that the vast majority of ordinary class teachers are called upon to teach them, particularly in countries where the full integration of a goodly proportion of children with special educational needs is already the norm. As seen in Chapter 4, effective integration of these children into ordinary classes requires high level professional skills on the part of teachers. The question arises as to how teachers can best acquire the skills needed.

Since the evidence shows that curriculum differentiation within ordinary classes is an essential feature of successful integration, and as it does not appear to be widespread, it seems that it is not an approach that develops ''naturally'', simply as a result of on-the-job experience. Some form of additional training is required during initial qualification as a teacher, perhaps after a period of teaching, and perhaps at various stages during a teacher's career. This chapter identifies forms of special training existing in OECD countries and considers their appropriateness.

Initial teacher training for special needs

General arrangements for initial teacher training vary widely across OECD countries. Iceland, Norway, Spain and the United States, for example, have a single, well-defined route: extended full-time study at university or training college, following graduation from upper secondary school. The pattern in the Netherlands is broadly similar, though more flexible study, involving some part-time provision, is on the increase. In France teacher training has since 1991 become the responsibility of the universities. Entry to training is by competitive examination; applicants must already hold a university degree or equivalent qualification. The United Kingdom offers a variety of routes: a four-year full-time undergraduate training, a one-year full-time postgraduate course, and various schemes with substantial elements of on-the-job training.

Five countries indicated that all students in initial training are introduced to special needs issues. In the New Brunswick Province of Canada all such students are introduced to "a wide range of teaching strategies and outcomes in order to help meet the needs of all students", and the university students taking courses in education are required to include one special education course. In France all the students follow a 42-hour module on special needs issues. There is some discretion regarding the content of these modules but all students are required to cover the Government's measures on integration and the adaptations to teaching that implementation of these measures entails.

Recent legislation in Italy has mandated the inclusion of special needs issues in initial teacher training. Since the early 1980s, students training for teaching in elementary and lower secondary schools in Norway have spent half a year studying special education. In the United Kingdom all students in training since 1989 have been "expected to have acquired a range of teaching strategies and skills suitable for a wide ability range and be able to identify pupils with special educational needs". In Ireland teachers training for primary education receive some instruction on special needs.

In 37 of the 50 United States, all initial teacher training students are required to take one or two courses or a university-designed experience in special education. In Iceland and in Spain there are as yet limited opportunities to study special education in initial training, although in Spain there are plans to include "basic training in special needs education" for all students training to teach in the primary phase. In Switzerland the regional directors of education suggested in 1985 that special education issues should be included in initial teacher training. Following this, an investigation of practice was conducted and a national commission is preparing proposals on how this might best be done.

While initial teacher training in Germany does not include instruction for special educational needs, there are moves to change this, and efforts are being made to include information, particularly with regard to integration. In Belgium and in Greece, similarly, there are moves to include some coverage of special needs issues in initial teacher training. In the Netherlands, initial training for ordinary education and for special education continue to be relatively separate, although in the curriculum of primary teacher training special emphasis is now being laid on handling children with SEN. This is in accordance with the policy of the Dutch Government to enhance integration of these children in ordinary schools and to stabilize the number of children in special schools.

Specialist training

While integration of children with special needs carries some implications for the training of most, if not all, teachers, there is in addition the necessity for a minority of teachers to specialise in this field. Some such specialists will work in special schools and some will provide support services for class teachers in ordinary schools. Special educators are faced with decisions concerning the conditions that should govern access to specialist courses, decisions about the nature of the courses provided and decisions as to whether there should be legislation requiring completion of such courses prior to work in special education.

Access

In most OECD countries, basic teacher training is a prerequisite for training to work as a special educator. This is stated explicitly in reports from France, Greece, Iceland, Ireland, the Netherlands, Norway and the United Kingdom and is implied for Belgium and Canada (New Brunswick). In Germany most special education teachers have been teachers in ordinary schools prior to training as special educators.

In Spain the usual route is by means of postgraduate study, of from one to three years, after basic teacher training. Some training colleges there, however, offer a special-isation in special education as an option in initial training, and this qualifies teachers to work as special education specialists directly on leaving college. In the United States, specialist training is through initial post-secondary courses, leading to bachelors' degrees. Most of these initial training courses are specific to one or other area of disability, although generic special education courses are now being developed in some regions.

Certain special education courses in Ireland and all such courses in the Netherlands have the additional requirement that the teacher be already working in special education; in the Netherlands this work has to be in a special school. This entry requirement is being debated in the Netherlands as the pressure for integration and more flexible training arrangements has stimulated a demand for teachers in ordinary schools to become trained as special educators. In France, teachers cannot be considered for specialised training until they have taught for three years in ordinary schools. In Greece, candidates for specialist training must have had at least five years' experience in ordinary schools and must pass an entrance examination.

The nature of the courses provided

In most OECD countries the provision of specialist training is on a postgraduate basis. In France, courses are offered at the university institutes for teacher training and at two national centres. The diploma obtained at the end of a course qualifies teachers to teach children with particular disabling conditions and in particular working contexts. There are six options: hearing impairment; visual impairment; physical handicap; psycho-logical problems; children experiencing difficulties at elementary school; and adolescents with difficulties. Spain has postgraduate courses of one to three years, concerned mainly with different disabilities, with diagnostic assessment and with therapeutic intervention.

In Norway, a comprehensive study of special education is organised over a four-year period. While each year builds on the preceding one, students can stop at any point. The first year is a general introduction to special education and is offered by several colleges throughout the country on a full-time or part-time basis. The second year is divided into different types of disability. The third and fourth years cover research methodology, communication, counselling and educational innovation. The Norwegian Postgraduate

College of Special Education plays a key role in this provision and also offers doctoral programmes.

In Germany the special education teacher's certificate is acquired after extended postgraduate study. The training requires study of at least eight semesters in an institution of higher education followed by a teaching practice, generally of two years, and a state examination. Specialisation in two out of a total of nine specialist areas is required. Switzerland has some ten higher education institutions running full-time courses of two to three years and part-time courses of three to four years.

Greece and Iceland each have a single institution at which a two-year full-time course is offered. The Icelandic institution also provides a four-year part-time variant of its course. In Ireland there are various full-time one-year diploma courses including one in special education, one for teachers of the deaf and one in compensatory and remedial education. Ireland also has some one-year part-time courses for teachers providing special education in ordinary schools. In the Netherlands, training for teaching in special schools is run by three institutions, with two-year evening courses organised at various locations throughout the country.

The United Kingdom has a large number of courses leading to a diploma or a master's degree in special education. These can be one-year full-time or part-time lasting two or more years, sometimes on a modular basis. These courses tend to combine theoretical and practical elements with course assignments and projects often based on initiatives in course members' schools. There is also a substantial provision of distance learning courses.

In Belgium there have been various legislative calls for further training for teachers working in special education but a comprehensive system has not yet been established. There have been initiatives to update a course available in both French and Flemish communities since 1924. In the French community a Decree in 1990 made regulations concerning in-service and continuing training of teachers. Courses were run for the first time in 1991-92. In the Flemish community a supplementary two-year course for young teachers in special schools has been developed within the framework of continuing training for all teachers. There has been formal pressure on school boards to organise such courses as a priority training initiative.

Legal requirements

It is increasingly necessary to have a specialist qualification in order to work in special education. In France the special education diploma is required, although teachers lacking this are allowed to take some classes on a temporary basis. In Italy support teachers must attend a two-year training course. In Norway special education training is required for teachers working in special classes, special centres and special schools and in Spain for those working with children with SEN in mainstream schools. Similar regulations apply in Iceland and Switzerland. In the United Kingdom specialist training is required for teachers working with children who have hearing or visual impairments, although teachers are permitted to work with such children, for a maximum period of three years, while acquiring the qualification. In several other countries where certification is not a formal requirement, in Belgium and in Canada (New Brunswick) for example, most teachers who work in special education do in fact have appropriate qualifications. In Iceland about half of those working in special education hold a one-year postgraduate qualification.

In-service training

In-service training is diverse, ranging from loosely structured on-the-job training to extended courses of postgraduate study. A distinction can be made between extended, award-bearing study and other forms of professional development. While the distinction is not a rigid one, particularly on account of the growing flexibility of arrangements with respect to certificated training, it is none the less a useful one. In special education, in-service training in the first sense is the principal source of professional training for teachers and has already been described. This section is confined to in-service training in the latter sense and considers its purposes, its prevalence and the nature of its provision.

Purposes

There is widespread endorsement among OECD countries of the significance of in-service training, sometimes referred to as professional development or as continuing education, and its key role in integration is well recognised. Reports from Finland, Germany and Greece, for example, stressed the importance of arranging in-service training for teachers before implementing plans for further integration.

Reports from Australia referred to in-service training concerned with integration within an ordinary school as being, not only a means of helping individuals develop the teaching skills needed, but also a means of fostering a sense of responsibility for helping children with special needs among all the staff of the school. The report from Canada (New Brunswick) referred to the need for teachers in ordinary schools to develop the skills of effective deployment of paraprofessionals assigned to help them in their work with children with special needs in their classrooms.

In the United States, much of the in-service training on offer in special education focuses on the implementation of Public Law 94-142, though there are also master's and doctoral degree programmes available to teachers who already have initial special education qualifications and who wish to progress to more advanced work.

The need for in-service training is not confined to those who work in ordinary schools and are relatively inexperienced in working successfully with children with special needs. Work with children with special needs in integrated settings can require skills not necessarily acquired by teachers trained to help these same children in special schools, where all the children on roll have similar disabilities and overall staff-pupil ratios are much higher.

In-service training is also required for purposes other than those of improving awareness of special needs and enhancing relevant teaching skills. Responses from Canada (New Brunswick), Iceland and Norway, for example, referred to their shortages of people skilled in planning, introducing, administering, supervising, monitoring and evaluating integration programmes.

Prevalence

It is not possible, on the basis of the present study, to estimate the prevalence of in-service training, though it is clearly a feature of the work of several OECD countries. An extensive and regularly offered national course in Iceland has involved some 10 per cent of teachers, and the 1991 professional development programme in the State of Victoria in Australia planned coverage of eight percent of schools, but these instances may be exceptional. Reports from Norway, Spain, the United Kingdom and the United States imply that in-service training is provided on a wide scale in these countries. Other countries mentioning that in-service training occurs include Belgium, Canada (New Brunswick), Greece, Ireland and the Netherlands.

Provision

Countries vary in the geographical scale on which in-service training in special education is organised. In the United States, a national clearing house and a computerised resource system enable teachers to locate research data relevant to special education. In Spain, the Ministry has set up a national network of teachers' centres, supported by and to some extent coordinated through the national special education resource centre. The regional centres provide some training of their own, facilitate training offered by other local providers and supplement courses initiated by universities. Similar arrangements exist in France. In Belgium, some of the in-service training is run through the adult education system. In Canada (New Brunswick) it is organised at provincial and school district levels.

In Italy, in addition to national and regional offerings, some of which are run by voluntary organisations, there are arrangements whereby individual schools can obtain funds to organize in-service courses for all their teachers. In the United Kingdom too, where much of the in-service training is organised at regional level, funds are often devolved to individual schools, where staff are encouraged to participate in defining their own training needs and in taking steps to meet them.

In the State of Victoria in Australia the Ministry has sought to support the realisation of its integration policy through a major professional development programme. This Inclusive School Integration (ISI) programme is designed to assist schools in developing and implementing a whole-school curriculum which ensures that all the children with special educational needs participate, learn and experience success. Seventy programme leaders have been trained; these include school support staff, representatives of parent organisations and others. A comprehensive evaluation of the implementation of the programme is taking place.

Range of course content appears to be broadly similar across OECD countries, though emphasis varies from one country to another. In France, many of the courses are designed to help teachers improve their knowledge of specific techniques, such as those of teaching sign language or Braille, though there are also more general courses for non-specialist teachers who are concerned with integration. In Iceland, a national course focuses on skills involved in teaching mixed ability classes. Some of the shorter special education courses in Norway are concerned with informatics and data processing.

Overview

Because teaching children of varying abilities is complex, in any country seriously intending to integrate a significant proportion of its children with special needs, there is an overwhelming case in favour of making some training for teaching these children an intrinsic part of initial training for all teachers. Among newly trained teachers, some awareness of special needs and some skill in differentiating the curriculum to make it suitable for children of varying abilities appear to be essential.

While special needs issues do not feature in all initial teacher training courses, the trend across OECD countries is clearly in favour of their inclusion. The proportion of initial teacher training that should be devoted to special needs varies from one country to another, depending for example on the extent of integration envisaged, on induction arrangements and support services available to new teachers, and on opportunities for in-service training.

For educators seeking to include appropriate coverage of special needs in initial teacher training, there are substantial difficulties to be overcome. Firstly, initial training curricula are already overloaded in some countries and special needs can only be included at the expense of something else. Secondly, there is a shortage of appropriate skills in the teacher training sector. Thirdly, many countries have different training arrangements for teachers of different age ranges. In particular, teachers of the upper secondary age range may have an ethos and expectations which pose a considerable challenge to introducing special needs issues.

While virtually all teachers have some experience of working with children with special needs, only a minority specialise in this field. Across OECD countries it is generally accepted that this specialisation requires training over and above that available to ordinary teachers, but the means through which this is acquired vary. These variations raise at least four basic questions.

Firstly, there is the question as to whether these specialists should first train and work as ordinary teachers. Often they do, and for most there are strong arguments that they should, particularly as the general trend is towards increased integration. However, there are also arrangements whereby some teachers can follow an initial training designed to equip them as special education specialists from the outset. This can be a valuable minority route, designed for those trainees with a strong early commitment to this field.

Secondly, there is the question as to whether advanced training should be available only to those already working in special education. While this experience is clearly advantageous, it may be hard to sustain as an imperative, particularly in countries seeking to increase the special needs support available to class teachers in ordinary schools.

Thirdly, there is the question as to whether all teachers working in special education should eventually complete advanced training. This is desirable but hard to achieve, and it would seem better for special educators to agree on the targets that appear to be realistic in their own countries.

Fourthly, there is the question as to the balance that there should be, in advanced training, between training for specific disabilities and more generic training geared to the requirements of integration. There has been a traditional approach to training for special educators, based on the assumptions that children with different disabilities require different teaching methods and that these children will be educated in segregated special schools. It would appear that a good deal of training is still provided in this way. If this is so, it constitutes a major challenge to those who would further the education of children with special needs in ordinary schools.

There are of course examples of teaching methods specific to disabilities, notably to hearing and visual impairment. Teachers need to be aware of these and some must be fully competent in the requisite skills. So, there is a role for elements of the traditional training. However, it is more generally the case that essentially the same repertoire of teaching methods is required, albeit at different levels, for children with different disabilities. More substantively, moves towards integration almost invariably require changes in teachers' attitudes, school policies and curriculum organisation. Training for those who will play a major role in integration programmes must not only enable them to translate their teaching specialisms into the ordinary school context but also equip them to be agents of change.

As many serving teachers do not have the attitudes, skills or understanding that effective integration requires, in-service training has a key role to play in any moves towards integration. The question arises as to whether schools should attempt to take on the education of children with special needs before they, the schools, are ready. If a principal reason for removing children from the ordinary school sector has been that their needs were not being met there, it makes little sense to return them unless substantial changes, notably through in-service training, have taken place.

But how much in-service training is necessary before integration commences? Integration is one kind of school reform and like all such reforms takes a lot of time. If schools wait until everything is ready nothing will ever happen, but equally each child's right to an appropriate situation must be safeguarded. It seems inescapable that integration moves should be preceded by, accompanied by and consolidated by training, with the type of in-service training on offer differing from one phase of innovation to the next.

While it is evident that in-service training is provided in many different ways across OECD countries, few reports referred to their in-service programmes as having been evaluated. Whether the concern be with effectiveness – securing the desired outcomes of training – or with efficiency – ensuring that the available training resources are used to best effect – high priority should be given to the systematic monitoring of training programmes. It looks as though in the majority of the OECD countries this has yet to be tackled.

Overall it is clear that there should be a continuum of training for teaching children with special needs, with some introduction for all teachers during initial training, followed up by in-service training, particularly as they are involved in integration programmes, and some form of advanced training for the minority of teachers seeking to specialise in this field. If these varieties of training are to combine to produce a coherent whole, then the people providing it should not be concerned exclusively with one type or another. Extensive co-operation between staff of academic institutions and those running special education support services in schools would appear to be an essential ingredient of an effective continuum of training.

Chapter 6

Parental Involvement

by

Harry Daniels, Don Labon and Mary Ann McGovern

Introduction

The phrase "parental involvement" is generally used, for example by Morgan and his colleagues (1992), to represent the ideally close working partnership through which parents and teachers can enhance their respective ways of helping the children for whom they share responsibilities. It acknowledges families' intimate knowledge of the children within them, teachers' experience of children in non-family settings, the overlap between parents" and teachers" skills, and the fact that parents and teachers have much to learn from each other.

The principle of "subsidiarity", whereby responsibilities and political decisions are best undertaken at the level of the smallest and most closely inter-related effective unit, is particularly relevant to issues of parental involvement. As children's closest relationships are generally found within family units, families bear the primary responsibilities for their support. Consequently, the roles of more powerful but more remote organisations such as public services can be regarded as subsidiary to those of parents.

Paradoxically, because parents in organised groups share such intimate concern, they are potentially well placed to engage in levels of international co-operation that more complex regional and national organisations have difficulty in achieving. Active members of parental organisations are not necessarily typical of parents more generally. Porter (1968), Baker and Stevenson (1986), and Lareau (1987), for example, have all demonstrated ways in which parents of higher socio-economic status engage more actively and more effectively in furthering their children's education.

The principle of "subsidiarity" is recognised in many OECD countries through formal representation of parents on the governing bodies of schools. Arrangements, however, across countries such as France, Germany, Italy, the United Kingdom and the United States, differ considerably. As Beattie (1985, 1987) pointed out in reporting international comparisons, parental representation does not guarantee parental participation.

In many countries parents have played an active role in the development of special education, sometimes by pressing for their children to attend special schools segregated according to disability, sometimes as proponents in the "normalisation" movement, whereby an increasing proportion of children with disabilities are being educated in ordinary schools. In these various developments parents have been active individually, as members of voluntary bodies concerned with particular disabilities, and as members of more broadly based civil rights organisations. Some national organisations concerned with disabilities, for example the German "Parents Against Separation" group described by Rosenberger (1988), have a significant number of members who are parents only of non-disabled children.

There is appreciable variation from one country to another in the extent to which parents have influenced integration practice. Denmark provides an example of parents' longstanding high involvement in developments. In the 1950s, following the government's invitation to parental organisations to participate in policy formation, parents were instrumental in securing changes which over the following decade resulted in increased educational provision for children with severe learning difficulties in ordinary schools and eventually to a transfer of responsibility for the education of these children from the Ministry of Social Affairs to the Ministry of Education.

Parents in other countries, such as Canada (New Brunswick), Norway, Spain, Sweden, the United Kingdom and the United States, have also been influential over many years in their countries' moves towards integration. As well as reflecting parents' wishes for their disabled children to participate as far as possible in normal living, their demand for integration stems from the belief that it helps reduce prejudice among ordinary people and enhances both educational progress and personal independence among the disabled.

Despite general moves towards integration, parents seeking integrated school placements for their own children can still experience considerable resistance. Evidence provided by a Danish parents' organisation, for example, referred to one outcome of increased integration there as being increased opposition to it among professionals. Muth (1988), surveying integration issues in Germany, found it common for parents seeking integrated placements for their children to have to meet quite formidable requirements. These included not only agreement of the school governing body and the district and regional education authorities, but also the unanimous consent of the parents of all the children in the receiving class.

Not all parents favour integration. The reports from Denmark, Ireland, the Netherlands and Norway, for example, referred to some parents as preferring segregated settings, and no doubt this is the case in other countries too. Reasons given included concern that disabled children may be lonely, neglected or victimised in integrated settings, that the ordinary children's learning may be impeded, and that ordinary schools may lack the staffing levels, expertise and material resources needed. More generally, they suspected that integration is being promoted as an economy measure rather than as a genuine means of improving the education of children with special needs.

There has in the past been evidence, reported by Hegarty and his colleagues (1981), that most parents who favoured segregation lacked direct experience of integrated programmes. However, this is not to say that such views should be dismissed out of hand.

Many of the reservations expressed by parents were with regard to children with severe disabilities, children who form only a small minority of those with special needs, and many professionals would agree that some children with severe disabilities might do better in a special school. Some of the reservations were expressed by parents of severely disabled children who were hardly manageable at home without some assistance and vacation relief, and for whom residential provision was often sought.

Reservations concerning integration were also expressed by parents of deaf children. Often they preferred their children initially to attend special schools specifically for the hearing impaired, to enable them to learn sign language and communicate with other similarly disabled children, and perhaps integrate into broader community activities at a later stage.

This chapter considers parents' involvement in the assessment and educational placement of their disabled children, their contribution to the children's day-to-day education, their response to educational programmes designed for them to implement, their support as the children mature and acquire adult status, their roles as advocates, and problems experienced. As well as drawing on OECD countries' reports, this chapter has made use of a comparative study, commissioned by CERI for this purpose, of parent groups advocating integration in Denmark, Germany and the United Kingdom.

Assessment

The extent to which parents are to be involved in the professional assessment and subsequent placement of their children is in some countries prescribed in legislation. In the United States, for example, since 1975, this has featured in Public Law 94-142, as amended in 1986 and 1990. As well as entitling children to multi-disciplinary assessment, an individualised education plan and placement in the most integrated setting thought suitable, the law stipulates that parents be consulted regarding the placement. If they object, they have a legal right to challenge the decision. Following placement, parents are also involved in the schools' periodic reviews of children's progress.

In several other OECD countries the position is similar. In the United Kingdom, following the recommendations of the Warnock Committee (DES, 1978) that parents should be involved as equal partners in the education of children with special needs, their active participation in multi-disciplinary assessment and their right of appeal in cases of dispute were written into the Education Act 1981.

In Belgium, parents sign an agreement which reflects their consent to the recommendations of the integration plan. Also they attend meetings where assessment is discussed and have frequent consultations with the teachers involved. In Denmark, parents must consent to every aspect of the integration plan before it is implemented and each year they are entitled to a re-evaluation of the plan. The report from France states that parents are involved in the creation of their children's curricula.

Despite some countries' firm commitment to partnership with parents, such evidence as there is regarding daily practice is less encouraging. Sonnenschein (1984) detailed the uneasy relationships that can exist between parents and professionals. Mittler (1990), referring to practice both in the United States and the United Kingdom, reported increasing evidence of a gap between rhetoric and reality. In a project commissioned by UNESCO (1988), responses indicated that many parents felt excluded from discussion and decision-making, particularly with regard to individualised educational programmes.

Various difficulties were reported. One was that laws were observed in such a way as to provide a symbolic reassurance of procedural fairness without enabling parents to affect the outcome of assessments. Another was professionals' use of technical jargon incomprehensible to lay people. Another was providing opportunity for parents to react to professionals' decisions but not to participate in the decision-making process. Professionals in different disciplines sometimes fail to consult fully between each other and may attempt to justify this by citing the need for confidentiality. In doing so, they may be going beyond the need to safeguard clients and be treating confidentiality as though it were an end in itself.

Provision

Parental involvement in the day-to-day provision of schools has been found, for example in the Northern Ireland study by Morgan *et al.* (1990), to take various forms. For convenience, these can be categorised as marginal, consultative, participative and managerial.

Marginal involvement is usually formalised and sometimes ritualistic, featuring in activities such as parent-teacher conferences, ''open house'' days and other parental visits to schools. School staff tend to speak to parents only in relation to the parents' own children. The business is largely to do with children's scholastic progress and, perhaps, ways in which parents can supplement teachers' efforts. In most countries with legislative provision for parents to be consulted regarding their children's placement the schools maintain ongoing involvement with parents at least at this level.

Consultative involvement is likely to be more frequent, more informal and more varied. Parents not only receive information and advice but also provide it. They talk of their children's interests as well as of their capabilities and they refer to their own attitudes and expectations. Meetings may take place at parents' homes, where they may feel more at ease, as well as at school. Discussion centres on ways in which home and school provision can best complement one another. Where appropriate, children as well as adults are included in the discussion. Good practice is likely to be characterised by a written account of any overall targets and educational programme agreed. Successive meetings include reviewing progress as well as planning further activities.

Participative involvement is also likely to be extensive and informal, though it may well occur within a structured framework. Parents are likely to work with teachers for the benefit of children in the school generally, not simply in relation to their own. They may serve on a Parents' Council, help teachers in the classroom, accompany children on school trips, and engage in fund-raising. For their work in the classroom to be effective, parents often require in-service training.

Not all parents feel comfortable with participative involvement, and it is common to some OECD countries only. The report from Greece mentions that parents are involved in children's social and sporting activities and that from France refers to parents' elected representatives as participating in the planning of school projects. In the United Kingdom at primary level it often happens that parents assist in classrooms. They may, for example, listen to individual children's reading or supervise small groups completing tasks set by teachers.

Managerial involvement requires the services of only a small proportion of parents, though a parent contributing to the management of a school is likely to be acting as a representative of the school's parents more generally. Because serving as a school manager can make many demands in terms of responsibility, time and particular skills, not all parents feel capable of undertaking it. It is, nevertheless, an important aspect of the running of schools and in some OECD countries is a legal requirement. Denmark, for example, has legislation stating that each school must have its own school board, consisting of approximately ten people, about six of whom are parents. Consequently, parents have the majority in making the overall decisions about the school.

Programmes

When parents participate in schools' classroom provision, whether in relation to their own children or to those of others, they are contributing to programmes chosen and supervised by the classroom teachers. Distinct from this kind of participation there are arrangements, more commonly at preschool stage but sometimes during the period of compulsory schooling, whereby parents implement their own programmes.

Several countries have their own preschool programmes designed for children with learning difficulties – France is but one example – but the most comprehensive and internationally disseminated of these is the Portage system. This was first developed in the United States in the early nineteen seventies and has since been adapted to meet the needs of many OECD countries. In recent years it has been extended for use in schools as well as in children's own homes.

Means through which parents are helped to use the programme at home are described by White and Cameron (1988). A trained home visitor and a parent (usually the mother, sometimes the father, occasionally both) engage the child in various activities. On the basis of these activities and of the parent's existing knowledge they jointly assess the child's skills in one or more of various areas, choosing skills set out in developmental checklists covering self-help, socialisation, language, cognition and movement.

The parent and visitor then decide together on short-term teaching targets. The visitor demonstrates the teaching methods and activities but the parent does the teaching. The parent records the child's progress on activity charts. Subsequent visits help the parent to review progress and decide on further activities. Volunteers, parents and a variety of professionals have been trained to be home visitors. Strengths of the programme include involvement and support for the family, but confining training to the home environment may limit more extended social contact for the child.

Most of the other programmes developed for use by parents at home or at school are concerned with the development of spoken or written language. As with Portage, care must be taken to utilize these programmes only with parents who are comfortable with a structured teaching role and who have whatever support they may need to function effectively.

Transition

Reports refer to ways in which parents have enabled adolescents with special needs to become more independent and set realistic goals for adulthood. Some parents, in the United States for example, have been instrumental in helping to establish work opportunities and group homes for students with learning disabilities who have not been able to continue their education in the secondary school. Others have lobbied successfully for policies that promote the hiring of disabled people more generally. As a result, some young disabled people have been able to find satisfying placements in workshops or other business environments.

Such placements offer young disabled people earned income as opposed to welfare money, enhance their self-esteem and enable them to increase their social contacts with non-disabled peers. A number of these young people are living in group homes, some of which may be under the supervision of "adult parents" from the community. While sheltered workshops and group homes may perpetuate a certain amount of isolation from the community at large, they offer opportunities for a degree of independent living that would be unlikely in large residential establishments.

Advocacy

Reports from Australia, Belgium, Canada (New Brunswick), Greece, Iceland, the Netherlands, Norway, Spain and the United States testify to the fact that many parents continue to be very active in lobbying for increased services for children with disabilities. Often it is the parents who force ordinary schools to implement already existing legislation in providing integrative programmes in such diverse curriculum areas as physical education, the performing arts, social development and community involvement.

In the United States, parents have established communication networks, both orally and in writing, to keep other parents informed about educational provision and material resources that exist within the community for people with disabilities and their families. These might include school or community educational programmes, social gatherings, sporting facilities or child-minding services.

Parents in some countries form groups that meet on a regular basis to provide support for one another and to discuss possible ideas for ameliorating the situation for children with disabilities. They sit on community planning boards to become better informed about community resources. They become involved in efforts to educate members of the community about disabilities and to promote their awareness of the rights of disabled people. This type of involvement allows parents opportunities not only to effect policy at local and national levels but also to influence procedural guidelines and perhaps ensure that there are means of monitoring them.

Reports from Canada (New Brunswick), Norway and the United States refer to parental participation in public hearings and regional advisory panels for the education of disabled children. In Norway, parents' participation in public events and their media representations has influenced recent political decisions in this field. In Iceland, similarly, parent groups were influential in the preparation of the Handicapped Act which was passed in 1983. Parents in Australia, Belgium, and Greece have also organised and lobbied to gain rights for people with disabilities.

Problems

While there are numerous examples of co-operation between parents and professionals, their perceptions of the children and their goals for them almost invariably differ to some extent. Because of this their relationships often have to bear a certain amount of tension. As Hegarty (1992) points out, the teacher who is concerned with providing expertise to a number of children has a professional involvement, while the parent whose focus is solely on one child has an emotional and personal involvement.

Teachers may feel that because parents are not professionals they cannot have the expertise to tell teachers how their children's special educational needs might be met. Mittler (1990) refers to teachers as sometimes devaluing active parental involvement, preferring their role to be one of benign passivity. If parents make demands of teachers, no doubt some teachers fear that their control of their own school territory is threatened and react accordingly.

Presumably, if polarisation is to be avoided, parents and teachers must get to understand each other as people rather than just as members of particular interest groups. Some of the complexities inherent in parental involvement can be considered in teacher training courses, perhaps through links with courses in social work or medicine. Mittler (1990) offers various suggestions, including opening professional workshops to parents and inviting parents to hold question and answer sessions with groups of teachers in training.

Overview

Across OECD countries, parental involvement has undoubtedly been a driving force in the development of special education. With regard to the majority of children with special needs, the force is in favour of integration, though this is not necessarily so where children's disabilities are severe. Parents' rights to be treated as partners in the assessment and educational placement of their children are recognised in some countries, though in practice professionals do not always ensure that these rights are respected.

The rights, needs and preferences of professionals, parents and children do not necessarily converge. Consequently, administrators contemplating changes to special education provision within their own countries may well wish to consider the balance they wish to achieve.

The extent of parental involvement in special educational provision varies considerably, ranging from token contact to full participation in classroom teaching and in school management. Given the fact that their participation can be highly influential for the good, and given the challenge of within-class differentiation outlined in Chapter 4 (Part I), their more extensive involvement in the work of schools should be welcomed. In tackling the technical and attitudinal difficulties to be overcome in achieving this, teacher training can play an important part.

Inevitably, given their differing priorities, there are tensions between administrators, teachers and parents, particularly when one or other group is seeking change. Such tensions can be minimized if professionals contemplating innovation consult with parent groups at the outset and if they respond constructively to parents' initiatives.

Chapter 7

Resources

by

Seamus Hegarty

Introduction

Even though integration can be beneficial, and even if it can be implemented effectively, its value can only be assessed if it is also considered in terms of its financial costs. So it is important to compare the costs of educating children with special needs in integrated settings with the costs of educating them in special classes and special schools. Such comparisons are possible but they are extremely difficult to make, partly because of the difficulties of identifying comparable groups of children, partly because of the complexities of funding arrangements in different countries.

This chapter considers comparative costs, outlines variations in countries' ways of allocating funding and takes up the point that some methods of allocating funding are more conducive to integration than others.

Costs

Children with special needs, irrespective of whether they are in integrated or segregated settings, cost more to educate than do ordinary children. In the United States in 1985-86, for example, the average per-child cost of special education was 2.3 times that of ordinary education, with costs for different disabilities ranging from 1.9 times to 10.6 times (Moore *et al.*, 1988). In the Netherlands in 1989, a child receiving special education cost in aggregate about four times as much to educate as an ordinary child in an ordinary school. Costs ranged from seven times as much for children with severe and multiple disabilities to two and a half times as much for those with moderate learning difficulties. These figures are not necessarily representative of OECD countries as a whole, but at least they provide some indication.

The present study provides no definitive answer to the question as to whether educating particular children with special needs costs more or less in an integrated system, although reports from two countries claim in broad terms that it is more economical. A response from Australia stated that "it is generally agreed that the education of a disabled student is less resource intensive in an integrated setting as compared to enrolment in a segregated centre"; the response from Ireland stated that "it is generally less costly to educate a disabled child in an integrated setting".

The general tenor of these responses supports the more specific findings of an earlier CERI study (OECD, 1994) in which responses from Australia, Denmark, Italy, Spain and the United States provided average annual costs per child in ordinary school education, in special schools, and for children with special needs in integrated settings. As a multiple of the unit cost of an ordinary child in an elementary school, the average cost of a special school placement ranged from four to fifteen times as much, whereas for an integrated placement it was only between two and four times as much. Special school placements cost between two and five times those in integrated settings.

Great care should be taken in interpreting these figures. Children in special schools are likely to have more severe and complex needs than those in integrated placements, and the demands they place on support services are consequently greater. Moreover, methods of calculating infrastructure and support costs of maintaining children in special schools may well differ from those in integrated settings. With the present state of knowledge these factors conspire to make global comparisons very difficult to make.

Allocation

Member countries of the OECD differ considerably in their methods of allocating funds for special education. The reasons for these differences, and their effects on the education of children with special needs, are not altogether clear. In the Netherlands, for example, ordinary and special education come under separate systems, whereas in the New Brunswick Province of Canada and in Norway they come under one.

The systems of financing ordinary and special education are likely to be separate in countries where education is funded partly at national level and partly at regional or district level. In Finland, where this applies, the government pays 70 per cent of education costs for most children but 86 per cent for some children with severe disabilities. In Iceland funding for special schools comes directly from the state while funds for SEN in ordinary schools, which also are provided by the state, is managed by the districts. In the Netherlands, where both ordinary and special education are financed nationally, there is in addition a national contribution to each district of 50 per cent of the cost of school counselling.

Irrespective of whether funds are allocated nationally, regionally or locally, at school level there is a range of possibilities whereby different amounts can be allowed for the different kinds of children on roll. At one extreme, the money can simply reflect the number on roll and the age distribution, allowing for the fact that it is assumed to be more expensive to educate students in the secondary phase than children in the primary phase. It implies that those with special needs are distributed evenly across schools, and this of course is not the case. Even in large schools it cannot allow for individuals with relatively rare disabilities that might make their appropriate education exceptionally expensive.

At the other extreme an extra allowance can be calculated for each individual with special needs. This should in theory match resources exactly to need, but it is exceedingly time-consuming and, even if feasible, the costs of its administration could well offset its advantages. A middle approach would be to make different allowances for different groups of special need.

While it is probably the case that most countries represent neither extreme, responses did not permit any precise analysis of methods for allocating funds at school level. For most countries, the information may well be inaccessible. It seems very likely, for example, that there are within-country variations to contend with. Moreover, the make-up of budgets allocated to schools may itself be complex; for example, money for buildings, equipment and staffing may come from different sources.

In the New Brunswick Province of Canada, funding is based on a block formula that assumes a given percentage of children with special needs, but there are exceptions under certain circumstances. Schools in the United Kingdom, similarly, receive core funding for children with special needs but also receive additional funding, on an individual basis in some cases, for those with statements under the Education Act 1981.

Unless allocation of resources makes due allowance for particular economic and geographical conditions, those with special needs may be penalised more than most. In a country such as Iceland, for example, special education support services and associated resources that can be shared by schools are only likely to exist in the major cities. The schools scattered through the surrounding sparsely populated rural areas are mainly very small. In such a school, it is very difficult for the teachers, dealing with an extremely wide spread of age as well as of ability, to meet individual special needs.

Whatever the arrangements for allocating funds to special education, there is the consideration as to whether the total allocated is sufficient for its purposes. Responses from many OECD countries, as different from one another as Canada, Iceland, the Netherlands and Norway, indicated that it is not. Shortages in money for human and for material resources were described.

Underfunding was reported to affect personnel such as teachers needing time to plan programmes as well as to teach them, teachers requiring in-service training, teachers to stand in for those temporarily absent while being trained, teacher trainers, and support service staff. Equipment referred to as being insufficient included sound amplifiers, computers and other technological aids. Adaptation of school buildings and classrooms to ensure that disabled children can have access to them was also identified as a problem.

Integration

The question arises as to which methods of allocating funding might best help or hinder integration.

At national level, the Netherlands system finances ordinary and special education separately, with substantially more money per head for children in special schools than for the same children in ordinary schools. This has left ordinary schools with few incentives to educate children with special needs and has made it attractive for special schools to take them on. This is changing: under certain conditions, a child returning from special to ordinary school can have some financial support and some extra help from a peripatetic teacher coming in periodically from the special school.

In Ireland, many of the special schools and associated services for disabled children are run by voluntary organisations. The funds raised by these organisations are then likely to be used to maintain the children in special schools rather than to encourage integrative programmes. In Norway, the national funding system may have a slight bias in favour of residential placements.

At ordinary school level, the extreme of allocating money per child regardless of educational need would clearly discourage heads of ordinary schools from taking on children with special needs. Whether or not the various methods of making an extra allocation for special needs provide schools with an incentive to integrate must depend to some extent on the size of the allowance. Moreover, if the allowance is not sensitive to different groups of children with special needs, heads of ordinary schools may only be encouraged to keep those children whose disabilities are minor. In any case, unless the allowance is linked with integration it may encourage heads to keep children with special needs in ordinary schools but place them in special classes.

In some countries there are districts in which the administrators have linked allocation of resources to children's achievements, thus providing incentive bonuses to schools with a high proportion of high achievers. Unless assessment takes account of the children's achievements on entry to the school and bases the bonuses on progress made thereafter, the arrangement inevitably discourages heads from taking on children with learning difficulties.

In several countries, there have been recent moves towards decentralisation of finances, with the bulk of the funding allocated directly to the schools, and this has the advantage of encouraging schools to look after their own affairs. One reported effect, however, has been the difficulty in financing those special education support services, counselling and advisory services for example, that can only be organised effectively at district or regional level rather than at school level.

Overview

While comparative costs of integrated and segregated special education are extremely difficult to estimate, such evidence as there is points consistently in the same direction. It appears that, for the vast majority of children with special needs, education in integrated settings is not inordinately costly and is in any case less expensive than their placement in special schools. Integration can be helped or hindered by methods of allocating funding. For example, funding to ordinary schools can be linked to integration programmes, can include realistic additional elements to allow for the extra costs of educating children with special needs, and can be sensitive to different levels of special need.

Chapter 8

Prospects

by

Peter Evans and Don Labon

Introduction

Over the past 30 years the trend across OECD countries has been to educate an increasing proportion of disabled children in ordinary schools. Research evidence has endorsed the benefits of integration, and countries' present policies favour a continuation of this trend. While there is a strong consensus with regard to pro-integrationist principles, however, practice across countries varies considerably.

In some countries the implementation of policies has been strengthened considerably through legislation, and these countries can provide many examples of success in educating children with special needs on an integrated basis in ordinary classes in ordinary schools. In these countries the main challenge is to develop the curriculum in such a way as to ensure that it can be made suitable for children across the full range of ability. In other countries the over-riding priority is to devise constructive means of reducing significantly the number of children educated in special schools.

In any one country, the extent to which integration is feasible depends to some extent on the ways in which education is organised generally. Countries differ considerably here, and within a single country there can be variations from one region to another. In some areas, for example, each secondary school provides comprehensively for children of a very wide range of ability, whereas in other areas some of the secondary schools are selective, providing only for the most able.

Other important variables influencing the feasibility of integration include the extent to which it has the support of parents and teachers, the extent to which teachers have the necessary skills and the extent to which administrators provide the necessary funding.

So, for each country, and perhaps for each region within a country, there is a unique combination of integration practice and prospects for further integration. It appears, though, that there is as yet no country in which that country's integration policy has been implemented completely.

This being the case, it is appropriate for each country to have a plan for further development. While it is for politicians and educators to design their own plans, relevant to their own countries' unique circumstances, the findings of this CERI study do point to at least some of the key features which any integration plan, whether it is at the level of a country, a region or a district, can usefully exhibit. These features are presented below in broadly, though not necessarily exactly, the chronological sequence in which they would be likely to be implemented in a typical integration programme.

A framework for planning

Identification

Basic to any country's development plan must be identification of the population under consideration and recognition of the educational provision currently available to it. While the Warnock Committee (DES, 1978) provided a useful delineation of the broader group of children with special educational needs as constituting some one sixth of the child population at any one time, in all member countries of the OECD the vast majority of children with special needs are already being educated in ordinary classes in ordinary schools. The focus for further integration, therefore, is likely to be on much smaller groups.

In the absence of an internationally agreed classification system, each country is likely to continue with its own sets of definitions of disability. In fact, different countries' definitions overlap considerably and in any case countries' records show the percentages of children educated in special classes and in different types of special school. Whatever the definitions, for many countries the focus groups must be among these children, or among their more recently born counterparts.

In some two thirds of the countries contributing to the present study, fewer than 2 per cent of children were said to be attending special schools, with a range from below 0.5 per cent to almost 5 per cent. For special classes in ordinary schools the reported range was much narrower, running from zero to about 1 per cent. Within a given country or area within a country, examination of this type of statistic should help preliminary decisions to be made as to which children warrant detailed consideration for further integration.

Consultation

Parents of disabled children, special education teachers, teachers in ordinary schools and staff of support services (both within and outside education) are clearly groups with whom early consultation should be undertaken, perhaps following some preliminary identification of the children concerned. In many countries, parents have in fact been prime movers of integration, and may already be organised into pressure groups. Not all parents, however, favour integration for their disabled children, and country reports mentioned some parents of deaf children and of those with severe learning difficulties as preferring special schooling for at least part of the children's time.

While there are clear arguments in favour of at least some consultation with groups representing a mixture of interests, these interests differ sufficiently to justify separate consideration as well. Within the teaching profession, for example, the attitudes and self-concepts of primary phase and secondary phase teachers may well differ, and the form which further integration takes will inevitably change from one phase to the other.

Assessment of existing strengths

It is clear that a key feature of successful integration is the skill of the class teacher in differentiating the curriculum; in presenting that which is to be learnt in such a way as to ensure that it makes sense to children of differing abilities. Consequently, an important part of any preliminary planning for integration must be some assessment of the extent to which ordinary school class teachers likely to be affected can do this already.

This assessment may also need to take account of the work of teachers in special schools. This is particularly the case if they are likely to shift into either teaching or supporting teaching in ordinary schools, as the knowledge and skills required there are not the same as those involved in teaching children with similar disabilities in special schools. Similar considerations may apply to staff of special education support services, including those employed by health or social work agencies.

Assessment also needs to take account of existing arrangements for teacher training, particularly in view of their strong implications for long term strategies for integration. For example, only some initial training courses for teachers intending to work in ordinary schools include consideration of children with special needs.

Target setting

Initial mapping of provision, supplemented by some preliminary consultation, will probably yield sufficient information to enable provisional targets to be set. Statistics gathered during the study suggest that for several countries the main target could be to increase the proportion of children educated in ordinary schools. For example, a country's main target could be to educate 99 per cent of its children in ordinary schools by 1999. Decisions about the time scale will no doubt be as important as those concerning the nature of the objectives.

For about half the participant countries, already with fewer than 1 per cent of their children attending special schools, the main target population for further integration may be children in special classes in ordinary schools. In this context, a working definition of full and effective integration into ordinary classes is necessary. Quality of teaching and of learning are clearly important features of such a definition, despite the fact that they can be difficult to measure. In situational terms, a criterion for full integration quoted as having been found useful is that of the child being taught in an ordinary class for at least 79 per cent of total lesson time.

In some countries, particularly in those in which relatively few children with special needs are taught outside ordinary classes, the main targets may be expressed in terms of ordinary class teachers' qualifications and skills, or in terms of the disabled children's achievements.

Implementation

Awareness raising is well recognised by those reporting integration programmes as constituting a crucial early phase in implementation. The emphasis is usually on reducing prejudices, unrealistic anxieties, and preoccupation with disabilities rather than with learning potential. The people involved include not only the parents and the teachers of disabled children, but also other teachers and parents concerned with the schools in which further integration is to occur.

It was reported that even in countries where integration programmes had been completed and success demonstrated, some members of the community continued to be sceptical. This indicates that anticipating expressions of negative attitude and reacting constructively to them have to be continuing characteristics of integration programmes, not just features required at the outset.

The training of teachers, usually on an in-service basis, is also well recognised as an essential feature of any integration programme. As curriculum differentiation is a necessary aspect of teaching in integrated settings, and as it requires high levels of skill, it is inevitably a key element. As with awareness raising, training is not simply a precursor to integration. Training can usefully precede, accompany and help to consolidate the introduction of children with special needs into ordinary schools. Training is also likely to be required for staff of support services and for those involved in supervising, monitoring and evaluating integration programmes.

One outcome of reported integration programmes has been a continuum of provision, whereby, should they become necessary, increasingly specialised learning programmes and increasing levels of support from specialist teachers can be made available to class teachers. This model has been strongly endorsed by educationalists in those countries in which it has been established. Unless support of this kind is made available it may be unrealistic to expect class teachers generally to persevere with integration programmes.

A successfully implemented integration programme may well result in a reduced special school population. If this is likely to be the case, dealing constructively with special school staff, the children still there and the material resources released need to be considered from the outset. In some countries, such schools have become specialist resource centres and bases for support services.

Evaluation

If planners are to assess the extent to which their integration programmes are successful, and if they are to understand the reasons for whatever is achieved, they need to invest time and expertise in monitoring processes and evaluating outcomes, making use both of short term and of long term evaluation strategies. Evaluation is likely to take account of all the main features of the programme, though this does not have to be the case. For example, in countries where there is already substantial experience of successful evaluation, uncertainties may be confined to specific issues.

Country reports indicated that in-service teacher training is an activity which is not generally evaluated, though it is not clear as to whether this is also a weakness of training contributing specifically to integration programmes. It suggests, though, that teacher training may be particularly difficult to evaluate.

Resourcing

Plans for integration programmes invariably include forecasts as to their resource requirements, and these are likely to include estimated costs of features such as making preliminary assessments, adapting buildings to ensure physical access for the disabled, providing training, and evaluating outcomes. These costs need to be set against anticipated savings, which may be appreciable if the resources freed through the reduced usage of segregated provision are managed constructively.

The findings of the study indicate that for the vast majority of children with special needs the costs of integrated provision are considerably less than those of segregated education. The financial benefits, however, may only appear eventually, as the new arrangements have to be set in place before the old ones can be altered; plans, therefore, need to be costed over a fairly long time scale.

References

BAKER, D.P. and STEVENSON, D.L. (1986), "Mothers' strategies for children's school achievement: managing the transition to high school", *Sociology of Education*, 59, pp. 156-166.

BEATTIE, N. (1985), *Professional Parents: Parent Participation in Four Western European Countries*, London and Philadelphia, Falmer Press.

BEATTIE, N. (1987), "Parents as a New Found Land: reflections on formal parent participation in five policies", paper presented to the Annual Meeting of the American Educational Research Association, San Francisco.

CANEVARO, A. *et al.* (1985), *Handbook for Integration*, Florence, La Nuova Italia.

DEPARTMENT OF EDUCATION (1992), *Statistics of Schools in England*, London, Her Majesty's Stationary Office (HMSO).

DEPARTMENT OF EDUCATION & SCIENCE (1978), *Special Educational Needs*, The Warnock Report, London, HMSO.

EVANS, P. (Ed) (1993), *European Journal of Special Needs Education. Special Edition on Integration*, 8(3).

GAYLORD-ROSS, R. (1987), "School integration for students with mental handicaps: a cross-cultural perspective", *European Journal of Special Needs Education*, 2(2), pp. 117-129.

HEGARTY, S. (1992), "Home-school relations: a perspective from special education", in Munn, P. (Ed.), *Parents and Schools: Customers, Managers or Partners?*, London, Routledge.

HEGARTY, S. and POCKLINGTON, K., with LUCAS, D. (1981), *Educating Pupils with Special Needs in the Ordinary School*, Windsor, NFER-Nelson.

LAREAU, A. (1987), "Social class differences in family-school relationships: the importance of cultural capital", *Sociology of Education*, 60, pp. 73-85.

MITTLER, P. (1990), "Prospects for disabled children and their families: an international perspective", *Disability, Handicap and Society*, 5(1), pp. 53-64.

MOORE, M.T., STRANG, E.W., SCHWARTZ, M., and BRADDOCK, M. (1988), *Patterns in Special Education Delivery and Cost*, Washington, DC.

MORGAN, V., FRASER, G., DUNN, S., and CAIRNS, E. (1992), "Parental involvement in education: how do parents want to become involved?", *Educational Studies*, 18(1), pp. 11-20.

MUTH, J. (1988), " Integration und gesellschaftliche Wertvorstellungen", in Zah, K. (Ed.), *Treffen deb undersarbeitsgemeinschaft eltern gegen aussonderung von kindern mit behinderugen*, Reutlingen.

OECD (1994), *The Integration of Disabled Children into Mainstreams Education: Ambitions, Theories and Practices*, Paris.

PORTER, J. (1968), "The future of upward mobility", *American Sociological Review*, 33, pp. 5-19.

ROSENBERGER, M. (Ed.) (1988), *Ratgeber gegen aussonderung*, Heidelberg, Edition Schindele.

SCHEERENBEGER, R.C. (1987), *A History of Mental Retardation: A Quarter Century of Progress*, Baltimore, Brookes.

SONNENSCHEIN, P. (1984), "Parents and professionals: an uneasy relationship", in Henninger, M.I. and Nesselroad, E.M. (Eds.), *Working with Parents of Handicapped Children: A Book of Readings for School Personnel*, Lanaham, University Press of America.

RUTTER, M., TIZARD, J. and WHITMORE, K. (Eds.) (1970), *Education, Health and Behaviour*, London, Longmans Green.

UNESCO (1988), *Review of the Present Situation of Special Education*, Paris.

WHITE, M., and CAMERON, R. (Eds.) (1988), *Portage: Progress, Problems, and Possibilities*, Windsor, NFER, Nelson.

WOLFENSBERGER, W. (1972), *Normalisation: The Principle of Normalisation in Human Services*, Toronto, National Institute on Mental Retardation.

WORLD HEALTH ORGANISATION (1980), *International Classification of Impairments, Disabilities, and Handicaps*, Geneva.

Appendix

Case studies

by

Peter Evans, Don Labon, Ingrid Lunt and Mary Ann McGovern

The appendices consist of brief accounts, on a country by country basis, of policies and population statistics relating to special educational needs. In each case, the country's own terminology is used for describing special educational needs, type of provision, and location.

While all 21 countries eventually joining the project are represented, the quantity of data for each country varies, partly in accordance with the different amounts of information available, partly because of differing methods of data collection. For example, only a limited amount of information is included concerning countries entering the project more recently.

Tables provide statistics as supplied by Member countries. Those labelled *a)* summarise information on the placement of children with different disabilities. Those labelled *b)* have been assembled in a common form and present numbers of children with specific disabilities, both as percentages of the population recognised in that country as having special educational needs, and as percentages of the total school population.

1. Australia

The Federal Government, through its Department of Employment, Education and Training, provides a special education programme which aims to improve the educational participation and outcomes for young people with disabilities by assisting government and non-government schools, organisations and parent groups to develop, implement and evaluate appropriate programmes. As the development of special education in Australia has been the responsibility of the State governments and non-government education authorities, rather than the Federal Government, State policies vary in detail, though all are supportive of integration. For example, in Victoria a review of education in 1984 produced a report which laid down 6 principles of integration:

1. Every child has the right to be educated in a regular school.
2. Provision to be organised on the basis of student needs rather than categories of disability.
3. Resources and services should be school-based.
4. Decision-making should be collaborative.
5. All children can learn and be taught.
6. Integration is a curriculum issue.

The total school population in Australia in 1990 was 3 341 657 and 5.22 per cent had SEN. 19 124 pupils, which represents 0.57 per cent of all school children were in special schools. Each state in Australia has its own system of education and policies vary between states. Statistics are collected on a variety of issues dealing with students with disabilities with each state applying its own categorisation criteria to its data collection. The following table shows the numbers and percentages of children with special educational needs in special schools, schools at establishments, special classes and ordinary classes for Australia as a whole. As can be seen from the table below, most pupils with special educational needs are educated in ordinary schools. The data in the table are based on figures from 1988 when the total school population was 3 336 957 pupils. The total of 22 200 pupils in special schools and 900 in schools at establishments represents 0.63 per cent of the total school population for that year. The total of 31 300 pupils in special classes represent 0.92 per cent of the total school population. In 1988, therefore, 1.55 per cent of pupils were educated in some form of segregated provision.

Table A.1*a*. **Placement of pupils (5-20 years) with special needs,[1] 1988**

Special need	Ordinary class	Special class	Special school	School at establishment[2]	Total pupils with SEN
Mental disorders	7 300 74.49%	2 200 22.45%	200 2.04%	100 1.02%	9 800 100%
Mental retardation	11 200 27.52%	16 500 40.54%	12 400 30.47%	600 1.47%	40 700 100%
Sight loss	4 300 84.31%	500 9.80%	300 5.88%	– 0.9%	5 100 100%
Hearing loss	15 200 80.00%	2 700 14.21%	1 100 5.79%	– 0.2%	19 000 100%
Nervous system diseases	14 700 63.91%	3 100 13.48%	4 800 20.87%	400 1.74%	23 000 100%
Circulatory diseases	1 700 80.95%	400 19.05%	–	–	2 100 100%
Respiratory diseases	31 700 92.42%	2 100 6.12%	500 1.46%	–	34 300 100%
Diseases of the musculo-skeletal system	11 600 98.31%	200 1.69%	–	–	11 800 100%
Other	22 200 77.35%	3 600 12.54%	2 900 10.10%	–	28 700 100%
Total	119 900 68.71%	31 300 17.94%	22 200 12.72%	1 100 0.63%	174 500 100%

Note: These statistics are collected by the Australian Board of Statistics (ABS) using the ''International Classification of Impairments, Disabilities and Handicaps'' as published by the World Health Organisation. They do not reflect the same classification schema used by each of the Australian States and Territories.
1. Pupils with a condition which has both a physical and mental component are counted within both categories in the table, although they are included only once in the total.
2. The word ''establishment'' in this context relates to the concept of institutions such as corporate institutions, hospitals, etc., *i.e.* places where school education may be provided, but where this is not the main objective of the respective environment.

Table A.1*b*. **Pupils (5-20 years) with special needs[1] by disability and as a percentage of total school population, 1988**

Special need	Total	% of pupils with SEN	% of total school population
Mental disorders	9 800	5.62	0.29
Mental retardation	40 700	23.32	1.22
Sight loss	5 100	2.92	0.15
Hearing loss	19 000	10.89	0.57
Nervous system diseases	23 000	13.18	0.69
Circulatory diseases	2 100	1.20	0.06
Respiratory diseases	34 300	19.66	1.03
Diseases of the musculo-skeletal system	11 800	6.76	0.35
Other	28 700	16.45	0.86
Total	174 500	100.00	5.22

Note: As this classification system is more general than the others, it is not possible to accurately break these categories down to fit all the categories in Tables 3.4 and 3.5. Hence there is a large ''other'' category.
1. Pupils with a condition which has both a physical and mental component are counted within both categories in the table, although they are included only once in the total.

2. Austria

In Austria, there has been a long tradition of developing a differentiated school system, with a number of types of school catering for different abilities and aptitudes. Special schools have been part of this tradition and at present there exist eleven types of special school, catering for a range of special educational needs. There are also a small number of children for whom schools cannot provide and who are provided for by the socio-medical services. It has been a highly segregated system.

Integrated schooling is a relatively new phenomenon and is being introduced by means of pilot projects linking special and ordinary schools. The impetus for this change came from professionals and parents, leading in 1988 to an amendment to the 1962 School Organisation Act and providing for pilot projects in integration at all levels of compulsory schooling. These pilot studies are being evaluated by the local education authorities in each area. Pilot studies of integration referred to the freedom for developing different curricula and teaching methods in schools with pilot projects. On September 1 1993 new amendments to the School Organisation Act came into force. These amendments allowed for improved co-operation between special schools and primary schools and adjustments to be made in class size where disabled pupils are present. Special schools are to be charged with the task of co-ordinating measures at regional level to ensure quality and the involvement of parents. Under the new arrangements schools must determine that there is a need for special education (in contrast to the earlier demand of special school attendance) and schools must make every effort to use the available school based arrangements to meet these needs. Parents' wishes must be fully taken into account by the District School Board in determining provision.

The total school population in Austria in 1991 has approximately 718 000, of which about 360 00 (50.14 per cent) are in primary school, around 340 000 (47.35 per cent) are in secondary school and about 18 000 (2.55 per cent) are in special school. There are 330 special schools with 2 500 classes. 2.55 per cent of the population has been classified as having SEN.

The integrative programmes currently being evaluated include 260 integrative classes, 30 co-operating classes, 35 small classes, and approximately 3 000 students in ordinary classes supported by ambulant special teachers. This accounts for approximately 4 285 students (0.60 per cent) of the total school population. The distribution between the different kinds of disabilities in special schools is shown in the following table.

Table A.2a. **Pupils (6-14 years) in special schools, 1991**

Special need	Number of pupils	% of pupils with SEN
Learning disabilities	11 934	66.30
Speech difficulties	576	3.20
Hearing impairment	144	0.80
Deaf children	378	2.10
Visual impairment	126	0.70
Blind children	54	0.30
Emotional/behavior difficulty	504	2.80
Physically handicapped	450	2.50
Mentally retarded	2 736	15.20
Severe sensory/mentally retarded	270	1.50
Schools in hospitals/clinics	828	4.60
Total	18 000	100.00

Table A.2b. **Pupils (6-14 years) with special needs by disability and as a percentage of total school population, 1991**

Special need	Number of pupils	% of pupils with SEN	% of total school population
Learning disabilities	11 934	66.3	1.66
Speech difficulties	576	3.2	0.08
Hearing impairment	144	0.8	0.02
Deaf children	378	2.1	0.05
Visual impairment	126	0.7	0.02
Blind children	54	0.3	0.01
Emotional/behavior difficulty	504	2.8	0.07
Physically handicapped	450	2.5	0.06
Mentally retarded	2 736	15.2	0.38
Severe sensory/mentally retarded	270	1.5	0.04
Schools in hospitals/clinics	828	4.6	0.16
Total	18 000	100.00	2.55

3. Belgium

An Act of 1914, which set up compulsory education in Belgium, stated that special classes should be provided in larger schools for pupils who were "poorly-gifted" or "abnormal". This, and subsequent legislation in 1924, 1931 and 1959, led to the development of a system of special classes based in ordinary schools. In 1970 an Act was passed which formed the basis for the present system. It identified three populations of children with special educational needs:

- children who could not meet the requirements of regular teaching;
- children with visual or hearing impairment, traditionally educated in special institutes;
- children with severe mental or physical handicap, who, up to then, had not attended school.

The 1970 Act had two basic principles:

- that as a general rule a child would attend a regular classroom and that attendance at a special school should represent an "exception" and should be justified by a professional assessment;
- that special education should be organised into eight types, or pedagogical settings, designed to provide the most appropriate response to particular needs.

The 1970 Act led to the closing down of all kinds of special classrooms located in ordinary schools and the setting up of a system of autonomous schools. There are very few links between ordinary and special schools. Integration into the mainstream of society is seen as the aim of education and a substantial proportion (at least 66 per cent) of children in special schools have the opportunity to gain qualifications and join the open labour market. There is a debate about integration which at present it is conducted mainly by professionals at the level of the school. There is some legislation but apparently little promotion at government level of the issue of integration.

The 1970 Act, modified in 1986, allows a child at a special school to attend an ordinary school on a full-time or part-time basis. In the Flemish education system, this is available for pupils with hearing and visual impairment. In both communities the integration figures are twice as high at pre-primary and primary level as at secondary level.

In the French community there have been some initiatives to set up special classrooms in ordinary schools, but the authorities generally dislike this arrangement, arguing that it is too much like the situation which prevailed before 1970, when generally poor quality education was offered to children with special educational needs in classes based in ordinary schools. The present system of separate schools was set up to overcome this problem.

The total school population in 1988/89 was 1 948 163 children. Of these, 59 914 (3.08 per cent) are in the eight types of special schools that are organised in Belgium. The proportions attending the different types of schools vary between the French and the Flemish communities. The table below gives the breakdown of pupils in the eight different types of school existing in the French and the Flemish communities. It should be noted that specific learning disabilities encompasses speech and language difficulties. At the secondary level, most children with specific learning disabilities transfer to ordinary school; a smaller number transfer to type 1 special school (for children with light mental deficiency)

Table A.3a. **Pupils in special schools, 1988/89**

Special need	Pre-primary		Primary		Secondary		Total and % of SEN population
	French	Flemish	French	Flemish	French	Flemish	
Light mental deficiency	nil	nil	2 755 (23.9%)	7 547 (44.1%)	8 119 (57.8%)	10 020 (66.2%)	* 28 441 (47.5)
Moderate/severe mental deficiency	204 (27.6%)	557 (41.6%)	1 286 (11.2%)	2 093 (12.2%)	2 233 (15.9%)	3 030 (20.0%)	* 9 403 (15.7)
Emotionally disturbed/ Autistic	45 (6.1%)	94 (7.0%)	1 379 (12.0%)	703 (4.1%)	2 651 (18.9%)	722 (4.8%)	5 594 (9.3)
Motor deficiency	148 (20.0%)	241 (18.0%)	579 (5.0%)	659 (3.8%)	617 (4.4%)	777 (5.1%)	3 021 (5.0)
Disease	198 (26.8%)	207 (15.5%)	451 (3.9%)	308 (1.8%)	37 (0.3%)	125 (0.8%)	1 326 (2.2)
Visual deficiency	35 (4.7%)	39 (2.9%)	113 (1.0%)	139 (0.8%)	148 (1.1%)	217 (1.4%)	691 (1.2)
Auditory deficiency	110 (14.9%)	201 (15.0%)	219 (1.9%)	446 (2.6%)	242 (1.7%)	248 (1.7%)	1 466 (2.4)
Specific learning disabilities	nil	nil	4 739 (41.1%)	5 233 (30.6%)	nil	nil	* 9 972 (16.6)
Total	740 (100%)	1 339 (100%)	11 521 (100%)	17 128 (100%)	14 047 (100%)	15 139 (100%)	59 914 (100%)

* These categories do not overlap exactly with those given in Tables 3.4 and 3.5. The representative of Belgium calculated the proportions placed into Tables 3.4 and 3.5. For example the figure of 40.95% given in column 1 of Table 3.4 is made up of 60% of the light mental deficiency category and 75% of the specific learning disability category.

Table A.3b. **Pupils (2-21 years) with special needs by disability and as a percentage of total school population, 1988/89**

Special need	Total	% of pupils with SEN	% of total school population
Light mental deficiency	28 441	47.46	*1.46
Moderate/severe mental deficiency	9 403	15.70	*0.48
Emotionally disturbed/Autistic	5 594	9.34	0.29
Motor deficiency	3 021	5.04	0.16
Disease	1 326	2.21	0.07
Visual deficiency	691	1.15	0.04
Auditory deficiency	1 466	2.45	0.08
Specific learning disabilities	9 972	16.65	*0.51
Total	59 914	100	3.08

* See explanation at foot of Table A.3a.

4. Canada
(New Brunswick)

All the information in this section relates to the Province of New Brunswick. Prior to 1986, the New Brunswick Schools Act made little or no provision for children with special educational needs. In fact, pupils with very special needs were provided with separate services and education under other legislation. During the 1980s there was a growing awareness of human rights and the recognition of a diverse society. The Canadian Constitution containing "The Charter of Rights and Freedoms" was proclaimed, guaranteeing that certain basic human rights and freedoms were to be protected, including the right to an education. Influenced by this, the New Brunswick Schools Act of 1987 now provides the framework for the provision of education for students with special educational needs. It contains the following three key components:

- it makes the Minister for Education and the school boards responsible for providing education for all students regardless of the exceptional nature of their needs;
- it requires school districts to provide individual programmes for students with special educational needs;
- it requires school boards to place students with special educational needs in mainstream classrooms, unless this proves detrimental to the education of the student or other students.

Subsequent legislation, the Schools Act of 1992, requires school boards to establish an appeal process for cases where parents disagree with school board decisions regarding placement, promotion, suspension and right to access to information. This legislation is intended to facilitate parental involvement in the decision-making process at the school and school district levels.

The total anglophone school population of New Brunswick for the year 1990/91 was 88 411 students. Of these, 9 137 (10.34 per cent) were receiving special educational programmes. There were also 163 visually impaired and 242 hearing impaired students served in ordinary schools and through resource centres by the Atlantic Provinces Special Education Authority (APSEA). This brings the total number of children with SEN to 9 542 or 10.79 per cent of the total school population. New Brunswick defines all special educational students as exceptional students; thus, this term includes gifted as well as disabled students. The only reason that students with hearing and vision impairments are distinct is because services are provided to them by an interprovincial authority which is governed under separate legislation.

Table A.4*b*.   **New Brunswick: pupils (6-15 years) with special needs by disability and as a percentage of total school population, 1990/91**

Special need	Total	% of pupils with SEN	% of total school population
Exceptional students (needs not specified)	9 137	95.76	10.34
Visual impairment	163	1.71	0.18
Hearing impairment	242	2.53	0.27
Total	9 542	100.00	10.81

5. Denmark

The main principle in Danish "Folkeskole" is that special pedagogical assistance cannot be prepared, decided or carried out without the parents' agreement. In addition, there are numerous possibilities for parents to seek advice and guidance about their child's possibilities and needs. Furthermore the choice of school is not binding for the entire school career. Parents are entitled to a re-evaluation, at least once a year, of their child's school situation. This could involve a change of school if the child had attended an integrated elementary school but, due to unforeseen problems, could not attend during adolescence. The most representative parental influence on school and education is stated in the legislation about the administration of the "Folkeskole". Each school has its own school board of normally five or seven parents, elected by the parents of pupils attending the school, two teachers, two pupils, and the head. Thus parents have the majority on the board, which is entitled to make most of the overall decisions about the school.

A fundamental principle of Danish educational policy is that everyone should have the same access to education and training that is basically free of charge from the time the child is 5 or 6 years of age. All children are entitled to instruction which must be adapted to the qualifications, the possibilities, and the needs of the individual pupil. Approximately 80 000 pupils (12-13 per cent of total number of pupils in the Folkeskole) are referred to special instruction for shorter or longer periods of a school year. 70 000 or 10 per cent of these receive special support in the ordinary class. Of the remaining 10 000 pupils, 6 000 attend special classes in ordinary schools, while only 4 000 pupils attend special schools (approximately 0.5 per cent of the pupils in Folkeskole).

Table A.5b.   **The school population and the percent of pupils with SEN**

	School population	% pupils with SEN
Public	554 000	
Private	60 000	
Total	614 000	13.03

6. Finland

Between the 1930s and the early 1960s the numbers of children in special education increased tenfold to 2 per cent and extended to include special classes and part-time provision. From the mid 1960s to the early 1980s there was a further considerable increase in special education with the result that one in six children in the state system was in receipt of some form of special provision. Since then there has been no further growth in special education and the aim for the 1990s is to develop the quality of teaching methods and curricula. Current policies emphasize the principle of integration which has been the subject of many committee reports since 1970. Their main thrust is to develop comprehensive schools for all children, supported by peripatetic teachers and resource room facilities.

The Secondary Education Act requires that all disabled persons be guaranteed an opportunity to receive vocational education. Vocational institutions are required to provide support for students with special needs and receive supplementary allocations for organizing special provision. It is also recommended that preschool children with special needs should be given formal preschool provision. Severely disabled children are entitled to two years of preschool provision.

In 1987/88, Finland had a total of 566 711 pupils in compulsory schooling. Of this total, 96 822 received special education of some kind. This represents 17.08 per cent of the school population. 14.3 per cent of the total school population received part-time special education in mainstream and 2.7 per cent were receiving education in special classes or schools. These were children for whom the school board had made the decision on the special education arrangements and who were studying according to some curriculum fitted for special education. A further 800 most severely mentally handicapped children were served by the social welfare authorities. It is planned to hand over this responsibility to the education authorities.

In Finland in 1987/88 there were 362 special schools. Much of the country, but especially the northern and eastern parts is sparsely populated which tends to increase the number of small, special schools. Education is arranged at first in the home municipality of the child to avoid long trips to school and boarding arrangements. Thus these special schools are small with only 1-3 special groups and special teachers. At this time there was a total of 3 700 special teachers, of which 2 300 were special class teachers and 1 400 special teachers in part-time education. Some of these part-time teachers were peripatetic teachers, some of them travelling across several districts.

Table A.6a. **Pupils with special needs integrated into mainstream, 1987/88**

Special need	Number of pupils	% of pupils with SEN	% integrated into mainstream
Visually handicapped	188	0.19	63.0
Aurally handicapped	864	0.89	25.0
Slightly mentally handicapped	8 096	8.36	9.1
Moderately mentally handicapped	2 362	2.43	4.9
Physically handicapped	1 171	1.21	21.0
Emotionally disturbed and socially maladjusted	11 951	12.34	63.8
Speech defect	25 553	26.39	100.0
Reading and/or writing difficulties	42 110	43.49	100.0
Handicap not specified	4 527	4.68	100.0
Total	96 822	100.00	83.00

Table A.6b. **Pupils with special needs by disability and as a percentage of total school population, 1987/88**

Special need	Number of pupils	% of pupils with SEN	% integrated into mainstream
Visually handicapped	188	0.19	0.03
Aurally handicapped	864	0.89	0.15
Slightly mentally handicapped	8 096	8.36	1.43
Moderately mentally handicapped	2 362	2.43	0.42
Physically handicapped	1 171	1.21	0.21
Emotionally disturbed and socially maladjusted	11 951	12.34	2.11
Speech defect	25 553	26.39	4.51
Reading and/or writing difficulties	42 110	43.49	7.43
Handicap not specified	4 527	4.68	0.79
Total	96 822	100.00	17.08

7. France

The education of children with special needs has been dominated by a medical model and legislation passed in 1975 to promote integration has been slow to influence provision. At present 68.8 per cent of children with special needs are educated in schools funded by the Ministry of Education and 29.7 per cent in institutions funded by the Ministry of Social Security. Around 0.5 per cent of children receive no education. These children are to be found in the institutions funded by the Ministry of Social Security.

Legislation passed in 1975 laid down procedures for providing for young handicapped persons. In this group were included those with a sensory or physical impairment or with severe intellectual handicap. It did not include those who were ill or who had emotional or behaviour difficulties. Circulars of 1982 and 1983 enlarged the population covered to include these groups. These circulars concerned the provision of support by health services to maintain children with difficulties, where possible, in their usual school and within their family.

Recent changes in the education system have been introduced by the Education Law of 1989. This has reorganised elementary education into three cycles and has set targets for school-leaving examinations. Two principles underlie the 1989 law. Firstly, the child is at the centre of the education system. Secondly, schools must be responsive to parents, local communities, other services and local employers.

There are approximately 10 million pupils in schools in France. Of these, 277 496 (2.70 per cent) receive special educational provision in special classes or special schools. 190 870 (1.90 per cent) are educated in establishments provided by the Ministry of Education. A further 138 084 are residential of whom 86 626 are educated in establishments funded by the Ministry of Social Security. Some proportion of these 138 084 children may receive their education in the ordinary school. A further 24 659 pupils with special educational needs are educated in mainstream schools. Of the 277 496 pupils educated in specialist establishments, 168 416 (60.7 per cent) are boys. The proportion of pupils educated in special schools and classes varies according to age: from 0.3 per cent at 5 years and under to 4.9 per cent at 13-14 years.

Table A.7 below shows the numbers and percentages of pupils in special educational establishments, including both public and private facilities. The overall percentage of pupils educated in special education establishments is 2.76 per cent.

Table A.7a below shows the percentages of children with special educational needs integrated into mainstream schools. The total number of integrated pupils is 24 659 (8 per cent of the total population receiving special education).

100

Table A.7. Pupils in special educational provision by disability, 1989/90

| | Ministry of Education, Youth and Sport | | Ministry of Social Security | | | | | | | | Total: Ministry Social Security | | Total of all establishment | |
| | | | Medical establishment | | Medical/Educational establishment | | Social/Educational establishment | | | | | | | |
	Number	%	Number	%	Number	%	Number	%			Number	%	Number	%
Blind	225	0.1	38	0.2	967	0.9	–	–			1 005	0.7	1 230	0.4
Partially-sighted	1 077	0.6	91	0.4	1 509	1.4	–	–			1 600	1.2	2 677	0.8
Deaf and partially-hearing	1 425	0.7	506	2.4	6 961	6.5	45	0.4			7 512	5.4	8 937	2.7
Motor deficiency	2 223	1.2	2 943	13.7	5 647	5.3	35	0.3			8 525	6.2	10 748	3.3
Physical handicap	888	0.5	8 355	40.4	689	0.6	15	0.1			9 059	6.6	9 947	3.0
Multiple handicap	12	–	1 030	5.0	7 445	7.0	43	0.4			8 518	6.2	8 530	2.6
Severe mental retardation	18	–	199	1.0	12 507	11.7	18	0.2			12 724	9.2	12 742	3.9
Moderate mental retardation	12 251	6.4	197	1.0	28 390	26.6	85	0.8			28 672	20.8	40 923	12.4
Slight mental retardation	92 461	48.5	234	1.1	13 834	13.0	138	1.3			14 206	10.3	106 667	32.4
Emotional problems	4 215	2.2	2 102	10.2	15 121	14.2	1 065	10.0			18 288	13.2	22 503	6.8
Psychiatric problems	818	0.4	3 778	18.2	6 817	6.4	92	0.9			10 687	7.7	11 505	3.5
Social problems	72 398	37.9	1 335	6.4	6 890	6.4	9 063	85.6			17 288	12.5	89 686	27.3
Non-handicapped	2 859	1.5	–	–	–	–	–	–			–	–	2 859	0.9
Total admitted	190 870	100.0	20 708	100.0	106 777	100.0	10 599	100.0			138 084	100.0	328 954	100.0
Total educated	190 870	100.0	8 313	–	72 694	–	5 619	–			86 626	–	277 496	–

Table A.7a. **Number and percentage of pupils admitted to mainstream schools by type of special educational need, 1989/90**

Special need	Number of pupils admitted directly to mainstream	% of pupils admitted directly to mainstream	Number of pupils admitted on the advice of a special commission	% of pupils admitted on the advice of a special commission
Blind	160	1.1	127	1.3
Partially sighted	1 389	9.4	854	8.7
Deaf	1 951	13.2	1 492	15.1
Partially hearing	1 364	9.2	464	4.7
Motor impairment	3 960	26.8	2 031	20.6
Emotional problems	3 210	21.7	1 050	10.6
Intellectual deficit	2 760	18.6	3 847	39.0
Total	14 794	100.00	9 865	100.00

Table A.7b. **Pupils with special needs by disability and as a percentage of total school population, 1989/90**

Special need	Number of pupils	% of pupils with SEN	% of total school population
Blind	1 517	0.43	0.01
Partially-sighted	4 920	1.39	0.05
Deaf and partially-hearing	14 208	4.02	0.14
Motor deficiency/physical handicap	26 686	7.56	0.27
Multiple handicap	8 530	2.41	0.08
Severe mental retardation	12 742	3.60	0.13
Moderate mental retardation	40 923	11.57	0.41
Slight mental retardation	113 274	32.03	1.13
Emotional problems	26 763	7.57	0.27
Psychiatric problems	11 505	3.25	0.12
Social problems	89 686	25.36	0.90
Other	2 859	0.81	0.03
Total	353 613	100.0	3.54

8. Germany

In 1975 the first integrated school was created in Berlin and further joint school experiments were set up and funded. Over the past 15 years there have been increasing numbers of experiments with different models of integration of children with special needs. In 1984, in the first report of the Federal Government, entitled "The Situation of the Handicapped", the positive effects of special educational support in schools were stated. In 1989 the second report of the Federal Government "The Situation of the Handicapped" reinforced principles of individual help according to need and the notion of integration in the education system in various forms. The intention is to develop a more flexible offering of different measures of support according to individual needs within a broadly integrated framework.

Over the past two decades those children previously deemed ineducable and excluded from schools have become integrated in schools. Considerable advances have been made towards the social integration of disabled persons. All political parties and important social groups have committed themselves to the humanitarian task of integrating handicapped persons into society. Germany is committed to the right of every child to education and training in line with their special needs. Although children are divided into categories according to their disability and often then placed in special schools, there is an increasing practice of "joint instruction", where handicapped and non-handicapped young people are taught together. There is also a continuum of support for children with special educational needs.

With respect to school legislation it should be mentioned that a growing number of *Länder* will modify their legislation for the support of handicapped students. Saarland has been the first land which introduced particular modifications to the school law. Meanwhile the Lander Hesse, Schleswig-Holstein and Berlin have also enacted new regulations. The concept of integration is applied in relation to the following principles:

- endeavours to promote handicapped young people in their development so that they can achieve an independent position in society;
- initiatives for joint instruction without any institutional separation;
- the range of preventive measures at the earliest possible stage.

In 1989, before the unification of the two parts of Germany, the Federal Republic of Germany had approximately 6.7 million students in general education schools, including about 248 000 in special schools (3.69 per cent). In 1990, after unification, the total number of students amounted to almost 9 million in general education, with 317 456 in special schools (3.52 per cent). The following tables show the situation in 1989, giving figures for the two parts of Germany separately. The figures relate to pupils in special schools. In the Federal Republic of Germany, back in 1990, an increasing number of pupils was supported by integrative measures.

Table A.8*b.i.* **Federal Republic of Germany: pupils with special needs by disability and as a percentage of total school population, 1989**

Special need	Number of pupils in special schools	% of pupils with SEN in special schools	% of total school population
Learning disabilities	136 422	55.00	2.04
Blind	1 277	0.51	0.02
Impaired vision	2 016	0.81	0.03
Deaf	2 734	1.10	0.04
Impaired hearing	4 834	1.94	0.07
Impaired speech	19 879	8.01	0.30
Physically handicapped	13 613	5.48	0.20
Mentally handicapped	37 970	15.30	0.56
Behavioural disturbances	8 788	3.54	0.13
Sick	7 453	3.00	0.11
Multiple handicap	13 025	5.21	0.19
Total	248 011	100.00	3.69

Table A.8*b.ii* **Democratic Republic of Germany: pupils with special needs by disability and as a percentage of total school population, 1989**

Special need	Number of pupils	% of pupils with SEN	% of total school population
Learning disabilities	50 571	79.50	2.27
Blind	220	0.34	0.01
Impaired vision	657	1.03	0.03
Deaf	601	0.94	0.03
Impaired hearing	1 746	2.74	0.08
Impaired speech	3 818	6.00	0.17
Physically handicapped	3 861	6.06	0.17
Mentally handicapped		No information available	
Behavioural disorders	1 355	2.13	0.06
Pupils in clinics or hospitals	809	1.27	0.04
Total	63 609	100.00	2.86

9. Greece

The first law concerning special education was passed in 1981 (1143/81) and this was elaborated and enriched in 1985 (1566/85). Special education is offered by the state free of charge at primary and secondary levels. The parents have the right to decide whether to accept the special education programme recommended for their child by the school or a medico-pedagogical centre.

The dominant philosophy of special education in Greece today concentrates on the provision of equal education opportunities for all the children according to their needs and abilities in a school for all which leads to integration not only in the school but also in society. Greece makes some forms of special provision for about 8.6 per cent (6.9 per cent in education and 1.6 per cent through the Ministry of Health and Social Affairs and through charitable organisations). About 66 per cent of children with special needs have those needs met in integrated settings. Over the past five years, there has been an increasing trend towards integration, with the development of a continuum of provision.

There are no national statistics at present collected on the exact number of people (adults and children) with disabilities or handicaps in Greece. In educational planning, there is a notional figure of 10 percent of the total school population assumed to have disabilities or learning difficulties and most of these are served in the ordinary school.

The total school population of Greece in 1990/91 was about 1.8 million children (aged 4/18 years). Of these, 12 383 or 0.68 per cent were receiving special education in special education units, mainly at the elementary level of schooling. Another 1 600 disabled persons over the age of 15 were attending workshops provided by the Manpower Organisation and 1 700 disabled persons aged 3-20 years were in institutions provided by the Ministry of Health and Social Affairs. Statistics of pupils with special needs in schools are collected by the local education authorities. The following statistics, which refer to pupils in special education units or institutions outside education, were gathered for the year 1990/91.

Table A.9b. **Pupils with special needs by disability and as a percentage of total school population, 1990/91**

Special need	Number of pupils	% of pupils with SEN	% of total school population
Blind/visual impairment	108	0.69	0.01
Deaf/hearing impairment	722	4.60	0.04
Physical handicap	430	2.74	0.02
Mentally retarded	2 400	15.31	0.13
Learning difficulties	8 723	55.62	0.48
Others (15+ in workshops)	1 600	10.20	0.09
Severely handicapped (outside education)	1 700	10.84	0.09
Total	15 683	100.00	0.86

10. Iceland

The Ministry of Education issued the first Circular on Special Education in 1977. This was based on the 1974 Primary School Act and ensured all pupils' education according to need. In 1983 a new Handicap Act was passed which aimed to facilitate the principle of normalisation through integration and equality of citizenship for the disabled. In 1988 the Law for Upper Secondary Schools stated that all those who have completed compulsory basic school have the right of entry to upper secondary school.

A new circular on Special Education took effect in 1990 with a strong thrust towards integration, stating that ''integration of handicapped and non-handicapped children shall be aimed at through systematic school development''. It defined the allocation of funds for special education not in terms of categories of handicaps but in terms of individually assessed need. The circular stipulated further that students should have the right to attend their local mainstream school. This move towards integration means a gradual decrease in the numbers of pupils in special schools. In addition it is intended that special schools be given an additional advisory role in relation to mainstream schools and parents.

The Law on Playschools 1991 states that disabled children and those with social-emotional difficulties who need special support shall receive such help in the playschool.

In Iceland approximately 6 600 children (15.71 per cent of the total school population) are receiving special education. Of these, 6 355 are in mainstream schools and 245 in special schools out of a total school population of around 42 000. Around 250-300 children receive some part of their special education in special classes set up within mainstream schools. There are seven special schools and four special units. Iceland is a small country with many sparsely populated areas which have small schools. Each district is allocated a certain number of teaching hours per week for special education and although additional hours are usually provided if a school justifies much an application it frequently falls short of the extra teaching hours that a school may request for as much as 20 per cent of its students. Special schools exist only in the main urban areas. The following table shows the numbers of children placed in these schools and units.

Table A.10a. **Pupils in special schools and units, 1990**

Special need	Number of pupils	% of pupils in special schools
Mentally retarded	109	44.4
Profoundly handicapped	66	27.0
Deaf	15	6.1
Psychiatric	17	6.9
Socially maladjusted	15	6.1
Autistic	8	3.4
Physically handicapped/communication problems	15	6.1
Total	245	100.0

Table A.10*b*. Pupils (6-16 years) with special needs by disability and as a percentage of total school population, 1990

Special need	Total	% of pupils with SEN	% of total school population
Mentally retarded	109	1.65	0.26
Profoundly handicapped	66	1.00	0.16
Deaf	15	0.23	0.04
Psychiatric	17	0.26	0.04
Socially maladjusted	15	0.23	0.04
Autistic	8	0.12	0.02
Physically handicapped	15	0.23	0.04
Others (not specified)	6 355	96.29	15.13
Total	6 600	100.00	15.71

11. Ireland

A Government Commission on Mental Handicap which reported in 1965 endorsed the then existing system of special schools and classes for mentally handicapped children and it became the model for educating children with other types of special educational need. However, in the 1970s the Department of Education began to prefer provision within the ordinary schools. Special schools have been set up by local communities or voluntary organisations and then recognised by the Minister of Education. Special schools and classes are recognised by the Minister under Rule 27 of the Rules for National Schools. A change in favour of setting up special classes rather than schools during more recent years was prompted by the lack of action on the part of such voluntary groups when provision was required in expanding areas of Dublin.

There has been little in the way of policy statements on special education by the Ministry. A 1980 White Paper on Education Development stated that: "while integration will be the first option considered, other options including that of complete segregation are being kept open". Ireland has also endorsed the 1987 statement of the European Commission which reaffirmed the importance of achieving the maximum possible integration of handicapped children into ordinary schools. A review committee on special education was established in 1991 by the Minister of Education with evidence to be taken from wide interests with integration as a major issue.

The total school population in Ireland in 1989 was 841 891 pupils. At present around 1.45 per cent of the total primary pupil population in Ireland receive special education, either in special schools or in special classes in ordinary schools. A third of the primary age pupils receiving special education are enrolled in special classes in ordinary schools, leaving approximately 1 per cent of primary age pupils enrolled in special schools. Approximately 1 per cent of the total post-primary student population receive special education either in special schools or in special classes in post-primary schools. Some 0.1 per cent of these are in special classes and 0.9 per cent in special schools. The table below shows the numbers of pupils in special schools and classes by disability.

Table A.11a. **Pupils in special schools and classes, 1989**

Special need	Special school	Special class	Total
Mild mental handicap	3 840	1 830	5 670
Moderate mental handicap	2 240	60	2 300
Severe/profound mental handicap	200	0	200
Physical handicap	500	0	500
Emotional disturbance	450	0	450
Hearing impairment	700	30	730
Visual impairment	150	0	150
Multiple handicap	48	0	48
Specific reading disabilities	150	0	150
Specific language impairment	0	20	20
Children of travellers	200	1 500	1 700
Deviant behavior	200	0	200
Youth Encounter Projects*	100	0	100
Total	8 778	3 440	12 218

* Youth Encounter Projects are four small schools that provide for young people who become seriously alienated from the conventional school system or who have become involved in minor delinquency.

Table A.11b. **Pupils (6-19 years) with special needs by disability and as a percentage of total school population, 1989**

Special need	Number of pupils	% of pupils with SEN	% of total school population
Mild mental handicap	5 670	46.40	0.67
Moderate mental handicap	2 300	18.82	0.27
Severe/profound mental handicap	200	1.64	0.02
Physical handicap	500	4.09	0.05
Emotional disturbance	450	3.68	0.05
Hearing impairment	730	5.97	0.09
Visual impairment	150	1.23	0.02
Multiple handicap	48	0.39	0.006
Specific reading disabilities	150	1.23	0.02
Specific language impairment	20	0.16	0.002
Children of travellers	1 700	13.91	0.20
Deviant behavior	200	1.64	0.02
Youth Encounter Projects	100	0.82	0.01
Total	12 218	99.98	1.43

12. Italy

The basis of recent developments in special education in Italy is the Law no. 118 of 1971, which states that "compulsory education must be provided in ordinary classes in public schools unless the pupil has such serious intellectual or physical difficulties that they prevent or make extremely difficult learning or attendance in an ordinary class". The Falcucci Commission was set up in 1974 to study the problems of pupils with handicaps. The Commission comprised specialists in child psychiatry, psychologists, members of institutions for handicapped people and social workers. The Report of the Commission called on the government to emphasise the key role of the school in collaboration with other services in overcoming the disadvantaged condition of handicapped pupils and in transforming schools so that they would be able to provide for the development of all pupils.

Government circulars since 1975 have promoted the idea of integration. A gradual development has taken place, so that classes do not become over-loaded with handicapped children. A law of 1977 abolished selection examinations and replaced them with a less competitive form of evaluation which supported the right to study. Laws passed in 1975 and 1971 provided for support teachers to be employed to work in mainstream classrooms with handicapped students. This has been difficult to put into effect, and a circular of 1979 attempted to set up criteria for the role of support teachers. This circular made it clear that the education of pupils with handicaps was the responsibility of the whole school community. Further, it advised that the identification and support of children with handicaps were not just the responsibility of the schools, but also of the local health services.

One of the crucial factors in the implementation of integration in Italy has been the training and retraining of teachers, and a series of laws and circulars have laid down regulations for this. A law of 1977 brought educational psychologists into schools to act as a link between the school and the local health and other support structures. Recent circulars (1985, 1987 and 1989) have stressed the importance of collaboration, but these have not always been applied and this has endangered the process of integration. Integration has become accepted as a reality in the nursery schools and the primary school, but is proving more difficult to accomplish at secondary and tertiary levels. This is partly because the legislative framework is not in place to support integration at this level, and partly because the training of teachers has not taken place.

Circulars of 1982 and 1988 stress the importance of providing a coherent and continuing educational experience for handicapped students. These circulars provide the basis for actions at the local level to encourage the integration of handicapped students in secondary schools and universities. These include adaptations to the curriculum which will allow students to follow a modified course of study. However, these courses of study do not provide certification and this makes them unacceptable to some parents. A permanent observatory was set up in the Ministry of Education in 1990 to examine the problems, both inter-institutional and inter-professional of the integration of handicapped students in general.

The total school population in Italy for the year 1990 was 8 510 622. Of these 107 709 or 1.27 per cent were identified as having special educational needs. The majority of pupils with special educational needs are educated in classes in mainstream schools. Students are not identified according to a type of disability, rather they are identified as having special educational needs which will be provided for in the ordinary classroom. The table below shows the percentage of pupils with special educational needs by stage of schooling.

Table A.12b. **Pupils with special educational needs in classes in mainstream schools, 1990**

	Number of pupils	% of total school population
Nursery school	6 822	0.86
Primary school	52 743	1.83
Lower secondary	45 156	1.99
Upper secondary	2 988	0.12
Total	107 709	1.27

13. Japan

In Japan there are three types of special school: schools for the deaf, schools for the blind and schools for the handicapped The schools for the handicapped are themselves divided into three: some provide for the mentally retarded, some for the physically handicapped and some for the health impaired, including the physically weak. For mildly handicapped children, special classes are established in ordinary elementary and lower secondary schools. There are seven types; the five already referred to with regard to special schooling, one for the speech handicapped and one for the emotionally disturbed.

The degree of handicap of children eligible for special schools is defined in the Order for Enforcement of the School Education Law (Article 22-2). The detailed stipulations of this Article are given in the notification of "Educational Placement of Pupils and Students Who Need Special Educational Treatment" (Notification of the Ministry of Education, Science and Culture's Elementary and Secondary Education Bureau Director-General, no. 309, 6 October 1978.) This notification also described the degrees of handicaps of children eligible for special classes. The School Education Law provides that every prefecture must establish special schools for the enrolment of all handicapped children of compulsory school age who are residents of the prefecture.

In May 1990, 93 497 children received education in 947 special schools, and 77 162 in special classes in ordinary schools. Of the total, 131 846 were within the compulsory school age range of 6 to 15 years. This constituted approximately 1 per cent of the total number of children, about 14.8 million, in this age range.

Table A.13a **Numbers of children enrolled in special schools, 1990**

Special need	Kindergarten	Elementary	Lower Secondary	Upper Secondary	Total
Blind	193	946	768	3 692	5 599
Deaf	1 531	2 456	1 748	2 434	8 169
Mentally retarded	55	16 217	14 864	23 321	54 457
Physically handicapped	106	8 183	4 640	6 319	19 248
Health impaired	3	2 622	2 240	1 159	6 024
Total	1 888	30 424	24 260	36 925	93 497

Table A.13*b*. **Pupils (6-15 years) with special needs by disability and as a percentage of total school population, May 1990**

Special need	Total	% of pupils with SEN	% of total school population
SC Mental retardation (mild)	55 001	41.72	0.37
SS Moderate/severe	31 081	23.57	0.21
SC Hard of hearing	1 488	1.13	0.01
SC Speech handicapped	6 114	4.64	0.04
SS Deaf	4 204	3.19	0.03
SC Visual impairment	203	0.15	0.001
SS Blind	1 714	1.30	0.01
SC Emotionally disturbed	11 315	8.58	0.008
Physically handicapped SC + SS = total	1 136 + 12 823 = 13 959	10.58	0.09
Health impaired SC + SS = total	1 905 + 4 862 = 6 767	5.13	0.05

SS = Special School.
SS = Special Class.

14. Netherlands

In 1985 a two track system of education came into force in the Netherlands: the Primary Education Act for most children aged between 4 and 12 and the Special Education Interim Act for those having a disability requiring more help than the ordinary primary or secondary school could offer. The Special Education Interim Act will remain in force until 1995. In its dual approach, the Act contains wherever possible provisions similar to those applying to ordinary primary and secondary schools while at the same time paying particular attention to the characteristic features of special schools. Links with ordinary primary and secondary education are important as the Interim Act aims to encourage the transfer of pupils from special to ordinary schools where possible. Recently the Minister of Education and Science has decided not to retain a separate law for special education but to subsume the rules under the Primary Education Act and to make it more flexible.

While there are 15 different types of special school, 70 per cent of special school children are provided for through three types: schools for children with learning disabilities, those for educable mentally retarded children and those for preschool children with developmental difficulties. During the last ten years there has been a considerable growth in these three types of school, and a decline in the number of pupils attending schools for children with sensory disability. The government encourages special schools to work according to a so called individual education programme, and several projects have been set up to establish this. In 1992 the Dutch Minister of Education and Science proposed further measures to improve possibilities for children with physical, sensory and severe mental retardation and for severely maladjusted children, and to improve the quality of specialised institutes for special education. In 1993 the government supported this by supplying computers to schools for children with physical, sensory and severe mental retardation.

The Netherlands has 1 001 special schools catering for approximately 105 000 pupils aged 4/18+ years. This constitutes 3.63 per cent of the total school population in special education. The proportions in the primary/pre-school and secondary phases were 4.56 per cent and 2.48 per cent respectively. In the compulsory age group (5-15), less than 0.1 per cent do not receive educational provision. The following table shows numbers and percentages of children by handicap in special educational provision.

Table A.14b. **Pupils (4-18+ years) with special needs by disability and as a percentage of total school population, 1989**

Special need	Total	% of pupils with SEN	% of total school population
Educable mentally retarded	33 200	31.69	1.15
Severely mentally retarded	7 314	6.98	0.25
Learning disabled	43 155	41.19	1.50
Deaf	847	0.81	0.03
Impaired hearing	3 977	3.80	0.13
Severe speech disorders	331	0.32	0.01
Blind	219	0.21	0.008
Partially sighted	295	0.28	0.01
Physically handicapped	3 355	3.20	0.12
Children in hospitals	879	0.84	0.03
Chronically ill	2 969	2.83	0.10
Severely maladjusted	5 485	5.23	0.19
Paedological institutes	1 095	1.05	0.03
Multiply handicapped	1 659	1.58	0.06
Total	104 780	100.01	3.63

15. Norway

In 1951 various Norwegian laws and regulations were gathered together into one act, the Special School Act. The period 1951-1976 saw great changes in school policy, influenced by pressures towards decentralisation and a strong lobby for the rights and privileges of all disabled children. There was a majority wish to remove segregation. In 1976 the Law on Special Education was amalgamated with the main school law to form one School Law to cover all children. Through the 1980s more than 50 special schools were closed and pupils transferred to local provision. Many local special classes transferred their pupils to ordinary schools and classes. The Norwegian school law states that "all children have the right to receive instruction in accordance with their abilities and aptitudes".

The Law on Kindergartens affirms the rights of "functionally disabled children" to priority admission to publicly supported kindergartens and preschools. The Law on Primary and Lower Secondary Education states that the municipal education committee is obliged to maintain a register of all those with special needs in order to be able to monitor provision to meet their needs. The Law on Upper Secondary Education entitles pupils aged 16-21 with special educational needs to "special education". Since 1987, their applications for upper secondary places have been given priority with a fixed number of places being reserved for students with special needs.

In line with a commitment to integration, with segregated provision now the exception rather than the rule, there is a reduction in number and a transformation of public special schools. There are at present 40 public special boarding schools. Following the White Paper of June 1991, most of these are being transformed into national public competence centres staffed by highly qualified personnel, offering services, nationally or regionally, to all age groups.

The total school population in Norway is 482 964 pupils aged 7-16 years with an additional 242 964 pupils aged 16-19 years making a total school population of 725 928 pupils aged 7-19 years. Around 0.6 per cent of pupils with special needs in Norway are educated in special schools and classes; the remainder are educated in mainstream schools. The table shows the breakdown of pupils with special educational needs in mainstream schools according to handicap. These statistics are based on 75 per cent of the population.

Table A.15a. **Percentage of pupils with special needs in mainstream schools, 1990**

Special need	Age 0-6	Age 7-16	Age 16-19
Visual impairment	3	2	2
Hearing impairment	4	3	3
Sensori-motor disabilities	10	4	5
General learning disabilities	16	15	28
Psycho-social disabilities	27	24	21
Language/communication	34	8	3
Subject related disabilities	–	41	28
Others	7	2	10

16. Spain

Spain has had substantial developments in legislation and policy in the field of special education over the past two decades. Following the launch of the Integration Plan in 1985 to cover an eight year period, there is a strong commitment to integration. This has been introduced gradually and started with younger pupils and those with less severe disabilities. Over the eight year period, the Integration Plan has aimed to develop in each local area at least one ordinary school which will be a centre for children with special educational needs. By the beginning of 1990/91 there were some 1 200 schools designated, providing for about 20 000 pupils with handicaps.

Alongside these changes in special education, the 1990 General Arrangement of the Education System (Organic) act redefined educational phases, established compulsory secondary education to 16 years, established post-compulsory education and "is open to dealing with diversity". It also proposes a new form of curriculum characterised by its openness and flexibility and permitting adaptation to the individual needs of the pupil. The act strengthens the implementation of the principles of integration and normalisation of "pupils with temporary or permanent special educational needs". Further it recognises the "interactive" nature of special educational needs. The Act obliges the education system to make the necessary resources available for pupils with special educational needs to be able to attain the general objectives established for all pupils within the regular system. It envisaged that within the next three to five years all primary schools would accept children with special educational needs and would have the appropriate resources to provide for them. There is also the intention of developing a new Integration Plan aimed at having secondary schools provide integrated facilities.

The statistics given below refer to the education system in force until 1992 and the data for 1989/90 school year in the MEC area (area that is managed by the Ministry of Education and Science) which covers approximately 45 per cent of the school population in Spain. In this area, there were about 1 900 000 pupils (6-14 years) in general basic education. There are no statistics on children outside the education system, but since education is compulsory for all 6-14 year-olds, and educational provision is made for pupils who are unable to attend school because of serious illness, it is likely that the numbers of such children will be very small.

In 1989 the MEC area of Spain had 215 special schools catering for 15 867 pupils. It had 660 special units in mainstream schools catering for 4 565 pupils. In addition there were 897 "Integration Project" schools which catered for 19 694 pupils with special educational needs. The overall percentage of children with special educational needs was 2.11 per cent. Of these, 40 per cent were in special schools, 11 per cent in units and 49 per cent in mainstream schools.

The "Others" category does not have the same meaning in special schools as it does in ordinary schools under the mainstreaming programme. In special schools the term includes pupils with syndromes that are difficult to classify, while in ordinary schools it reflects a "fuzzy" category of "pupils with learning difficulties" as well as students with poorly diagnosed syndromes, along with pupils from ethnic minorities and socially disadvantaged families.

At the end of the 1990/91 school year, the Ministry of Education and Science replaced most of the special units within ordinary schools. In the 1991/92 school year, only 53 units were still operating. As with other countries, those units are in rural areas where there are so few children with severe difficulties that a special school is unjustifiable. They are then, units' that work as substitutes for special schools. The average number of pupils per unit is eight. The difficulties of the pupils are mainly linked with mental retardation or multi-handicaps.

The following table gives a breakdown of pupils by placement and special needs.

Table A.16a. **MEC area: pupils (6-14 years) with special needs in special schools, units and mainstream schools, 1990**

Special need	Number and % in special school	Number and % in special unit	Number and % in mainstream	Total and % SEN
Sight impairment	229 (40.03)	37 (6.47)	306 (53.50)	572 (100)
Hearing impairment	1 208 (52.68)	230 (10.03)	855 (37.29)	2 293 (100)
Mental handicap	10 790 (48.06)	2 686 (11.96)	8 976 (39.98)	22 452 (100)
Physical impairment	1 680 (56.26)	250 (8.37)	1 056 (35.37)	2 986 (100)
Personality disorders	906 (30.15)	325 (10.82)	1 774 (59.03)	3 005 (100)
Autism	411 (80.12)	29 (5.65)	73 (14.23)	513 (100)
Other disabilities	643 (7.74)	1 008 (12.14)	6 654 (80.12)	8 305 (100)
Total	15 867 (39.54)	4 565 (11.38)	19 694 (49.08)	40 126 (100)

Table A.16b. **MEC area: pupils (6-14 years) with special needs by disability and as a percentage of total school population, 1990**

Special need	Total	% of pupils with SEN	% of total school population
Sight impairment	572	1.43	0.03
Hearing impairment	2 293	5.71	0.12
Mental handicap	22 452	55.95	1.13
Physical impairment	2 986	7.44	0.15
Personality disorders	3 005	7.49	0.15
Autism	513	1.28	0.03
Other disabilities	8 305	20.70	0.42
Total	40 126	100.00	2.03

17. Sweden

In Sweden, there has been a growing trend towards integration over the past decades. Since the enormous growth in the 1960s and 1970s of segregated provision particularly in the form of remedial classes, there has been a shift in attitude towards a view that children's special needs are more appropriately met in ordinary school in integrated settings. However, integration has not been universally successful. For example, almost all blind, visually impaired and motor impaired children now attend ordinary classes, whereas deaf and partially hearing children tend to attend special school. Mentally retarded children tend to be locationally integrated in ordinary schools but in separate teaching groups.

In 1978 the government appointed a committee, which reported in early 1981, to study the integration of pupils with functional impairment. Sweden has been divided into five regions for planning support services for pupils with severe handicaps since 1984. Extensive advisory services have been developed in these regions. The integration Commission also proposed the development of resource centres to provide support for disabled children, their parents, teachers etc. Four of these have been set up and receive State grants. Regional co-operation and the resource centres have made it possible to offer almost all children with a handicap education in the ordinary school system.

There has been a marked change of attitude towards special education and pupils with difficulties. This involves a shift in conceptualisation and a basis for identification and allocation of resources. Previously resources were allocated on the basis of a definite and limited diagnosis, labelling and categorisation; now, the principle of the pupils' need for support determines resource allocation. There has also been a shift in terminology from handicapped (acknowledged now to be a relative term) to functional impairment or special needs. The new curriculum for the compulsory school (Lgr 80) which was established in 1982/83 is based on three guiding principles within special education: handicap is relative; non-segregation; a holistic concept of the pupil with special needs. It strongly emphasises the responsibilities of schools towards all pupils and the special responsibility towards those with special needs. It emphasises the school's responsibility to attempt to alter its working methods to meet pupils' special needs and the duty of the local education authority to allocate resources to meet these needs.

The total compulsory school population for Sweden in 1990/91 was 900 961 pupils. Within mainstream, children with difficulties can be taught in small groups within the regular classroom or in a separate teaching group. There are some separate special schools for children with severe physical or sensory impairment and for children who are mentally retarded. Some 90 per cent of classes for mentally retarded pupils are on the sites of mainstream schools. The numbers in the following table are estimates, and the percentages are percentages of the total school population.

Table A.17a. **Pupils with special needs in special schools and mainstream schools**

Special need	Number and % in special schools and classes	Number and % in ordinary classes
Hearing-impaired	360 (0.04)	990 (0.11)
Deaf	450 (0.05)*	0
Partially-sighted	0	900 (0.1)
Blind	0	45 (0.005)
Physically disabled	360 (0.04)	1 440 (0.16)
Mentally retarded	8 110 (0.9)	1 800 (0.2)

* In special schools for the deaf.

18. Switzerland

Although the education system in Switzerland is organised separately by the 26 cantons, there exists a coordinated committee of Directors of Public Instruction (CDIP). This body has avoided a polarisation of integration versus segregation and has called for a special education which is differentiated, flexible and remains open to integration. In 1985, the CDIP produced the following recommendations:

- Schools should respond as much as possible to the needs of all their pupils. This means to take into account and to provide especially for pupils who have learning difficulties.
- The special provision to meet the needs of pupils with learning difficulties must reflect the individual needs and the available structures within the canton. The objective is to enable the children to live as rich and independent lives as possible.
- The legal basis for provision must be flexible and allow maximum interaction between special and ordinary schools.
- Pupils with handicaps must be educated in ordinary schools where this seems practical and justifiable.
- Special education can take the form of support in an ordinary class, extra support either in class or outside it, placement in a special class or in a special school.
- Initial and in-service training of teachers should take account of the needs of pupils with learning difficulties.
- There should be regular exchanges in the area of special education between the different regions of Switzerland.

The law on Invalidity Assurance provides funding for children with severe disabilities if they are in segregated provision. Some of the cantons are beginning to move towards some integrative provision but, if this is to occur, the law on Invalidity Assurance must be revised. The total school population in Switzerland is approximately 715 000 pupils. Of these, 34 995 pupils (4.9 per cent of the total school population) are educated in special classes (66 per cent) or special schools. The proportion varies from canton to canton (1 per cent up to 10 per cent). Special classes are attached to the main school system and are attended by children with learning disabilities, behavioural problems, motor disabilities, speech problems, and those speaking a foreign language. Of the pupils following a special education programme, almost one in three is not a Swiss national. The following statistics do not take account of children with special needs who are being educated in ordinary classes.

Table A.18*a*. **Pupils with special needs in special classes and special schools**

Special need	Number and % in special class	Number and % in special school	Total and % SEN
Learning disabilities	18 303 (52.3)	–	18 303 (52.3)
Behaviour problems	3 150 (9.0)	1 820 (5.2)	4 970 (14.2)
Foreign language	1 785 (5.1)	–	1 785 (5.1)
Motor disabilities	35 (0.1)	630 (1.8)	665 (1.9)
Speech problems	140 (0.4)	700 (2.0)	840 (2.4)
Mental retardation	–	7 069 (20.2)	7 069 (20.2)
Visual handicap	–	210 (0.6)	210 (0.6)
Hearing disabilities	–	735 (2.1)	735 (2.1)
Chronic illness	–	105 (0.3)	105 (0.3)
Others	–	–	313 (0.89)
Total	23 413 (66.9)	11 269 (32.1)	34 995 (100)

Table A.18*b*. **Pupils with special needs by disability and as a percentage of total school population, 1989/90**

Special need	No. of pupils	% of pupils with SEN	% of total school population
Learning disabilities	18 303	52.3	2.56
Behaviour problems	4 970	14.2	0.70
Foreign language	1 785	5.1	0.25
Motor disabilities	665	1.9	0.09
Speech problems	840	2.4	0.12
Mental retardation	7 069	20.2	0.99
Visual handicap	210	0.6	0.03
Hearing disabilities	735	2.1	0.10
Chronic illness	105	0.3	0.02
Others	313	0.89	0.04
Total	34 995	100	4.90

19. Turkey

Since 1951, the Ministry of National Education has had the responsibility to provide for children who are in need of special education. The Education Act of 1983 created the legal framework to this effect. Within this ministry, a General Directorate on Special Education and Guidance has been set up. Staffing of the existing special schools has been improved and regular professional training courses in special education are organised for teachers. Special departments have been set up at the universities to teach new educational methods and to research in the field of special education.

In 1991 there were some 7.5 million handicapped people in Turkey. Some 3.7 million of them were aged 0-18 years, constituting 14 per cent of the total number in that age range. Only 21 910 children, out of a total population of approximately 2 960 000 however, all within the age range 4-18 and constituting 0.74 per cent of the handicapped children in this age group, had access to special education. There were 65 special schools, with a total teaching staff of 933 and 8 206 pupils on roll: 9 schools for the visually handicapped, 33 for the hearing impaired, 2 for the orthopedically handicapped, 11 for the educable mentally handicapped and 10 for the trainable mentally handicapped. In the 851 special classes in regular schools there were 851 teachers and 9 770 students. A further 3 934 students with special needs were being educated in integrated classes.

Table A.19a. **Pupils (4-18 years) in special settings, 1990/91**

Special need	Number in special schools	Number in special classes
Visual handicap	935	49
Hearing impairment	5 918	691
Orthopaedic handicap	219	0
Educable mental handicap	668	8 949
Trainable mental handicap	466	81

Table A.19b. **Pupils with special needs by disability and as a percentage of total age 0-18 population, 1991**

Special need	Number aged 0-18	% of pupils with SEN	% of all 0-18s
Visual handicap	52 742	01.4	0.2
Hearing impairment	158 266	04.2	0.6
Orthopaedic handicap	369 194	10.0	1.4
Educable mental handicap	527 420	14.3	2.0
Trainable mental handicap	79 113	02.1	0.3
Speech/communicative difficulty	922 985	25.0	3.5
Chronic illness	263 710	07.1	1.0
Physical/behavioural/emotional difficulty	263 710	07.1	1.0
Gifted	527 420	14.3	2.0
Other*	527 420	14.3	2.0

* Ward of state; children who need protective care.

20. United Kingdom

The education of children with disabilities in the United Kingdom has been influenced markedly by the work of a Committee of Enquiry set up in 1974 to consider the Education of Handicapped Children and Young People. This committee published its report in 1978 (known as the Warnock Report after its Chairwoman, Baroness Warnock) and its recommendations laid the foundation for the Education Act 1981, which required that children with special educational needs should be educated in ordinary schools subject to account being taken of the wishes of the parents and three other factors. These are that the required special educational provision can be offered; that the arrangement is compatible with the efficient education of their children; and that the arrangement makes efficient use of resources.

"The Education Act 1993 will, when fully implemented, add to the arrangements set up by the 1981 Act in several ways:
- a new Code of Practice will provide clear guidance for the role of authorities and schools in making arrangements for pupils with special educational needs;
- a new independent Tribunal will be established to hear parents' appeals against authorities' decisions about the special education for their children;
- any maintained school, named in an SEN statement will be required to admit the child;
- the Secretary of State will have power to make regulations to enable special schools (which are currently run by local education authorities) to become self-governing."

The 1988 Education Reform Act introduced a national curriculum and national assessment arrangements, a new system of funding education through greater delegation of budgets to schools and greater choice for parents over the school they send their children to. The Warnock report and resulting legislation recognise that as many as 20 per cent of pupils might at some stage in their school life have special educational needs, and that, for the vast majority of these children, their needs should be met in mainstream schools. There would always be, however, a smaller group, possibly about 2 per cent of the child population, whose needs could not be met from resources in ordinary schools and who might need a formal assessment of their needs and specification on a "statement" of their needs for extra resources.

In 1990 the United Kingdom had 1 873 special schools, catering for 117 600 pupils; 1.3 per cent of the total school population. Within this, the school population of England and Wales was 7 555 300. Of these pupils 93 100 (1.23 per cent) were being educated in special school, either part-time or full-time. The majority of these had a "statement" of their special educational needs. A total of 139 779 pupils had a "statement" of their special educational needs. This amounted to 1.85 per cent of the total school population. 17 963 pupils with statements were being educated in special classes or units in mainstream schools. 36 336 pupils with statements were being educated in mainstream classrooms. The remainder were being educated in special schools. That is, of the total population of pupils with special educational needs, 63 per cent were being educated in special schools, 12 per cent in special classes and 25 per cent in mainstream classes.

Table A.20*b*. **England and Wales: pupils with special needs in special schools, special classes and mainstream schools and as a percentage of all pupils, 1990**

Special need	Number and % of pupils in special schools	Number and % of pupils in special class	Number and % of pupils in mainstream school	Total and % of all pupils
All	93 100 (63)	17 963 (12)	36 336 (25)	139 779 (1.85)

21. United States

While much of the legislation enacted to ensure the rights of individuals with disabilities in the United States has been in place since the mid 1970s, the configuration of rules that guide educational practices has continued to evolve. Local, state, and Supreme Court litigation has modified and re-interpreted the legislation set forth for the implementation of Public Law 94-142 and its successors, public Law 99-457 and Public Law 101-476. The rulings of the courts of the United States apply only to local jurisdiction, while decisions of the Supreme Court are upheld throughout all 50 states and United States territories. The law regarding the education and integration of students with disabilities continues to evolve. The most encompassing legislation is the Education for All Handicapped Children Act (1975), amended to the Individuals with Disabilities Education Act (1990); it has six major principles.

1. *Zero rejection.* The intention, arising from racial segregation issues, is to prevent schools from excluding any children with disabilities. School districts are obliged to conduct an annual child census and evaluate the education of those with disabilities.
2. *Testing, classification and placement.* Evaluation materials and procedures used in placing children with disabilities must not be racially or culturally discriminatory.
3. *Individualised and appropriate education.* The individual educational programme must include statements of the child's present levels of educational performance, of annual goals and short-term objectives, of the specific educational services to be provided and the extent to which the child will participate in regular educational programmes, the commencing date and duration of these services, and the criteria for annual or more frequent evaluation of the objectives and their achievement. "Appropriate education" defines the extra provision required to meet the requirements of the individual educational programme.
4. *Least restrictive appropriate educational placement.* State education agencies must ensure that, to the maximum extent appropriate, children with disabilities are educated with children who are not disabled.
5. *Procedural due process.* Parents are entitled to notice, consultation and hearings. They are free to be part of state advisory panels, they should have access to system records, and they are entitled to protection of their children's records.
6. *Parent participation and shared decision-making.* Parents must be given opportunities to present complaints relating to their children's identification, evaluation, placement, or right to a free appropriate public education. They are entitled to low-cost legal assistance.

The educational placement of children with special needs varies considerably from one disability to another. In 1988-89, the most likely placement, for 79 per cent or more of their time, for those aged 6-21 with speech and/or language impairment, was in the regular class; 77 per cent of them were so placed. Similarly, 39 per cent of children with visual impairment and 31 per cent of children with health impairment other than orthopaedic impairment were placed in regular classes. By contrast, 56 per cent of those with a specific learning disability were withdrawn for 40 per cent or more of their time to resource room education. Separate classes were the most likely placements for those with mental retardation (61 per cent), serious emotional disturbance (37 per cent), hearing impairment (32 per cent), multiple disabilities (44 per cent), and orthopaedic impairment (35 per cent). Among the deaf/blind, 30 per cent were in separate classes and 45 per cent in special schools, often on a residential basis. Type of placement also varied with age, as can be seen from the following table.

Children and young people with disabilities in the age range 3-21 receiving special education and related services in 1989-1990 constituted approximately 7 per cent of the estimated total resident population, of 67 721 000, in that age range. The following table shows the number in each category of disability, in the age range 6-21, receiving such services in 1990-91. Over 4.4 million received services, 96 per cent of them under the Individuals with Disabilities Education Act and the remainder under the Education Consolidation Improvement Act.

Table A.21a. **Placement of children with SEN, 1988/89**

Type of placement	3-5 year-olds (%)	5-12 year-olds (%)
Regular education	42	31
Resource room	16	38
Separate class	26	25
Separate school	13	5
Residential/home/hospital	< 3	> 1

Table A.21b. **Pupils with special needs by disability and as a percentage of total school population, 1990/91**

Special need	Number in age range 6-21 years	% of pupils with SEN	% of total school population
Specific learning disabilities	2 144 377	49.11	3.17
Speech or language impaired	990 186	22.68	1.46
Serious emotional disturbance	392 559	8.99	0.58
Mental retardation	552 658	2.66	0.87
Multiple disabilities	97 625	2.24	0.14
Hearing impairments	59 312	1.36	0.09
Orthopedic impairments	49 393	1.17	0.07
Other health impairments	55 312	1.27	0.08
Visual impairments	23 686	0.54	0.03
Deaf/blind	1 522	0.03	0.002
Total	4 366 630		

Part II

CASE STUDIES

Summary

This report describes good practices in integrating disabled children into mainstream schools based on 64 case studies from 19 OECD countries. In the appendix, single page abstracts of each country's case studies are provided. The studies were based on schools within their administrative contexts or "units", as they came to be known, in the realisation that good practice will inevitably entail support from agencies outside of the direct administrative control of the school and its education authority. Information was gathered from documentation, questionnaires and interviews with a wide range of professionals as well as parents and children.

The chapters in the report are organised around the different levels of development that are necessary to stimulate integration as they emerged from the case studies. Thus, information is reported on the development of individual learning programmes, the relationships between the actors involved, whole school approaches, parental and community involvement, the role of special schools, support from external services and issues relating to training. Problems and solutions raised by the case studies are then discussed. The report concludes with a chapter that brings together the work presented in the reports from both the first and second phases of the study. These are supplied in the form of desiderata in the formulation of policies and practices intended to promote integration.

The work demonstrates that integrating disabled pupils can be academically beneficial for children with special needs as well as leading to social gains on the part of teachers and non-disabled children. Although it must be pointed out that disabled children may become socially isolated unless the appropriate support is provided. Training is a key component. Programmes need to develop a wide range of skills covering the development of individual teaching programmes and classroom arrangements as well as appropriate school organisation. They must also create attitude change and a new form of professionalism which encourages working constructively with other professionals as well as parents. The development of successful integration strategies requires careful planning and long-term commitment. All of the parties concerned must be involved with the aim of developing "ownership" and confidence that the new arrangements will work, while in the process overcoming fears that standards will be threatened. Resources, in the form, for instance, of curriculum materials, will need to be supplied and teachers should be given time to reorganise their work. Evaluation, of both process and outcome, is seen as a key feature in successful implementation and maintenance of integration programmes.

Chapter 1

Orientation

Introduction

By 1991, 19 OECD Member countries were involved in the CERI project concerned with the integration of children with special needs into the primary and secondary phases of ordinary schooling. The aims of the project were to trace progress in integration across OECD countries, to identify good practice and to report findings. The purpose of reporting findings would be to help OECD Member countries review their implementation of their own policies and plan further developments.

The first phase of the project, which had involved compiling data on the basis of country reports, had been implemented, and analysis of findings had begun. In 1991, representatives of the 19 OECD countries met to arrive at basic decisions concerning methods of complementing and extending their recently compiled country reports, using a case study approach. They agreed to identify, evaluate and report specific examples of approaches to integration already established within their own countries.

At least one case study was to be undertaken in each country, with some countries reporting on several. Reports were to include description of the processes through which integration occurred as well as evaluation of outcomes. The processes were to be reported in sufficient detail for readers of the reports to be able to replicate these approaches, after adapting them to suit local conditions.

The emphasis of a case study could be on some aspect of integration practice, for example on a programme followed by an individual child, on the curriculum followed by a class containing a few children with special needs, or on the training provided for teachers implementing such a curriculum. Each study, however, was also to consider and report on the context of this innovation. The context was to include any factors directly influencing the effectiveness of the innovation.

For example, were the study to focus on an innovatory programme within a classroom, the report might have to take account of and describe the attitudes of teachers other than the class teacher implementing the programme, the school's policy with regard to integration, and the working of support services external to the school.

Units

The collective term for the *innovation in its context* was to be a *unit* of study. It was recognised from the outset that the key unit for the introduction of innovatory practice in integration was likely to be the school, as the success or failure of an integration programme would depend on the attitudes and support of the whole staff of the school, influenced strongly by the leadership of the head. It was thought, though, that collectively the case studies would be at their most informative if they sampled units of varying size.

Units were to be selected on the basis of their likely-hood to yield examples of good practice, useful to people planning similar endeavours in other countries. For the benefit of readers contemplating similar developments, reports were to include details of obstacles encountered, and of attempts to overcome these, as well as of successes experienced. Videotape recordings would be accepted as particularly useful means of enhancing reports. The units were to be sufficiently well established to provide illustrations of the processes involved, not only in initiating and implementing innovatory programmes, but also in maintaining them in more everyday circumstances.

In most cases the country representatives already knew of significant developments in their own countries, often through reports they received as a matter of course from national or regional inspectorate services, and in some instances the representatives themselves had taken some responsibility for the initiation and supervision of such developments. The distribution of units selected across different countries can be seen from the table on the next page.

Altogether there were 64 case studies, the majority of them focusing on either a single school or a group of schools, with external support services relatively under-represented. Most of the information on teacher training was produced by just one country. While there was some unevenness in the sampling, the overall spread of units, ranging from within-class studies to those embracing the work of many schools, was satisfactory.

Methodology

Representatives of Member countries agreed on the core questions to be answered through the case studies, devised a format for reporting and considered various approaches to evaluation. The framework appears in full in Appendix I. It was thought important in all cases to sample the perspectives not only of the teachers, administrators and others serving as providers of integration but also those of the children and parents acting as its consumers.

Employment of researchers as external evaluators was recognised as being valuable and in several cases necessary, particularly where country representatives themselves had been proactive in initiating the developments selected for study. Some of the evaluation was to be through collaboration across Member countries, and this was considered a particularly fruitful means of enhancing the project's comparative perspective.

Distribution of case study units across countries

COUNTRY	UNITS				
	Classroom	School	Group of schools	External support	Training
Australia					9
Austria	1				
Belgium			4	2	
Canada			1		
Denmark			1		
Finland			1		
France		4			
Germany		5	2		1
Greece	2	2			
Iceland		3			
Ireland			2		
Italy	2				
Netherlands			2		
Norway			2		
Spain	2			1	
Sweden	4				
Switzerland	1	1		1	
United Kingdom	7				
United States	1				

General approach

In all cases information concerning a unit was gathered through perusal of relevant documentation. In most cases this was followed up through discussion with people already familiar with the development, either through their being involved directly in the activities or through their having advised on, organised, supervised or monitored programmes. Much of the discussion occurred within the context of on-site visits.

Discussions took place with children and with their parents as well as with professionals, though meetings with parents were not always easy to arrange. Visits almost invariably involved a certain amount of observation of integration classes and groups at work, though this tended to be informal and involving for example participant observation rather than a structured sampling of events.

The following extract, from a report concerning integration arrangements stemming from a special school in Greece, broadly reflects the kind of approach adopted with respect to the majority of the study units:

"The school was visited on a number of occasions. Semi-structured interviews were conducted with those members of the staff who were involved in integration programmes, including the head teacher and the school psychologist. Other members of staff were also interviewed about their contribution to the curriculum and their views on integration. Opportunities were given to attend classes, participate in activities, watch videotapes of integration programmes, look into the school records and examine documents on integration; less were the chances to talk to parents. There were informal talks with pupils, and sixth formers were asked to write a short paragraph on their experience in the integrated gardening programme."

The extent to which country representatives, and research or inspectorial staff deployed by them, went beyond critical analysis of documentation was in part inversely related to the extent to which evaluation had already been incorporated into the design of the study units under consideration. Evaluation built into the study units themselves, as opposed to that conducted as part of the OECD project, is reported in Chapter 9 (Part II).

Variations

In some cases the approach was basically that of the majority but, as the following extract from a case study of an Icelandic elementary school illustrates, it sometimes took a more structured form:

"Participant observations were conducted in regular and special education classrooms, in the teachers' lounge, the halls, and other places where students and personnel spend their time during teaching hours and breaks. In-depth interviews were conducted with school administrators, special educators, students and parents. Interviews were tape-recorded and then transcribed, and participant observations resulted in detailed field notes. Before the visits to the school a list of open-ended questions was sent to school administrators. Written answers to these questions provided a wide range of information about the school. To collect contextual information, the District Education Office was asked for information about special education in the school's district. Finally, a number of documents about the school were collected during visits to the school. These diverse sources of data were analysed inductively."

Structure and administration of interview schedules varied according to task. In Ireland, for example, researchers were commissioned to evaluate the use of computers as aids to integration. Firstly, they devised an interview schedule and pilot-tested it in two of the 50 project schools that had been granted money to buy computer systems. Then the Inspectorate of the Department of Education arranged for the inspector of each of the remaining 48 schools to use the schedule in interviewing staff in that school.

Similar variations also occurred with respect to questionnaires. In a Norwegian in-depth study of two elementary schools, whereas the younger children responded to structured interview questions, the older children were presented with the same questions in the form of a written questionnaire. In another Norwegian study, this time of the effectiveness of a support service for the visually impaired, four different but complementary questionnaires were used. Administrators, psychologists, teachers and parents were asked to rate different aspects of the service on the same five point scale.

The overall range of approaches can be demonstrated through two further examples, each atypical. Evaluation of the Netherlands case study units was contributed to through visits by two foreign experts, one from Norway and the other from the United Kingdom, who discussed their impressions with staff of the research team conducting the case studies and who later presented their conclusions in the form of a joint written report.

Another distinctive variation in approach was that leading to the case study report from the United States. Here, a panel of experts in the field of integration drew on their collective experience to develop a composite description of a fictitious school, reflecting the extent of integration typically achieved so far in that country.

Themes

In the body of the report, little distinction is made between the implications for integration of the phases of primary and secondary education. Undoubtedly, however, as was well recognised in the report of the first phase of the project, barriers to integration are harder to negotiate at the secondary level than at the primary level. Various factors contribute to this: the organisation of secondary education becomes more segmented as students move into academic or vocational courses, differences in attainment between the average and the less able tend to increase as they get older, and attitudes of teachers towards integration may be less positive at the secondary level. It was noticeable, in fact, that where the case studies focused exclusively on one phase of schooling, the focus tended to be on the primary phase.

Nevertheless, there were examples of good practice in integration at the secondary level, and their essential characteristics were just the same as those found at primary level. In principle, then, the distinction is an artificial one, and such differences as do exist appear to be of degree rather than of kind.

In subsequent chapters, accounts of selected case studies are clustered in accordance with size of unit, starting with the smallest and working outwards. Chapters 2 and 3 (Part II) focus on the individual classroom, first by looking at ways in which teaching can be adapted to meet special educational needs, and second by considering the implications of these adaptations for relationships among teachers and children.

It is not until Chapter 4, when these elements are placed in the context of schools as a whole, that the overall shape of integration developments begins to emerge. Chapter 4 ends with a series of statements on conditions which have been seen to facilitate the implementation of successful whole school policies.

From this point the report moves on to consider ways in which integration arrangements in schools can be influenced by factors outside ordinary school. Chapter 5 illustrates the contributions of parents and other members of the community at large, and Chapter 6 demonstrates the ways in which staff of special schools are playing an increasing part in assisting the progressive integration into ordinary schools of children who formerly might have been educated in special schools. At the end of Chapter 6 there is a series of statements concerning conditions which appear to be conducive to the success of this kind of work.

Chapter 7 outlines ways in which services based outside schools can support integration and Chapter 8 identifies constructive modes of facilitating integration through in-service training. Staff running such training could be based in ordinary schools, special schools, external support services or teacher training establishments, with each group having particular kinds of contribution to make.

The last two chapters draw the experiences of the case studies together. Chapter 9 presents an account of the problems which were found to present obstacles to integration, distinguishing between those characteristics of the processes of initiation, implementation, maintenance and evaluation, and considers possible solutions. Chapter 10 takes account of the country reports contributing to the first phase of the project as well as the case study reports prepared for this second phase. This final chapter summarises, through a series of brief statements, what appear to be the main features of good practice in integrated education. One page abstracts of the case studies carried out, organised by participating countries, are included in Appendix II.

Chapter 2

Learning Programmes

Introduction

By definition, a child with special educational needs within a class of mostly ordinary children of the same age requires learning experiences different in some way from those of the majority. It may be that:

- the same content can be learnt more slowly;
- the content is learnt at a more superficial level;
- only a proportion of the content is learnt;
- there is some means of facilitating the child's access to the learning materials;
- the child receives extra teaching help; or
- there is alternative content.

If there is alternative content, it may be within the same area of the curriculum as that pursued by the majority, but at an earlier level. If children are applying skills or knowledge already acquired, rather than engaging in new learning, similar variations apply.

In order to sustain a child in ordinary school and ensure a fair degree of participation in the ordinary curriculum, it may be necessary to arrange for phases of withdrawal from the normal classroom. During such a phase a child with special needs, either individually or in a small group, receives intensive help, usually designed to enable that child to integrate more satisfactorily during the rest of the time. The work undertaken during phases of withdrawal may be quite different from that engaged in by the rest of the class, for example if it takes the form of training aimed specifically at overcoming a particular disability.

Most of these departures from the programmes designed for the majority are not mutually exclusive and at any one time a child may participate in more than one of them. The case study reports referred to all these variations and described some in detail. The remainder of this chapter is devoted to presentation of an array of examples, all of which, within their particular settings, were judged to constitute good practice.

139

Reducing content

In any ordinary classroom, where the content of a lesson is appropriate to the majority but where no particular attention is paid to the range of abilities within the class, there will be some children who do not understand the whole of it. Those who are slower or less attentive may only grasp the introductory aspects, and consequently only have a hazy idea of what is required, their output may be relatively small, and they are likely to become discouraged.

One well-known method of overcoming this difficulty is to plan the curriculum in such a way that children with special needs are presented with only those aspects of the ordinary curriculum that they can manage. For instance, they may be offered education on an integrated basis in selected subjects only (such is an example of a French project). The following extracts, from Belgian and Irish case studies respectively, provide examples:

"At mainstream school A, a class of hearing-impaired pupils is integrated with a class of children with normal hearing, but only for certain activities and practical courses:

– intellectual awareness activities, four afternoons per week;
– painting and handicraft, two 90-minute periods per week;
– physical education, one hour per week; and
– play (in nursery school), one afternoon per week.

In some cases at primary level, pupils in special classes and ordinary classes receive instruction together in some subjects of the curriculum but not in English, mathematics or Irish. Pupils with a hearing impairment are integrated with pupils in ordinary classes for art and craft and physical education. Their difficulties in language and reading mean that they are not integrated for other subjects, however. Some of the pupils in the special classes for mild mental handicap are considered able to manage the more ''aesthetic'' aspects of the curriculum and are integrated for music, singing and nature study. Also, if pupils with special needs are interested in, or excel at, sports they are integrated in team games.''

Similarly, in a French project swimming was one starting point for the integration of children with visual impairment. In a Greek study, environmental studies provided the vehicle for developing contacts between a special school and an ordinary school. Some of the children from the two schools worked together on a once weekly basis in a garden created in the grounds of the special school.

In another Greek case study, a secondary age special school student regularly attended the carpentry workshop of the adjacent vocational training school. Also on the roll of this special school were other students, carefully selected as being co-operative and as having good learning potential, who spent part of three days each week in a neighbouring ordinary school. One girl, for example, attended ordinary classes for history, social and political education, ''life in school'', religion, arts and craft, geography, and music.

The following extract, from a report on the work of a unit for students with specific learning difficulties in a United Kingdom secondary school, provides a useful example of the changing nature of curriculum modification arranged for the students as they moved up through the school.

"In their first year in the unit, pupils joined their mainstream classes for technology, physical education and pastoral sessions. Otherwise, the unit teachers had regard for the National Curriculum areas but admitted that, for a term or so, the time spent on the non-statutory curriculum might exceed the time spent on the statutory curriculum. The imbalance was thought necessary in order that the pupils concerned might return to the full National Curriculum as soon as possible. The school was making considerable efforts to cover the National Curriculum by topic work within the unit, by extra input for science and by an intensive modern language course late in the summer term. Disapplication* was therefore not considered necessary. Pupils returned to mainstream classes as soon as they were able – the scheduling of this depended on the individual's difficulties and progress. However, by the end of Year 7, the unit pupils would only be withdrawn for English and modern languages, and by the following year they only went to the unit for help with individual difficulties. It was considered that pupils for whom this staged integration would not be possible would not be suitable candidates for the unit."

Facilitating access

When a child has difficulty in reading a word, pairing the written word with a picture that helps the child guess its meaning has for many years been a way of facilitating access to print. This principle has been applied successfully in Australian trials of a learning package, "Compic in the Classroom", that includes a set of 1 200 pictographs, with accompanying written words colour coded to indicate whether they are being used as verbs, nouns or adjectives. As well as being useful in teaching reading skills, the pictographs can be mixed into written instructions assigning children to activities in any subjects of the curriculum, thus making the instructions easier to understand.

Even quite severe physical disabilities can be compensated for, through mechanical and electronic aids, sufficiently well to enable the children concerned to participate in the normal school curriculum. In the following example, illustrating the requirements of a ten-year-old Swedish girl with cerebral palsy, the Bliss-board referred to is part of another system which uses pictographic or diagrammatic symbols to aid communication:

"Because of her very soft muscles, Malin needs to be tied to her wheelchair. She can handle her electric permobil very well and is good at pointing to her Bliss-board. As she has great difficulty in speaking she is communicating via a computer. Malin needs assistance when eating. In the classroom Malin has a special desk with

* Disapplication – a legal provision given in the 1988 Education Act (UK) to allow children with SEN to be exempted from part or all of the national curriculum.

upholders for her arms, and the assistant has to lift her from the wheelchair to the desk.''

Providing extra help

The provision of extra teaching help in the ordinary classroom is extremely widespread as a means of meeting special needs. It is generally considered to be an essential feature of integration projects, with significant educational advantages over the more traditional means of either withdrawing children periodically or placing them in special classes. One of the Swiss case study reports referred to a careful comparison undertaken there of costs of in-class support versus costs of special class provision. Overall, costs were about the same, with the extra costs of staffing for the integrated classes balanced by the extra costs of premises for the special classes.

The in-class support teacher usually works with individuals or with small groups either on the same tasks as those engaged in by the rest of the class or on some modification of these tasks. On occasion, though, the support teacher may look after the class as a whole while the class teacher takes the opportunity to carry out some more intensive work with those with special needs.

The help is often provided by a teacher who has had extra training in special education, thus enabling some in-service training for the classroom teacher as well, but this is not always the case. The help may be provided by a member of another profession, for example, or by an unqualified person who works under the direction of the class teacher. The following extract from a Belgian study of the integration of visually impaired children into ordinary classes illustrates the point:

"For visually impaired pupils, a weekly credit of two extra hours is provided by law; for visually handicapped children who use Braille, a weekly credit of four hours is allocated. (...) In practice it may become necessary to devote some of these credit hours to consultations about both planning and assessment. (...) First of all, the handicapped pupil is given direct support consisting of: searching for adaptations and solutions whenever the handicap acts as a brake on the child's activities; offering adequate materials; teaching the pupil how to use them; giving extra support during some of the lessons. The transcription of textbooks and other material is done in co-operation with a specialised institution (the Helen Keller Institute). A physiotherapist comes in and helps the blind child to acquire greater autonomy and mobility.''

Similar means of securing integration through in-class support teaching were seen in a Spanish case study involving a boy with mild learning difficulties and some problems of motor coordination. Throughout the school day the boy was in the ordinary class, following basically the same subject timetable as his peers. The support teacher was present for just over a third of the time, for some of the language, science and mathematics lessons, with the different subjects managed by different teachers. The flexible nature of the extra help provided is visible from the following extract:

"In general, Daniel, his present support teacher, is providing Victor's tutors with material or adapted programmes, for instance in the areas of social and natural sciences, so that sometimes Victor partakes fully in some assignments of these areas with his classmates, while at others he performs ones which have been adapted specifically for him according to his needs. However, it is also true that the sole and excessive importance that has been given to the conceptual subject matter in the upper cycle and the large volume of this means that the work rate is very high and therefore the support work in the classroom occasionally proves very tough going. Victor receives some support outside school through a private teacher engaged by his parents to reinforce his school work."

While the help provided by the support teacher is often general, occurring with respect to any difficulty the child experiences, in some instances it may be confined deliberately to specific skills, as can be seen from this extract from a report concerning the integration of Belgian children with hearing impairment:

"Depending on the pupil's ability to communicate and understand the teacher, an interpreter helps him for one or more hours per day using cued speech or sign language. The interpreter, a member of staff of the rehabilitation centre, is present in the classroom only to 'translate' what the teacher says or, where necessary, the pupil's questions and answers."

The French studies show that these different forms of help cannot be ruled out but must remain in place to meet a variety of ever present special needs.

Introducing alternative content

One of the problems traditionally facing the ordinary classroom teacher wishing to set alternative work for the two or three slower children in the class has been that of finding time to show them how to use the alternative materials provided. This problem is increasingly being solved through the use of computers, particularly if their software is interactive and the programmes can use children's initial responses as a basis for setting tasks at appropriate levels of difficulty. The Irish case study of computer usage in fifty schools provides some idea as to the areas of the curriculum in which programmes tend to be concentrated:

"Pupils in the project (...) spend on the average just over 1.5 hours per day at the computer. (...) The computer is used in most schools by pupils with special needs and by other pupils for reading, writing, mathematics and computer games. Writing is the learning activity for which the computer is used in the greatest number of schools both by pupils with special needs (N=43) and by other pupils (N=41). It is followed closely by mathematics (...) and reading (...) and finally by computer games (...)."

The greater a child's learning disability, the greater the likelihood that an individual learning programme will be required. An extreme example of ways in which such programmes can be developed in ordinary classroom settings is provided through an

Italian case study of the integration into an elementary school of an eight-year-old autistic boy with serious learning and behavioural problems.

On entry to the school he had been unable to establish relationships with either people or objects, had made stereotyped movements which were difficult to interpret, had uttered the same sound repeatedly without producing recognisable speech, and had been hyperactive without any apparent cause.

A teacher, usually but not always the same special education specialist, was assigned to the child. Carefully targeted programmes were designed to enable him to follow the work of the class at certain times; at other times he would work individually with the specialist teacher or play outside. He gradually became able to toss balls into baskets, listen to speech, leaf through illustrated books, identify named colours, and cut with scissors. He also began to approach other children and teachers, and learned to wait before satisfying a need.

Some idea of the kinds of programme the boy followed can be seen in the procedure used to help him identify a named colour. Saying "take the red one" the teacher guided the boy's hand to the red object. Later, the teacher used gesture rather than physical assistance as the extra prompt, and eventually relied on the verbal prompt only. Then the teacher introduced distracting elements, such as a black object as well as a red one, repeating the request. Successful performance was rewarded, sometimes by praise, sometimes by pleasurable activities such as drawing.

Arranging withdrawal teaching

While in-class support generally has educational advantages over withdrawal teaching, there are some instances in which the latter is preferable. The report from the United Kingdom, summarising the work of seven case studies, refers to four types of instance in which children were withdrawn temporarily from ordinary classes:

i) structured programmes of work necessary to meet pupils' needs but irrelevant to the mainstream group – for example, conversation training for hearing impaired pupils, speech therapy, structured language work for specific learning difficulty, life skills for pupils with severe learning difficulties;

ii) programmes of work that were common to mainstream classes but which were offered in the unit so that a high degree of support could be offered – for example, some project work, or mathematics. This might occur when, although there were no conceptual problems, there were conditions which interfered with learning – for example, communication for hearing impaired pupils, literacy skills for pupils with specific learning difficulties;

iii) programmes of work that were of a significantly lower level than those offered in mainstream classes – particularly for basic language and number work; and

iv) when it was considered that the pupil would be socially or emotionally uncomfortable in the mainstream situation.

In some instances, withdrawal from the ordinary class is prompted by the limited availability of specialists or of material resources rather than by the child's curriculum needs as such, as can be seen from the following extract concerning provision for students with physical disabilities in a United Kingdom secondary school:

"For example, various therapists might only be able to visit during class times; and the necessity for regular treatment for some conditions (for example, muscular dystrophy) or the need to engage in specific therapeutic activities (such as swimming) meant that pupils had to be withdrawn to use specialist facilities as and when they were available or necessary. On account of pressures on the mainstream timetable, it was often difficult to make arrangements to make up the work that they had missed."

In addition it may not always prove possible to facilitate a child's access to the ordinary school curriculum entirely within the confines of the mainstream school. It may be thought necessary, as the following extract from a Belgian case study illustrates, for the basic access training to occur in a special school:

"In most cases parents will opt for integrated education in order to avoid having to send their child to boarding school. Although their preference is shared by all parties involved, in special education and in the special supportive services the experts say that blind children and children with a major visual handicap would do better if they attended the first year of primary education at Ganspoel. First year pupils there get a good grounding in Braille; at Ganspoel, there is a lot of scope for mobility training, learning to be self-reliant and acquiring social skills. Even with the help of a support teacher, it is difficult to acquire these skills while attending a regular school, as no intensive training is provided there."

Overall planning

While many of the programmes described here can be and may need to be arranged on a short-term basis, there is also a need for long-term planning, particularly if integration is to be partial and if the child will be dividing time between ordinary and special schooling. The French report, for example, laid particular stress on this. The following extracts, from a report on a service for the visually impaired in Finland, demonstrate one such approach:

"The regional secretary of the Central Federation or the rehabilitation instructor sees to it that the appropriate school authorities are informed about each visually impaired child during the year that child reaches the age of five. Notification is sent to the local school board, the family of the child, the Jyvskyl school and the regional teacher (if there is one in that municipality) (...)."

"The educational plan for a visually impaired child is made during the spring of the year that the child reaches the age of six. The education is planned jointly by the regional secretary or rehabilitation instructor in charge, representatives of the local school authorities, day-care, the preschool teacher at the Jyvskyl school and the parents of the child (...)."

"A further education plan is made during the spring of the year that the child starts school. The plan is made by a team including the regional teacher, the itinerant preschool teacher of the Jyvskyl school, the child's future teacher (if known, as is to be hoped), a representative of the local school authority, a representative from the social service in charge of the afternoon care of the child and the parents of the child. The education plan is re-evaluated whenever necessary and at certain regular intervals (*e.g.* when the child moves to another stage in school) (...)."

"The Central Federation employs an educational secretary. She organises courses for pupils in the highest class of comprehensive school, and students in vocational schools and colleges; these courses are aimed at improving their technical abilities in study and giving them a better command of daily living skills."

In France, programme planning is often supported by contracts or through annually renewable agreements made by the various parties concerned. These are usually built into the working plans that schools are required to draw up by law.

Chapter 3

Relationships

Introduction

The truism, that the success or failure of integration schemes is dependent on the quality of the relationships among the people concerned, is largely supported by the literature review carried out as part of the Australian project. Evidence from research undertaken in Australia and in the United States indicates that:

- the extent to which disabled children are integrated into ordinary classes is closely related to the attitudes of teachers and other staff;
- for many schools, positive attitudes are the result rather than the cause of integration;
- most school-based initiatives in integration are over-dependent on the goodwill and personalities of dedicated and creative staff;
- children in ordinary schools providing for the disabled have more positive attitudes towards disability, girls are more accepting than boys and the older children are more accepting than the younger; and
- enhanced attitudes toward people with disabilities dissipate rapidly without sustained exposure.

This chapter draws on case studies to illustrate the importance of positive attitudes in securing successful integration, the beneficial effects successful integration can have on relationships, the social hazards of integration, and systematic approaches to avoiding or overcoming these hazards.

Conditions

Several case study reports stressed positive attitudes towards disability as being among the most important conditions required for successful integration. The following extract is from a Belgian case study of the work of a team of support teachers concerned with visual impairment:

"The success of integrated education depends to a large extent on the attitude of the school, particularly of the class teacher. Individual teachers generally tend to have a supportive attitude towards the integrated pupils. They feel motivated enough to

147

make both the extra effort and the organisational adjustments required. They think of the presence in their class group of a visually handicapped child as a challenge as well as an enrichment."

Positive attitudes are required, not only towards disabled children and the extra effort they may entail, but also towards the fact that their presence is likely to make the teacher's work more open to public scrutiny and accountability, as the following extract from an Icelandic case study illustrates:

"To have students with special educational needs in a classroom means increased pressure on the classroom teacher. This pressure is twofold. First, having students with special educational needs means that there will be a special educator in the classroom for parts of the day. Teachers in Iceland are used to teaching alone and may be uncomfortable with the presence of a special educator in the classroom, not knowing how to put his skills to use or how to collaborate with him. Second, having a child with special needs in the classroom, with or without the assistance of a special educator, also creates added pressure on the classroom teacher, who must then attend to the needs of a more diverse group of students."

The significance of positive attitudes across the school as a whole, not just as characteristics of an individual teacher, can be seen in the following extract from a Spanish study of the effectiveness of a within-school support system:

"A constant factor at this school (...) is the existence of a *good climate of social relations* between most of the teaching staff and, therefore, the existence of a pleasant working atmosphere. The work of the support team (like the co-ordination of the tutors between one another) time and time again calls for a constant relationship, which has to be professional, but is also social. If this relationship is tainted by negative feelings (indifference, mistrust, rejection, etc.), It is very hard for it to prove satisfactory. (...) It is a group with *credibility* amongst fellow teachers, *i.e.* they have shown themselves to be sufficiently qualified and to be capable of performing the task entrusted to them. (...) Undoubtedly, the fact that the headmistress forms part of this team has helped their work to have the consideration and relevance it deserves."

Benefits

As integration succeeds, various social benefits begin to emerge among the children. A Danish report referred to a much lower incidence of the bullying of children with special needs in ordinary schools than in special schools; the sample was small, however, and the phenomenon may have been specific to these schools. Similarly, in the Irish study of the introduction of computers to meet special needs, skill in using computers won for disabled children the respect of their peers, but this effect would not necessarily occur once all children had become adept in their use. Reports also referred to the social benefits for ordinary children, as the following extract, from a different Irish case study, indicates:

"From the point of view of social development, both principals and teachers generally regarded integration as having positive effects not only on pupils in the special classes but also on pupils in ordinary classes. Teachers in primary schools noted the protective and caring behaviour some of the pupils in ordinary classes displayed in the school playground towards pupils with special needs."

In fact, most of the references were to social benefits for ordinary children rather than for those with special needs. In the Greek study of integration through a gardening programme, several of the ordinary school students expressed their surprise to find that those with special needs were not noisy, distractible or odd-looking, and that they got on well with their tasks. In the United States compilation of a typical school, ordinary children became more tolerant and, because they could see special education occurring in the ordinary classroom, less likely to stigmatise it or imbue it with some kind of mystique.

One of the Belgian case studies referred to ordinary children as learning to work more independently, presumably because of teachers' efforts to help disabled children do this, as well as learning to be more considerate. The following extract, from one of the United Kingdom elementary school studies, gives some indication of the extent and nature of this social learning:

"Assemblies united all pupils (...) and pupils from the special classes mingled with those from mainstream. No notice was taken of, for example, pupils with profound and multiple difficulties who could not control utterances or behaviour: with the perspicacity they often possess in large measure, children were able to distinguish between 'bad behaviour' and behaviour which could not be controlled. One child would accept reprimand for talking out of turn while another would be calling out nearby, unrebuked. An incident was cited of how a former Glanaber pupil complained of the distracting behaviour of some of his class at secondary school. When reminded that he had been exposed to interruptions and so forth from pupils at Glanaber, he replied that his Glanaber friends were 'just handicapped' – there was nothing wrong with them – whereas the pupils of whom he was complaining were rude and disruptive."

Reports also included many references concerning the social benefits of integration for teachers. One of the Belgian reports referred to the extra attention given by teachers to disabled children as creating special emotional bonds between them, and to teachers as becoming more likely to prepare their lessons with care, to the benefit of all the children in the class. An Australian package helping teachers develop their techniques for managing children with social and emotional difficulties enhanced these teachers' relationships with ordinary children too.

There were also examples of integration as helping teachers' relationships with one another, with particularly constructive relationships developing between class teacher and support teacher. One of the Spanish case studies referred to this collaboration as enhancing class teachers' teaching and evaluation skills, encouraging them to perceive children more positively, reducing their isolation, and enabling them to share decision-making. Similar gains are referred to in the following extract, this time from a Swiss case study report:

"Having a second teacher in their classroom working with one or two children has altered their situation somewhat. Most of them, however, view this change very positively: they have to co-operate with the special education teachers, which means that they plan and deliver the lessons together. The regular teacher is no longer solely responsible for all the pupils and all the lessons. The special education teachers, through the way they work, relieve the regular teachers of some of their responsibilities and also give them valuable advice on, for example, how to deal with problems within their classes or what approach to adopt with respect to a particular pupil."

Disadvantages

There were some references in the case study reports of apprehensions, occasionally with justification, among non-disabled children and adults concerning disadvantages to them of the integration of children with moderate or severe difficulties into ordinary schools. One of the Irish studies, for example, reported concern among teachers and parents that during break or lunch periods younger children may have reason to fear teenage students with moderate mental handicap.

The composite report from the United States referred to some intolerance among ordinary children, concern among parents that meeting the needs of disabled children would cause teachers to neglect the rest, and fear of the more severely disabled children among children and adults unfamiliar with them.

One of the Swiss case studies reported a controlled experiment, undertaken following public concern that able children might suffer as a result of integration arrangements. The researchers compared academic and social progress of able children in classes offering special education support with that of equivalent children in classes without this arrangement, found no significant difference and concluded that such fears were unfounded. Similarly, in a German secondary school comparison, non-disabled children in integration classes did just as well academically as did their equivalents in classes without disabled children.

As indicated in the previous section, case study reports provided more evidence of social benefits of integration for ordinary children and for teachers than for disabled children. In fact, reports from almost a third of the countries referred to disabled children in ordinary school settings as being socially isolated, with their individual educational programming perhaps exacerbating their isolation, though it was usually unclear as to whether they would have been any less isolated in special schools. Swedish and Swiss reports referred to systematic consideration of this phenomenon and their findings can usefully be detailed further here.

A Swedish study of the social integration of 16 mentally disabled children aged 7 to 15 in eight ordinary schools used interviews with staff and questionnaires and a projective test with children to assess the latters' feelings. Whereas the teachers generally thought the older and the younger children to be well adjusted, across the age range the majority of the children did not see themselves this way. They tended to lack friends, suffer teasing and find school boring.

Sociometric measures used with 215 Swedish children with hearing impairment indicated that younger children in ordinary classes received more friendship choices than did older students. The majority of the teenagers perceived themselves to be outsiders, and almost half of them were never selected as preferred companions, either inside or outside the classroom. While no direct comparison could be made with segregated education, the social situation of deaf children at a special school appeared more favourable than that of the hard-of-hearing in ordinary schools.

The following extract, concerning a severely physically disabled Swedish girl already referred to in Chapter 2 (Part II), is informative:

"The social network around Malin has been rather good until recently, when the staff noticed a decrease in peer relations. Malin is acting very slowly and her classmates seem not to have time to wait for her to get ready. She has a close relationship with another orthopaedically impaired girl in a parallel class and with her own brothers in the same school, but she is withdrawing more and more from her classmates. Malin is very tired after school and she prefers sitting alone in her own room in the afternoon."

One of the Swiss researches, comparing children in the 9 to 11 year age range in different settings over an 18 month period, went some way towards answering questions as to whether integration can socially disadvantage children with special needs. The popularity of children with learning difficulties, both in 27 ordinary classes with educational support and in 47 ordinary classes without educational support, was appreciably lower than that of other children, mainly because of their prickly behaviour, the extent of their learning difficulties and their associated lack of self-confidence. As the same characteristics made children unpopular in special classes, the researchers did not think that the less popular children's problems would be solved by transfer.

Children in the 42 special classes that were involved in the research, partly because they did not necessarily attend the schools nearest to their homes, had fewer opportunities for social contact with ordinary children from their own villages. Whereas for children with special needs in ordinary classes there was a slight tendency to come to like school less over the 18 month period of the enquiry, this was not the case for children in special classes.

The children in the special classes perceived their scholastic abilities more positively than did those with special needs in ordinary classes, with those receiving support in ordinary classes perceiving themselves particularly negatively. This was the case despite the fact that children in ordinary classes, whether with or without support, made far more progress, particularly in mathematics, than children in special classes.

One hazard for children with disabilities in ordinary schools is that of being with people who do not know how best to handle them. There was little reference to this problem in the case studies, no doubt because they were selected largely as reflecting good practice. The following extracts, however, from a study of physically disabled students in a United Kingdom secondary school, are salutary:

"One member of the special educational needs staff (...) had noticed, for example, a member of staff taking the hand of a year 7 girl of restricted growth 'to help her along in the corridor'. Although the teacher clearly did this out of kindness and it was a warm-hearted reaction, yet it merely served to separate this pupil from her peers for the teacher would not have done this had the girl not been disabled."

"One girl, in her second year at Fingal following a special school primary education, (...) tended to reject her peers by body language, always seeking adult interaction and physically turning her back on other pupils with whom she might be grouped. The special educational needs teacher (...) had done an analysis of teacher talk distribution within the class and found that ten percent of it in one situation was focused on this particular girl: staff generally 'seemed to be making up to them for the physical disability'. It was noticeable that pupils did not help her – they left her to pick up her crutches, for example. According to members of staff, this was because the pupil had rejected the advances of peers when they were all new to the school the previous year and, 'because they're only 12-year-olds after all', other pupils had 'given up' and accepted the girl's social isolation."

Systematic approaches

It is clear that, for various reasons, children with disabilities can easily find themselves isolated and can easily think ill of themselves in ordinary schools. Some of the case studies referred to strategies for circumventing these problems. In a Belgian study, for example, staff of an ordinary school arranged for the school's hearing-impaired children to sit together at lunchtime, so that they could communicate comfortably with one another and share common experiences.

The United States composite school arranged social skills training for the more severely disabled children, provided opportunities for children without disabilities to tutor those with disabilities, and began a "special friends" programme, whereby disabled and non-disabled children were encouraged to interact in and out of school.

Of the nine professional development packages sampled in the Australian project, one of those found to be highly successful dealt specifically with social skills training. It was designed to enable teachers to assess the social skills needs of children with disabilities in their classes, to teach the required social skills to individuals and small groups, and to evaluate the success of the training provided. Positive features included:

- demonstration of the need to teach social skills directly to children with disabilities and not assume that they will develop spontaneously;
- establishing with all children the need to recognise and value their own feelings and those of others;
- the use of strategies for incorporating social skills into whole class learning – for example, modelling in pairs, practice in small groups, and inclusion in whole class lessons in personal development; and
- emphasis on increasing peer acceptance and tolerance of children with disabilities.

Chapter 4

Whole School Approaches

Introduction

"Integration of handicapped students should be the responsibility of the whole school and not only of a few teachers."

"At the level of the school, it is important that not only the teacher is involved, but the whole school team show a supportive attitude towards the integration of the handicapped pupil. All parties should be involved in the decision-making process."

These quotations, from Norwegian and Belgian case study reports respectively, reflect more general findings. The French report, for example, emphasised the necessity for collective decision-making at various stages in an integration project. Co-operation of staff as a whole becomes particularly important when, as is the case in most secondary schools and as may occur to some extent in elementary schools too, individual children go to different teachers for different subjects.

The research reviewed as part of the Australian project identified various features of ordinary schools, in Australia, the United Kingdom and the United States, that were related to successful integration. Some were concerned specifically with disabled children and their teachers. Others, however, were concerned with the schools more generally, including:

- catering for individuals rather than just offering standard programmes;
- involving members of the broader school community in decision-making;
- recognising social and life skills, as well as academic achievement, as contributing to the success of the school;
- providing leadership through role models and clearly stated goals;
- organising activities designed to achieve the stated goals and periodically to assess progress made towards these goals; and
- offering a responsive programme of staff training.

The Australian project included three packages designed to be used in training the whole school staff to accept and contribute to the integration of disabled children within the ordinary school. The packages, all tested successfully, included manuals for presenters, reading materials, videotapes, overhead projection transparencies and workshop activity sheets. One was concerned with raising people's awareness of the needs and aspirations of the disabled, by involving staff in discussing issues about disability, and with helping them to plan classrooms and other areas of the school with disabled children in mind. Another aimed to help teachers develop skills in managing difficult behaviour. The third engaged them in planning and implementing a curriculum which would be conducive to the integration of children with special needs.

While these research findings and staff training packages can be useful in showing what whole school approaches might entail and how schools might go about developing them, they do not in themselves provide examples of good practice. Several Member countries' case studies described attempts to implement whole school policies for integration. The fact that these attempts were often only partially successful probably reflects the difficulty of the enterprise. They were, nevertheless, highly illuminating, and cumulatively they provided various examples of good practice.

The remainder of this chapter presents aspects of different case studies and then draws together what appear to be conditions that need to be met if a whole school policy for integration is to be effective.

Practice

With varying degrees of success, attempts to implement whole school policies for integration exist in many OECD countries. The examples chosen here, occurring in Iceland, Switzerland, the United Kingdom and Canada (New Brunswick) respectively, are not necessarily representative either of the individual countries concerned or of OECD countries in general.

One of the Icelandic case studies was of a school for children aged 6 to 16 years, with 490 on roll and an overall pupil-teacher ratio of 17.5 to 1, in a socially mixed urban area of a district with a declared educational goal of full participation of all school-age children in their local neighbourhood schools. The school had a reputation for being innovative and providing good services for children with special needs.

In practice, nine of the school catchment area's children registered as disabled attended the school and six attended special schools or units elsewhere; two children registered as disabled and living outside the school's catchment also attended the school. In addition, a further 61 of those on roll were judged to have some form of learning difficulty and to need minor extra assistance. Two full-time and one part-timer teachers were designated special educators, and another teacher worked as a part-time counsellor.

Planning, monitoring and evaluation of provision for special needs was carried out through weekly meetings of the school's welfare committee, membership of which included the school principal and the leading special educator. There was no systematic external monitoring of the school's special needs services. The school's special educators spoke of giving priority to preventive work with the younger children, to flexibility in offering a mixture of in-class support and withdrawal, and to close co-operation with class teachers. The general atmosphere in the school was relaxed and friendly, and children with special needs were accepted or at least tolerated.

While every child was on the register of an ordinary class, over the past four years three special units had been established. Attendance varied considerably, with some joining for just a few lessons, others going regularly for a year or more, and a few placed there full-time for several weeks:

"Sometimes it appears to be a matter of an on-the-spot decision by the special educator rather than a matter of a plan as to whether an individual is withdrawn from the regular class or taught in the classroom itself."

Within ordinary classes those unable to keep up with the rest were given individual rather than group assignments and they often appeared to be socially isolated. Some of the school's teachers thought that the children with the more severe disabilities were better served through the separate special units.

All the children with special needs interviewed said they liked the school, and most of the parents were very supportive of the school, but staff of outside agencies had doubts about the school's capacity to deal with children with disabilities and expressed the view that those with more severe disabilities were better placed in special schools. When children were placed in special schools, the cost of placement was met from the national budget and not from within the district, and from the point of view of integration this served to some extent as a disincentive.

The second example selected here is that of a Swiss elementary school in a largely middle class suburban catchment area. It was one of many schools in the region to be involved in an integration experiment, evaluated by university researchers over the period 1985 to 1989, the results of which have led to more widespread developments in integration.

The experiment had been triggered partly by a declining number of children of school age in the region and partly by criticisms of the then predominant system of segregated special classes, which constituted about 5 per cent of the total number of classes in the region. People advocating the experiment had included parents, special class teachers and university researchers. The experiment did not include many children with severe disabilities, most of whom continue to attend special schools.

By 1992, arrangements in this school had evolved to the extent that teaching staff operated in teams of four, each team consisting of three class teachers and one special needs specialist, referred to within the school as the "small class teacher". Designation of children as "educationally disadvantaged" was undertaken in consultation with the local educational psychologist, who was assigned to the school but employed externally:

"Educationally disadvantaged children who are put under the prime responsibility of the small class teacher are given an essential part of their education (from 18 to 22 lessons) in the mainstream classes assigned to them. Some of the mainstream class children are monitored by the small class teacher, who gives them some individual coaching, inside or outside the mainstream class (...). This teacher may also help children who were at some earlier time in small classes. As part of the 'option branch' project (one afternoon a week), the four members of the team provide instruction in fine arts and music for mixed groups of pupils."

Maintenance of this pattern required extensive co-operation within each team. Formal arrangements for consultation included weekly planning meetings among the four concerning the option branch project and weekly meetings among the three class teachers concerning particular subjects. In addition, the special needs expert met each class teacher fortnightly to discuss the children generally and at six month intervals to discuss and write reports on each of the children with learning disabilities. All the school staff attended weekly meetings concerning general school matters.

Each class teacher and the special needs expert met quarterly with the educational psychologist to plan support arrangements for children with special needs, and met periodically with parents. Other meetings with people from outside the school included six-monthly regional meetings of teachers engaged in integrated education.

Evaluators identified several beneficial outcomes of this degree of integration, following some seven years of evolution from a predominantly special class system. For children with special needs these included advantages in being taught by more than one teacher, better social and educational progress, and less likelihood of their being disruptive. The arrangements helped to diminish disagreements among teachers and helped them to see some behavioural difficulties among children as stemming partly from shortcomings in the school. Co-operation among staff, despite the extra work involved, facilitated sharing of expertise and enhanced the quality of their working lives more generally.

Continuing difficulties included the complexities of the arrangements, the extensive time commitments required, the domination by children's chronological ages of their class groupings and of the standards expected of them, the need for further training in teaching integrated classes, and a pay structure that discouraged periodic exchange of class teacher and special needs expert roles.

The United Kingdom example is of a an elementary school on the fringe of an industrial town with a relatively high level of unemployment. The school had a history of having provided, through special classes, for special needs across a geographical area beyond that of its own catchment area.

At the time of the OECD project visits in late 1991, there were 14 full-time teaching staff, 6.5 nursery nurses and two special support assistants. There were nearly 300 children on roll, of whom 46 had statements of special need. Many had physical disabilities as well as some learning difficulty, and a few had severe learning disabilities. Ten were fully integrated in ordinary classes and the remaining 36 were distributed across five special classes. Individual structured integration programmes operated in each special class. The school also ran a nursery, offering 46 part-time places, three of which were taken up by preschool children with statements.

The head was successfully encouraging class teachers to take on children from the school's special classes, thus progressively implementing one of the school's main aims, as stated in the school handbook:

"Through the shared activities it is hoped that understanding of one another's strengths will occur as well as acceptance of one another's weaknesses."

An important aspect of school ethos was an emphasis on integration as a means of educating children, rather than as marking stages at which those with special needs had "caught up" with the rest. A striking feature of the school was the very real acceptance among ordinary children of those with special needs. Both within the classroom and outside it, children would spontaneously and unostentatiously give a helping hand to those needing it. The flexible integration arrangements necessitated complex and ever-changing timetables, and these were facilitated considerably by the fact that special and ordinary class arrangements were all actively managed by the head of the school:

"(...) pupils would go individually to the nursery with a nursery nurse – it was felt that it was beneficial for them to see other, more advanced, children playing and thereby have the opportunity to copy them. Those with less severe difficulties would join a mainstream class for an hour's activities in the afternoon. Mornings were usually devoted to specific language and number work throughout the school and the special classes operated their own curriculum with individual programmes operated through individual and group work. At times, just one or two pupils would be in a mainstream class; at others, a whole special class would be out in mainstream with or without a nursery nurse. Some pupils joined another mainstream class and were taught by their teacher, while others would accompany their special class teacher while she went to a mainstream classroom and taught the class, freeing the regular class teacher to go elsewhere (for example, to teach a specialist subject). Some of the most severely handicapped pupils in the special unit would integrate with another special class."

The Canadian example comes from a New Brunswick district with a strong commitment to integration and a long history of integration practice, including closure of the district's two special schools in the early 1980s and, in accordance with explicit district policy, subsequent shifts from special to ordinary classes. All children, including those with special needs, then had right of access to education in their own local schools.

By 1993 an important feature of the organisation of each school in the district was the student services team, consisting of the school head or deputy head, a guidance counsellor, a methods and resource teacher, and teaching assistants. The district's allocation of staffing to schools was largely on the basis of number of children on roll, but varied to some extent according to the nature of the catchment area. For example, one methods and resource teacher would be allocated to every 200 or so on roll. In the elementary and secondary schools visited as part of the OECD project, pupil-teacher ratios generally were between 16:1 and 21:1, with between 300 and 600 on roll. From the point of view of integration, a key role appeared to be that of the methods and resource teachers:

"The methods and resource teachers' primary duty is to assist classroom teachers in developing instructional programmes for exceptional students. Their role focuses on providing collaborative consultation, teacher to teacher support, and assistance with problem solving. Teacher assistants provide the one-to-one support needed for individual students with severe disabilities, and the overall classroom assistance teachers may require for less intensive situations. Guidance counsellors focus directly on personal student problems as opposed to instructional issues and are part of the student services team in the school. Co-operative education co-ordinators at the junior and senior high school level also serve on the student services team. They assist in arranging job placements for exceptional students. This is an essential part of the overall integration programme, although it is based on integration into the community.''

Another important aspect of the methods and resource teachers' work was receipt of in-service training, on a bi-weekly basis, run by district support services based externally to the school. Topics included multilevel instruction, co-operative learning, problem solving and non-violent crisis intervention. Part of the methods and resource teacher's job was then to help other members of staff acquire these skills too. All staff with integrated children in their classes were allocated ''school enhancement days'', which enabled them to consult other adults, plan assignments, visit other schools and so on.

Networks

Ordinary schools are unlikely to be isolated in their development of whole school policies for special needs, and in the case studies referred to in the previous section the schools concerned had various links with members of the local community, with other schools, with external support services and with district or regional education authorities.

Sometimes links across schools developing integration policies become formalized, and the networks thus created can be powerful aids to the dissemination of good practice. In the Swiss example, the periodic regional meetings of teachers concerned with integration served such a purpose, as did the arrangements in Canada (New Brunswick) for in-service training. One of the Irish studies reports collaboration concerning special education within a region across a group of five ordinary schools.

Extensive networking is reported in a Netherlands study of 28 co-operating elementary schools aiming to maintain children with special needs within the ordinary school system. The schools were relatively small, averaging about 100 on roll, each school had a teacher concerned particularly with special needs, and their co-operation was co-ordinated by the region's education advice centre.

If a school was unable to provide effectively for a particular child, placement in another of the schools was negotiated through the advice centre, thus enabling the child to have the opportunity of a fresh start. With regard to their work generally, the staff of the schools operated a common policy, collaborated in working groups concerned with various aspects of curriculum development (at the time of the OECD project there were 16 such groups in operation), shared materials, agreed on teaching methods and attended in-service courses run at the education advice centre.

As with the implementation of the whole school policies referred to in the previous section, these arrangements fostered extensive co-operation among teachers, provided mutual support, facilitated exchange of ideas, and enabled teachers to develop the attitudes, confidence and skills required for the successful teaching of children with special needs.

Conditions

It can be seen from earlier chapters that integration is only likely to thrive in a school if staff generally are convinced of its value and if they have the personal and material resources needed. The examples presented in this chapter demonstrate the extra impetus integration can have if there is an explicit whole school policy favouring it. They also demonstrate some of the difficulties encountered in implementing such a policy.

From these examples, and from others thrown up through the case studies, there emerges a fairly clear picture of a range of conditions facilitating the successful implementation of a whole school integration policy. They include the following:

- national legislation requiring, or at least promoting, integration;
- regional and district policies supporting integration;
- allocation of national and local special education resources in a manner conducive to integration;
- wholehearted promotion, monitoring and evaluation, by the school's senior management team, of the school's integration policy and its implementation;
- flexible organisation of classes, permitting groupings of various kinds and some interchange of staff roles;
- learning programmes at various levels, for individual and for group work, programmes to develop social as well as academic skills, time to develop, evaluate and modify these programmes;
- staff with general credibility and with special needs expertise, able to offer in-class support and withdrawal teaching, and able to provide consultation and in-service training for class teachers; and
- arrangements, such as the legally binding school working plans that operate in France, enabling all staff to consult, to co-operate, to plan, and to develop and maintain appropriate attitudes and skills.

As indicated above, whole school integration approaches are helped considerably if national and local policies and means of allocation of resources are conducive to their development. They can also benefit greatly from other sources of help external to the school: parents and other members of the local community; special schools; support services; training establishments. It is to these sources we now turn.

Chapter 5

Parental and Community Involvement

Introduction

While the case studies revealed many examples of parental and community involvement in integration arrangements, the focus of the OECD project enquiries was generally on what was happening in the schools themselves. Within the context of a few visits to the schools, it was generally not easy for the enquirers to gather evidence and opinion directly from many of the parents and other community members involved. Consequently, their contribution to the education of children with special needs may be under-represented here.

The Australian project's review of relevant literature in Australia and the United States highlighted a significant positive correlation between disabled children's success in school and the active involvement of their parents in their education, and stressed the importance of securing the genuine inclusion of parents in integration projects. There was also ample evidence of the difficulties experienced by parents in getting themselves to be taken seriously by professionals. There was reference to training programmes designed to help parents overcome such problems, for example by developing negotiating skills.

The case studies, as well as illustrating attempts to involve parents in integration projects, demonstrated some of the difficulties in securing such involvement. In the Greek studies, for example, while no parents reacted negatively to the programmes, only a few were supportive to the extent of working actively with their children at home. Such passivity is not necessarily a function of apathy, as the following extract from one of the Icelandic case studies demonstrates:

"(...) parents interviewed seem to view the school as the 'expert' in their child's education and are reluctant to ask questions, interfere, complain, or make suggestions, even when they do not agree with the school. Therefore, parents rarely confront the school openly and the messages to the school are often subtle and informal. This reluctance on behalf of parents is not because they find the school unapproachable; on the contrary, all of the parents emphasize that they find the school personnel, both administrators and teachers, accessible and easy to talk to."

Judging from the case study reports, the parents were very positively disposed towards integration. However, they were not necessarily representative of parents of disabled children generally, as they had agreed, presumably, to their children's inclusion in integration programmes which by and large were seen as successful.

The most enthusiastic parental endorsement of integration arrangements appeared in responses to a questionnaire follow-up to one of the Swiss projects, but this must be seen against a background of publicised evidence that children in special classes in that country underperformed, and many parents expressed that they were formerly "sold" places in special classes.

Parents may be influenced by factors other than that of quality of education provided. In Belgian and Netherlands studies, for example, the alternative of weekly boarding was a powerful disincentive; even when placements are day placements, travelling times can be excessive.

Parents whose children were not disabled were reported as mainly being either positive or neutral in their attitudes towards integration, recognising its value in helping ordinary children understand special needs. Some were said to express reservations, mainly on the grounds that ordinary children might not get their fair share of attention.

The responses of the heads of 48 elementary schools to an attitude questionnaire, presented as part of one of the Irish case studies, puts this usefully into context. There were indications that although the majority of parents favoured having children with special needs in their schools, they were not quite as favourably disposed as teachers, and the non-disabled children were even more favourably disposed than either parents or teachers.

Advocacy

It can be inferred from the above that only a minority of parents of children with special needs are likely to be highly active as advocates of improvements in the education of their own children, or of children with special needs generally. Nevertheless, the case studies provided many examples of parents as having been highly influential advocates, usually as a result of their seeing their own children as not receiving a fair deal rather than out of a desire to gain advantage. The following extract, again from an Icelandic report as it happens, conveys the general spirit:

"The parents of students with special needs, who were interviewed, were overwhelmingly pleased with how their school had responded to their children's educational needs. Many of them, however, pointed out that they – not the school – had been the ones who discovered the child's problem. They had also been the ones who pressured the school to respond to the child's needs. The parents emphasized the importance of advocating on behalf of their children. They agreed that if parents do not advocate for their children they run the risk of not receiving proper educational services."

A case study report concerning another Icelandic school referred to the school as only having begun to provide for children with special needs as a result of the parents of a disabled child having pressed their son's right to be in a local school; their success had been made possible through administrative support from the school and through the work of a teacher committed to integration. In fact, community involvement generally in this school was exceptionally strong, so much so that parental resistance to a former head's attempted enforcement of a change in policy had precipitated that head's resignation.

In a German study, integrative classes in a city's elementary schools were established by the education authority following a motion initiated by the Parents' council. In a Belgian case study, parents were reported as the driving forces behind the establishment of a support service organising integrated education for visually impaired children, initially having to combat reticence on the part of teachers both in special schools and in ordinary schools. Another Belgian study, concerned with the integration of children with severe learning difficulties in ordinary schools, referred to members of a parents' association, formed originally in the 1970s by parents of five children with Down's syndrome, as having joined forces with professional staff of a child guidance centre to establish such provision.

In a Greek study, there was reference to a teacher's attempts to aid children's transition from a special school by establishing a special class in an ordinary school. There was resistance among the school's parents and teachers until enlisting the support of an influential parent generated a change of attitude. One of the Irish studies found that co-operative arrangements for special education among five ordinary schools had stemmed from initiatives started in the 1960s, when the parents of children with learning disabilities, in the absence of a special school in the area, had set up special classes in local elementary schools. The composite report from the United States referred to parent advocacy groups as having pushed the district education authority to move towards the elimination of segregated schools.

Co-operation

While parents may act as advocates by attempting to influence public service provision from the outside and/or by setting up alternative provision themselves, they may also aid improvements by contributing within existing arrangements. Case studies reported various ways in which parents had contributed to day-to-day school activities.

Some of the case studies referred to attempts by school staff to encourage parents to learn about their children's work in school and supplement this through activities at home. In one of the United Kingdom case studies, these involved teachers in extensive home visiting, which was generally welcomed by parents, though some perceived it as intrusive. In some schools, home-school diaries were used, again not altogether successfully.

In one of the Spanish case studies, teachers of children with hearing impairment prepared holiday work for parents to undertake with the children. In a Belgian project, parental help at home was considered a necessary part of meeting the extra demands of the integration programme, and parents' agreement to this was obtained formally.

Other case studies referred to involvement of parents more directly in the work of the school. In Iceland, some of the parents did voluntary work as classroom assistants. In New Brunswick, Canada, one of the most successful strategies for sustaining parental involvement was thought to be including them as partners in the teachers' problem-solving meetings. In some cases these meetings also included parents whose children did not have disabilities.

In some cases the parents' needs to develop skills as educators were recognised to the extent that they were offered training programmes. In the Spanish case study referred to above, parents were put in touch with sign language classes. In one of the United Kingdom case study schools, staff had run parents' workshops on spelling and reading, including a course on paired reading. One of the Australian packages was designed to train parents and other community volunteers to work with disabled children, singly or in small groups, within the ordinary classroom.

In the French studies, parents (who have the right to be involved in educational decisions concerning their children) participate at meetings, involve themselves in decisions concerning the individualised programmes for their children and are sometimes members of the schools' governing bodies. Usually the schools' working plans will build in regular meetings between parents and professionals and will identify a range of methods for keeping parents informed about their children.

Management

In a number of studies there were references to parental contributions to the work of schools as going beyond in-class support of their own or other disabled children and entering into larger scale organisation and management activities.

Parents of children on the roll of a Belgian special school for children with visual impairment acted on behalf of the school in deciding which ordinary school to approach with regard to their children's integration, and in initiating contacts. Similarly, in a Belgian special school for children with learning difficulties the parents played a major role in securing integrated placements. In the former, the parents also arranged the children's day-to-day transport to and from school and ensured that textbooks were transcribed into Braille when needed.

Fund raising is an activity in which parents were often, and successfully, involved. Funds raised by an Irish voluntary group concerned with children with severe learning difficulties were used to cover the costs of classroom equipment, transport, and in one instance the building of a school extension. In one of the Greek studies, the parents' association also employed a part-time psychologist and a speech therapist for the school. In Finland, a parents' association ran courses and camps for children with visual impairment. The following extract from the United States report gives some indication of the range of parental and community involvement there:

"The school organises foster grandparent, parent volunteer, and peer tutoring programs which are available to all students. Students with moderate or severe disabilities have a big brother/sister program available on a limited basis, particularly for students labelled severely emotionally disturbed. Parent support groups offer some assistance to parents of students with moderate and severe disabilities."

"Some local business and community organisations have donated equipment for students with severe disabilities. Local religious and athletic organisations offer community recreation programs, especially for older students who need career or vocational experiences. The local mental health agency is involved with a few students with moderate and severe disabilities."

"Some businesses and business organisations provide opportunities for students with disabilities who are in financial need. In addition, other organisations often provide opportunities for students with moderate and severe disabilities to attend summer camps or local recreation camps, and will under certain conditions purchase or loan to families necessary equipment."

Chapter 6

Roles of Special Schools

Introduction

As more children with special needs are educated in ordinary schools, so the proportion attending special schools declines, and one type of response to this situation has been to develop the special schools as resource centres, continuing to educate the children with the most severe disabilities but also providing support for children with special needs attending ordinary schools. The resources made available may take the form of equipment or of staffing, and may be for helping the children directly or for training ordinary school staff.

In the Australian project, ten packages demonstrating links of this kind were submitted. While none were evaluated as part of the project, they were described as being of interest and their claims were considered in the light of relevant research findings. The report concluded that special schools could provide valuable help to ordinary schools, subject to certain conditions, including the following:

– special school and ordinary school staff carefully negotiate what support is required and how it is to be offered;
– special school staff have the teacher training and consultancy skills needed; and
– the teaching strategies being advocated are demonstrated, not just talked about.

Several case study reports mentioned aspects of special school support for ordinary schools, but only in a few instances did it provide a major focus for the study. Three of the studies considered here were concerned with visual impairment. In addition, there were services based on a special school for children with moderate learning difficulties and on one for children with severe learning difficulties. All five schools demonstrated successful provision, yet inevitably there were difficulties still to be overcome.

Supporting children with visual impairment

The case study report from Finland was of the work of a school for children with visual impairment. The school also served as the national resource centre for this aspect of education, running in tandem with a smaller but equivalent school for children whose first language is Swedish. As with many special schools, the number of children on roll at the school had declined since the 1970s, in this instance from over 100 in 1976 to 35 in 1992.

The vast majority of the country's children with visual impairment were being educated in ordinary schools, and at the time of the OECD study the special school was maintaining records concerning some 478 such children, some one in seven of them being blind and the rest part-sighted.

The country's approach to identification of and educational planning for these children was highly systematic. Staff of the school were kept informed of developments for all such children from identification onwards and were involved in educational planning as each child reached statutory school age. School records of children's subsequent progress, however, lacked this level of detail.

Links between the special school and ordinary schools were maintained mainly through eight peripatetic teachers, based at the special school. Their work in their assigned areas included helping teachers in ordinary schools, meeting parents, advising local authority administrators, and liaising with the country's 11 regional teachers for the visually impaired. As the peripatetic teachers and the regional teachers exercised very similar functions, there appeared to be a need for their relative contributions to be considered further, to ensure that best use was made of their respective skills.

The special school organised on-site support courses, some for preschool children and some for children integrated into ordinary schools. The courses, usually lasting for a week, were used, for example, to teach mobility, Braille, or the use of other visual aids. They were sometimes used for diagnostic, counselling or advisory work.

The school ran on-site courses for ordinary school teachers with visually impaired children in their classes and for the children's parents. Programmes contained information about the effects of visual impairment on learning, about study techniques and about the use of visual aids. There was some need for systematic assessment of the results of the training given. The school evaluated, devised, displayed and distributed teaching and learning materials in various school subjects and ran a library, supplying books in Braille and sound recordings.

In the Netherlands, an all-age special school for visually impaired children had a similar background, similar organisation of outreach services, and was one of three such national institutes. There too the number on roll had declined markedly as more children with visual impairment were being educated in the region's ordinary schools.

At the time of the OECD study the school had about 150 on roll, with some twenty peripatetic teachers providing a certain amount of support for over 200 children in the region's elementary and secondary schools and almost 100 in various types of special school. The basing of the peripatetic teachers in the special school, while enhancing links between the special school and ordinary schools, was also thought to carry the potential disadvantage of providing too ready a channel along which problematic children in ordinary schools could be transported to segregated specialist provision.

For almost half the region's children with visual impairment the class teachers in the ordinary schools were the main sources of help in school. The peripatetic teachers were allocated support time of from one and a half to seven hours weekly per child, depending on a child's age and severity of disability. While this form of allocation had the advantages of being predictable and easy to administer, its lack of flexibility led to some difficulties in securing appropriate provision.

Support could include assessing, teaching, planning an individual education programme, ensuring the appropriateness of technical aids, and advising teachers and parents. As with the Finnish school, there was a need for more evident independent monitoring of children's progress. The peripatetic teachers also provided training courses, based at the special school:

"Essential for the success of ambulant support and integration as a whole is the training centre (...). Children as well as parents and teachers can rely on an ample supply of different courses. These courses provide information and training but also give the participants the opportunity to exchange experiences, problems and solutions. The training is considered as important for teachers dealing with visually handicapped children. Special courses are provided for arithmetic teachers, teachers of physical education and so on. The courses are free to all participants."

One of the problems experienced at the school was the fact that the teachers selected for peripatetic work were generally the more experienced, whereas the proportion of children with more complex disabilities in the school was increasing. Furthermore, as advisory and training roles of peripatetic teachers differed appreciably from their previous teaching roles, there was a need for their training and induction into their new styles of working.

As part of Norway's plan to convert its special schools to resource centres, the case study school for children with visual impairment was established as one of the country's 13 national competence centres, providing a service across the whole of the country for visually impaired children aged 7 to 13 years. In addition the centre carried some regional functions with respect to adults.

Accommodation included residential facilities for parents, children, teachers and others attending courses. Staffing, up to a full-time equivalent of 87 people, included researchers as well as teachers and teacher trainers. Over the year prior to the OECD study, the centre had undertaken advisory work in relation to between 600 and 700 children with visual impairment.

Resourcing, diagnostic, advisory and training functions were broadly similar to those in the equivalent centres in Finland and in the Netherlands. Rather than relying on a school-based force of peripatetic teachers, however, staff of the centre sought to work in close collaboration with the special education support services run by regional and district authorities, supplementing and extending their provision rather than duplicating or replacing it.

Case study researchers evaluated the centre's provision by selecting a sample of 150 children and asking almost 600 people associated with these children – school administrators, educational psychologists, teachers and parents – to rate various aspects of the centre's provision on a five point scale.

With respect to most of its functions the centre was generally regarded as successful, exhibiting high levels of competence, and the enquirers concluded that provision for children had not deteriorated as a result of the closing of the segregated special school. Many of the children about whom advice was sought, not surprisingly, had disabilities additional to that of visual impairment. This raised the question as to whether individual national centres should specialise in single disabilities, or whether each should deal with a more comprehensive range.

There were some criticisms of the centre's production and supply of adapted text-books and other specialist materials. Consumers' dissatisfactions related to the delay in their delivery rather than to their quality. Children with visual impairment were said seldom to receive their books at the same time as the rest of the class received theirs.

There were significant criticisms, particularly among parents, of the local support services on which the centre relied. Criticisms were aimed at educational psychologists and health visitors rather than teachers, and the educational psychologists themselves expressed some dissatisfaction with the service they were able to offer to the visually impaired. The enquirers concluded that, despite its high competence, the centre could not be fully effective unless local support services could be made effective too.

Supporting children with moderate learning difficulties

The United Kingdom school under consideration here was one of a number of the country's special schools for children with moderate learning difficulties to run outreach services. As with other case studies, the development of this service was in part a response to falling rolls in special schools; in this instance, two special schools had amalgamated.

As well as providing for its 120 children aged 5 to 16 on roll, the school offered two kinds of outreach service, which altogether supported 189 children in ordinary schools. Firstly, three teachers based at the school ran a support and advice service available to staff of all the 60 or so ordinary schools in the area. Secondly, the school had more structured arrangements with seven of the local ordinary schools, termed "cluster schools". Each cluster school admitted children with officially recognised diagnoses ("statements") of special needs arising from moderate learning difficulties. Each had a teacher from the special school attached, on a full-time basis, to help the school provide for up to 10 children with statements.

Both types of outreach service enabled special school staff to support the part-time integration in ordinary schools of children on roll at the special school as well as to advise on means of helping those with special needs on the rolls of the ordinary schools. Advisory work, in-service training and provision of materials were broadly of the kind already described in relation to other case studies, though this service did have particular features worth mentioning here.

Access to the special school's advisory service was conditional on some special support already having been provided in the ordinary school and on discussion with the parents already having been undertaken. Decisions on how best to help were made through a panel, which was led by senior staff of the school and which members of local authority advisory services were invited to join. Any help offered by the school was expressed in the form of short-term contracts. Meetings were held annually with local professionals as means of assessing the services' effectiveness.

In the ordinary school, a support teacher would go through the class teacher's plans for the whole class, not just for those with special needs. The support teacher would take the class, giving the class teacher a chance to observe particular children in action. The two would together draw up further plans, ensuring that they would be differentiated to allow for the full ability range in the class. On occasion, support teachers would provide an in-service training course for the staff of a department or of a school as a whole.

Both types of outreach service were regarded as successful, with the cluster arrangement being the more powerful but also having more difficulties in maintenance. One of the problems of the cluster model was the reputation acquired by cluster schools. On the one hand, some parents saw them as stigmatised by taking on problem children and avoided placing their own children there. On the other hand, some parents placed their children there "on the quiet", hoping that any problems they had would be treated.

One of the less successful features of the model was the slowness with which the special school reduced its number on roll, and there was some question as to whether more could be placed successfully in cluster schools. The extent to which any resistance to this might stem from ordinary school or special school staff was not clear, though the fact that children with statements were being fully integrated into classes of 30 must have had some relevance. Certainly there was resistance among staff of ordinary schools to the idea of extending the model to include children with severe learning difficulties.

Supporting children with severe learning difficulties

While outreach services based on schools for children with severe learning difficulties are not common, a few exist as this successful case study from the United Kingdom illustrates. The school was situated in a market town surrounded by close-knit village communities and provided for some 45 children aged 2 to 19. In addition to their severe learning difficulties, a number also had physical disabilities and/or sensory impairment.

The special school had the advantage of sharing a site with an elementary school in which staff were positively disposed towards children with special needs, partly because the school made special arrangements for a number of such children on its roll, including some with specific learning difficulties.

About half the children on roll at the special school attended the elementary school on a part-time basis, each group being accompanied by a nursery nurse who would help out generally in the classes in which these children were integrated. In most cases this extra help more than compensated the class teacher for the extra work involved in providing for the disabled children. Integrated activities were chosen carefully: play, lunch, physical education, dance, and a few other practical activities in which their earlier levels of development would not be unduly disadvantageous.

The special school children ceased to attend the elementary school once they had passed beyond its chronological age range, even though they were young developmentally, as the special school staff were concerned to engage them in age-appropriate activities. As they reached the age of about 15, however, they participated in structured activities arranged for them in association with secondary students of a similar age, who visited the special school for this purpose, helped out at lunchtimes, and sometimes took the older special school students off on short outings. In addition, some special school students attended the secondary school as a separate group for technology and some were integrated into ordinary classes on an individual basis for home economics, physical education and music.

One of the special school teachers also ran an outreach service, visiting children with learning difficulties in surrounding elementary and secondary schools, and offering teaching, assessment, advice, and preparation of teaching materials. In keeping children with special needs in ordinary schools this service was found valuable, particularly as there was a predominance of small rural schools and a strong village community ethos favouring integration. As in the previous example, the outreach teacher provided the service on the basis of specific short-term contracts.

Conditions

As the examples supplied in this chapter illustrate, outreach work can be a successful response to the diminishing special school population, can form an integral part of the implementation of a region's or country's integration strategy, and can enhance partial integration arrangements for children on the rolls of special schools. Success, however, is not easy to achieve, and certain conditions which are conducive to it can be identified. Case study findings indicated the following:

- the children, parents and teachers concerned, teachers in the special school as well as those in the ordinary schools, are motivated towards integration;
- facilities exist to ensure that the special school teachers undertaking outreach work develop the assessment, training and advisory skills needed;
- if those advising in ordinary schools are based in the special school, their work helps teachers to cope for themselves, rather than to rely on special schools to look after the children presenting significant difficulties;
- if those based at the special school undertake extensive advisory work in the ordinary schools, they have appropriate arrangements with local authority services, thus avoiding duplication of effort;
- if those based at the special school rely on local authority based advisers to undertake all but the most specialised support work, rather than take it on themselves, it is essential that staffing and expertise in the local authority services are sufficient for this to occur;
- outreach staff and staff in ordinary schools have sufficient flexibly allocated time to negotiate, plan, evaluate, and develop their skills further as well as to teach;
- outreach staff negotiate specific and finite arrangements, including learning targets, for the support they are to provide;
- special school staff arranging integrated placements take due account of staffing levels in the ordinary schools as well as of the expertise and goodwill available;

- special school staff constructively take account of any effects their outreach work may have on the reputation within the community of the ordinary schools with which they are concerned;
- special school staff monitor both the progress of children for whom they undertake outreach work and the professional development of the teachers they help, using the results to evaluate and revise their provision;
- outreach staff develop and maintain a stock of appropriate support materials, ensuring that ordinary school teachers and children can have access to them when they need them;
- allocation of special school staff time and expertise to the school's various teaching, resourcing, advisory and training functions is such that all these functions remain viable;
- special school staff consider carefully the range of expertise they are to offer, attempting to tailor this to meet local needs;
- to organise and manage all of these aspects, the co-ordination of the various systems is imperative, whether this will result (as in France) or not in the creation of contracts, agreements or other local arrangements.

Chapter 7

External Support Services

Introduction

For teachers providing for children with special needs within their ordinary classes, such support as is available comes mostly from within the school, and within-school support services have been outlined in earlier chapters, mainly in Chapters 2 and 4 (Part II). Occasionally, support occurs across schools, and various kinds of support provided for ordinary schools from some special schools have been considered in Chapter 6.

There is in addition a multiplicity of sources of support which are external to schools altogether, though the impact of any one of them on the average class teacher may well be minimal by comparison with that of support coming from within the school. Most of these external support services are run by district or regional education authorities, some are managed through health or social services, some by voluntary bodies and some are organised nationally, for example by a government's ministry of education.

Case studies from the majority of the countries involved in this phase of the study acknowledged the existence of external support services, but acknowledgement mostly took the form of passing references in reports concerned essentially with within-school matters. The general impression given by these references was that support services were offered by many people, with varying kinds and levels of expertise, but that they often had only marginal influence on the schools.

Personnel

The Austrian case study report provides some indication of the range of personnel likely to be involved in an external support service based on a local educational authority. The report referred to the establishment of an advisory team, appointed at district level to help heads and teachers in ordinary schools, along with parents of children with special needs, arrive at decisions as to whether the individual children concerned should be educated on an integrated basis in ordinary schools.

Meetings of the advisory team were to be chaired by a representative of the local education authority and membership, in addition to those likely to be involved directly in a child's education, could include school inspectors, educational psychologists, therapists, peripatetic and advisory teachers, directors of relief hostel accommodation (if planned), and doctors (if medical factors influenced educability).

Similarly from the point of view of personnel involved, the Canadian (New Brunswick) report referred to the education district's policy makers as being closely involved with the work of the district's student services team, which consisted of two methods and resource teachers, a school social worker, a school psychologist and a speech therapist.

Similar personnel but a rather different basis for organisation was featured in a Belgian early-help service, established to advise on integration and funded partly by a parents' association and partly through local and national level public services. Staff consisted of a physiotherapist, a speech therapist, three psychologists, a remedial teacher, a social worker, a neuropaediatrician and a parent. A similar constellation of personnel contributed to a network of mobile support services run for young disabled children across a region of Germany.

Accessibility and function

Several of the case study reports referred to external support services as being in existence but not very accessible. For example, one of the Greek case study reports commented on a district peripatetic diagnostic team as having insufficient time to undertake detailed assessments. An Irish report cited few children being referred for assessment, following cutbacks in psychological services, and mentioned a need for greater input from speech therapists and medical auxiliaries. An Icelandic report mentioned limited availability of educational psychologists but reasonable access to health services.

These passing references to external support services gave the impression that the multi-disciplinary services were largely concerned with diagnosis and advice on children's educational placement rather than with help with teaching methods. There were some references, however, to peripatetic teachers and to special education advisers as providing support broadly of the kind attributed to special school outreach staff in Chapter 6 (Part II). Also, as the following extract from a case study report of a school in the United Kingdom shows, some local education authorities (LEAs) vigorously promoted in-service education and training (INSET) aimed at curriculum development:

"There was a considerable amount of activity in the LEA as regards INSET on matters relating to provision for pupils with special educational needs. There were various curriculum guidelines and teachers were working across discrete special needs areas. There was also a 'special educational needs and the National Curriculum' forum organised by the special needs inspector and there were meetings for every special school teacher, service staff and special needs co-ordinators. There had been a lot of work on the whole curriculum."

A striking example of a successful special education support service emerges from the Canadian (New Brunswick) study, touched on earlier in this chapter and considered in more detail in Chapter 4 (Part II). This showed the work of a district's student services team to be highly valued in schools, primarily because it concentrated on helping teachers develop their own skills rather than focusing on assessment and placement of individual children:

"(...) the School District Number 12 student services team supports the schools in a variety of ways such as by providing professional development training, bi-weekly meetings for the methods and resource teachers, and indirect and direct interventions, and by problem-solving. School staff and parents indicated that district office staff have been a strong support team and their leadership has influenced the development and success of integration in the schools. Many school staff felt that integration would not have happened without the leadership, commitment and support from the School District Number 12 student services team."

The fact that the district had nailed its colours to the mast several years previously by closing its two special schools and firmly adhering to a total integration policy must have helped schools and their support services get away from a preoccupation with assessment as a possible gateway to placement outside the ordinary system. It would be simplistic, however, to assume that this policy implementation was the sole cause, or even a necessary condition, of the evident success of the district's external support service.

At this point it will be useful to look at three other external support services, one from the Netherlands, one from Spain and one from Switzerland, none of which had closed the door on special schooling.

Three examples

The network of 28 co-operating elementary schools in the Netherlands has already been referred to in Chapter 4 (Part II), and mention was made there of the fact that this network was co-ordinated by the region's education advice centre.

Within a total pupil-teacher ratio of 21.4 to 1 and a child population of 2 789, it was claimed that the network had succeeded in maintaining 260 children with special needs, some 88 of whom might otherwise have attended special schools, within the elementary school system. Furthermore, more children had moved from special schools to these elementary schools than in the other direction.

Visiting as part of the CERI study confirmed claims that the proportion of children in segregated education was well below the average for the country, that the children with special needs in the ordinary elementary schools were progressing well, and that teacher morale was high.

Each school implemented a whole school policy for special needs and had a teacher designated special needs expert. It should be mentioned that these were small village schools and that placement in a special school would be a particularly large step, as the country's existing special schools were all situated outside the region.

The education advice centre (the OAB) employed educational specialists, consultants and teachers. A main aim, agreed with the schools, was to help them maintain children with special needs in ordinary schools. The centre co-ordinated the development of an education policy common to the elementary schools, ran in-service training in special education for the teachers and supplied them with materials. One of its roles was to negotiate agreements between elementary schools to move problematic children from one school to another, in order to give these children fresh starts:

"Teachers were uniformly positive about it, finding in it a source of mutual support, an opportunity for sharing experiences and problems, and a major arena for professional development. The network seems to have a non-competitive ethos, with staff building on each other's strengths and learning a great deal from each other (...)."

"The network is not confined to special education. Indeed it seems to operate across a wide range of the functions of the schools – curriculum policy, staff deployment and resourcing, indicating that a wider process of innovation is taking place in these schools. Thus, the school co-operation which permits the degree of integration that is taking place is not defined in terms of pupils with learning difficulties; to that extent the integration initiative is a normal part of the life of the schools (...)."

"The OAB appears to play a critical role. Without its animating influence it is unlikely that the school networking or the integration initiative would have developed."

The Spanish example was a pedagogical orientation centre, a district's education support service which incorporated a special education element and promoted its integrational stance. It was selected for study as being the most highly rated among 22 such services evaluated through interviews and the use of attitude scales with teachers and other professionals involved.

Within the centre a multi-professional special education team of three, along with two speech therapists, serviced 25 schools, 10 of them secondary. To that extent the service was similar in organisation to that of external support services already referred to. It differed, however, in that it also included eight assistants who worked to the multi-professional team but who were located in the schools, serving as support teachers.

Each member of the team had a cluster of schools assigned and visited each school in the cluster once every two or three weeks as a rule, more often if necessary. A visit would often involve observing a child, administering tests, perhaps interviewing parents, discussing the child with the class teacher, preparing a report, and discussing this with class teacher and support teacher. The three would then jointly prepare an action programme.

Team members also contributed to the centre's in-service training programme, very much welcomed by teachers and fronted by an annual seminar, offered to all the teachers in the district, with content based on a prior enquiry concerning their interests and needs. The annual seminar led to further seminars and workshops, run through the following year.

School staff generally implemented whole school policies favouring integration, expressed positive attitudes towards integration and made good use of special education materials and special education staff based there. They appeared, however, to make less effective use of external support.

Job satisfaction was reported as being very high among the assistants based in the schools, but less high for the external support staff, who found their extensive travelling between centre and schools a problem. The main needs overall appeared to be for more training in special education for class teachers.

The third example, from an isolated and sparsely populated region of Switzerland, is of a peripatetic support service for the 10 per cent or so of the ordinary school population considered to have special educational needs. Prior to the development of this service, children with relatively rare disabilities, from Italian-speaking families, had to be educated in residential establishments in regions where the dominant language was either French or German. At the time of the CERI study, 1.5 per cent of the region's school age population attended special schools, a much lower percentage than that in the country as a whole.

The case study focused on two groups, both with relatively rare disabilities: children with visual impairment, and children with brain damage.

The initiative for the service for children with visual impairment came from a parents' association pressing for day schooling in Italian. The roles of the special educator appointed were to help parents in their work with their preschool children, to consult with staff of the residential establishments in other regions with a view to organising children's return, to arrange placement in local schools and advise on provision, and to maintain contact with residential institutions, obtaining their continuing specialist advice as necessary.

An evaluation found the service to be successful, with some 15 children being helped in this way and only one child placed residentially. In addition to advice from the peripatetic special educator, support for the ordinary schools concerned included allowance of additional teaching and preparation time in these schools, access to training courses, and computer-based production of Braille texts and visual aids. The main problem encountered was that of securing the necessary liaison among a multiplicity of specialists responsible to a variety of employers.

Initiative in developing the service for brain-damaged children was more recent and came from the regional education authority. From an educational point of view one of the main problems was that when children and young people had to be hospitalised outside the region, following accidents or for operations on tumours, they were eventually sent back to school without sufficient preparation for the new challenges to learning that they and the schools would have to face.

The strategy adopted was similar to that used for children with visual impairment. Staff of the region's peripatetic special education support service consulted hospital and convalescence establishment staff, made contact with the children during hospitalisation if appropriate, undertook preparatory work with the children, their families and the schools, and arranged any extra teaching help necessary in the schools.

As before, liaison across professions presented problems but these were mainly surmountable. At the time of the OECD study a dozen young people, mainly adolescents involved in road accidents, had been helped in this way and the service was functioning satisfactorily.

Discussion

Some of the conditions conducive to the successful implementation of integration policies by external support services are broadly the same as those listed at the end of Chapter 6 (Part II) as being needed among outreach staff of special schools. For example, external support service staff need to work in a climate positively disposed towards integration, they need to be able to develop the appropriate assessment, training and advisory skills, they need to help teachers to cope for themselves rather than be overdependent on outside agencies, and they need to collaborate with other advisers.

A crucial difference between external support service staff and support staff based in schools is that the former are unlikely to have direct responsibilities for educating children, and can therefore be considered able to take an impartial view of the children's educational needs. In practice this is rarely the case, as they are generally employed by district or regional education authorities, which have their own priorities. Nevertheless, if they have the appropriate assessment skills and credentials they are likely to serve as gatekeepers to special schools.

If teachers in ordinary schools feel overwhelmed by the problems presented by children with special needs, the external support service staff may then spend a great deal of their time exercising this gatekeeping function, at the expense of their training and advisory roles, and may themselves become overwhelmed. Yet, as the case study reports referred to above illustrate, it is support services' training and advisory functions, particularly if they can have impact at the level of the whole school, that are so much appreciated.

Given this problem, it is tempting to think, following the example from Canada (New Brunswick), of closing the special schools, but doing this is not necessarily either feasible or advisable in other countries, and in any case it was an action arrived at after many years of negotiation and educational development in the ordinary schools. But it does bring us back to the perception of the whole school as a key unit for innovation and development.

In exercising training and advisory functions, external support staff, by virtue of their professional diversity, may well be able to offer skills less common among teachers. The helping skills workshop package featured in the Australian case study report provides some indication as to what these may include. The package, designed for use by support service staff working with teachers, aimed to enhance people's existing communication and problem-solving abilities. Topics included developing assertiveness skills, managing stress, understanding family problems, and clarifying roles.

As well as identifying the school as a key unit for development, this chapter also identifies training as a key mechanism for change. It is to this topic that we now turn.

Chapter 8

Training

Introduction

As the many references to training in previous chapters indicate, case studies from the majority of the countries involved in the CERI study acknowledged access to appropriate in-service training as being an essential feature of successful integration programmes. Most of the references were to teachers as the recipients of training, though this was not invariably the case. For example, several training programmes for parents were mentioned in Chapter 5 (Part II). Training for contributions to special education integration programmes may also be useful to other groups, such as inspectors, advisers, social workers, volunteers, care workers in residential schools, and classroom assistants not qualified as teachers.

Because of the nature of the case studies, the references made in earlier chapters to teacher training have been to in-service training for people already qualified as teachers, rather than to initial training. This should not be taken to imply that initial training in special education, when it occurs, is not of value.

As the case studies were generally school-based, the references to trainers have been to people employed in ordinary schools, special schools or local authority support services. This should not be taken to negate the value of the substantial in-service training courses offered by teacher trainers employed by universities and colleges. By way of compensation, examples presented below have been selected so as to include some indication of the nature of their contribution.

Foci

The focus of training may be on an individual teacher, on selected teachers within a school (for example, on heads), on the whole staff of a school, or on various groups of professionals employed in external support services. It may be that all the teachers in a school need to undertake short-term training for a specific purpose, but not all at the same time.

In these circumstances a free-standing training package, consisting perhaps of a handbook supported by audio and/or video material, can be of particular value. The following extract, from the report of a United Kingdom case study of a secondary school with a unit for children with hearing impairment, illustrates the point. The teacher offering the training referred to had herself attended a substantial special education course run by teacher trainers employed in a higher education establishment:

"Each teacher, on appointment to the school, was invited to visit the unit and learn about its methods and equipment. A new teacher was able to listen to filtered speech, the kinds of sounds that a hearing impaired child ordinarily experienced, and become familiar with the effects of amplifying speech. The same opportunities were arranged for all pupils entering year seven, and this experience was most instructive in understanding the situation of pupils with a hearing loss. Teachers and pupils were able to recognise the difficulties experienced by hearing impaired pupils and, more importantly, to realise that they had ordinary learning needs which could be met through special help (...)."

"This facility had been offered to each established teacher who admitted a hearing impaired child to class, and further training was arranged also. The teacher was provided with written guidelines on special teaching methods and the ways of supporting pupils in the classroom. This covered the best positions for teacher and learner, the teacher's use of the radio microphone and the pupil's use of the hearing aid, clarity of speech and lip movements, contextual cues and the ways of strengthening language structures. For example, there were indications about the kinds of sounds that were heard most distinctly, the degrees of difficulty in hearing vowels and consonants and the ways in which the pupil could develop a mental set which governed the anticipation of what was to be heard next (...)."

"The teachers' recollections were that this kind of help was invaluable when they had first taken responsibility for a handicapped child's learning. They remembered being initially uncertain about what was required of them, and being anxious in case they were not able to do what was best for the pupil or the others in the class. Their first problem had usually been one of self-confidence, and the specialist teacher's help had been necessary at this stage to reassure them about their own usefulness".

As well as illustrating training organised within a school, the above extract also demonstrates the cascade element so useful in training, whereby the training of one person (in this instance on a course in a higher education establishment) itself generates training for others.

A similar cascade effect was inherent in the Canadian (New Brunswick) training, already described in Chapters 4 and 7 (Part II), whereby the district's student services team provided ongoing in-service training for groups of methods and resource teachers from the district's schools, with each methods and resource teacher then running similar in-service training within that teacher's own school. It should be noted that this provision did not consist simply of information-providing. Joint problem-solving constituted an important feature of the training, to which people other than teachers, notably parents, were invited.

In-service training at district level was also a feature of a city-wide development of integration classes in Germany. Here, as part of the plan, integration class teachers had in-service training time of two hours per week allocated in their first year and one hour per week in the third. In some instances the training offered, while focusing on teachers within a school or on representatives of schools across a district, may be part of a larger scale plan, conceived at regional level. The following extract reports in-service training undertaken in the United Kingdom by teachers in an elementary school and a secondary school, linked for various purposes, including that of staff development. It illustrates local and regional aspects of the training offered, and includes national elements:

"The regional policy on learning difficulties, adopted in 1983, was innovative and the rapid training of learning support staff in primary and secondary schools was necessary in order to implement it. The main area of in-service support was, until recently, a two year part-time course leading to a Diploma in learning difficulties (...). The course was prepared jointly by the Regional Council and a college of education and was validated by the Council for National Academic Awards (CNAA) (...). The course was taught mainly within the region and involved face-to-face teaching, tutor supervision and distance learning, with the aim of preparing staff to fulfil five professional roles:

– co-operative teaching;
– direct teaching of pupils with learning difficulties;
– supporting pupils who needed to overcome temporary difficulties;
– consultancy to mainstream colleagues; and
– in-service training of mainstream colleagues."

"Some of the teachers in the primary and secondary school had undertaken the diploma and were now qualified. The acting principal teacher of the secondary learning support department was currently following a diploma course offered by the Open University. The course involved mainly distance learning and was nationally recognised. Following a reconsideration of the cost implications of training, the region now recommended the Open University diploma as the main route for obtaining specialist qualifications in learning support (...)."

"Learning support teachers from the primary and the secondary school were invited to be members of a District group, formed to respond to the national guidelines on English. Another secondary learning support teacher was a member of a local 5-14 mathematics working group. These groups will be involved in the in-service training of mainstream staff of primary and secondary schools and other 5-14 groups will be established at a later date, and will include learning support staff."

Several references to in-service training described it as part of a national plan. For example, the national training in the education of children with visual impairment in Finland, based on a special school, has already been referred to in Chapter 6 (Part II). In one of the Spanish case study schools, most of the teaching staff were taking part in an in-school training programme sponsored by the Ministry of Education, with more than 400 schools participating, whereby staff analysed their needs, prioritised, and then drew up and implemented their own training plans.

The Icelandic report referred to a national strategy, for training special educators, which combined a university-based course offering with school-based opportunities. The university-based course, followed on a two year full-time or four year part-time basis, led to a certificate qualifying its recipients to teach children with special needs both in special schools and in ordinary schools. As the national need for these teachers, however, was such that it could not be met through this course's output, averaging some 25 teachers annually, the course was revised to encompass the following extension:

"Linked to the revision of the program for special educators was the running of so-called Professional Skills courses, focusing on how to respond to special needs in regular schools, which 5 to 600 teachers have attended since. The course model is a cascade one where teachers are trained as facilitators to lead a self-education course for their fellow teachers at school, using material which they themselves have written. The facilitator courses lasted 15 weeks followed by a two year part-time course in the schools. These courses have been evaluated positively by most of the participant schools, not least the schools which have found it hard to free their teachers for in-service courses at the University College of Education, on account of long distances, shortage of staff and high costs."

An action research package

Most of the nine training packages successfully tested in the Australian project have been mentioned already in this report. One not yet considered, an action research package designed as a vehicle for in-service training for the individual teacher in the ordinary school, is particularly useful for presentation at this point, as it embodies several features of effective in-service training.

A key characteristic of the action research package was that the teacher undertaking the work was able to draw on the expertise of a support group of some three or four people, identified at the outset as being able to provide help and advice specifically relevant to the tasks envisaged.

In one trial, for example, the teacher had elected to work individually with a six year old boy with reading difficulties. Her support group consisted of a special education support teacher, a university lecturer and a special programmes co-ordinator. Following an initial planning meeting of the group, the teacher attended a workshop on action research run by the lecturer, then worked with the lecturer to plan a teaching programme. The programme involved extending the child's phonic ability, establishing a sight vocabulary and using this vocabulary in story writing.

The teacher was released from class duties sufficiently to undertake daily half hour or one hour sessions with the boy over a seven week period. As well as being given time to teach the child, the teacher allocated time to meet periodically with the members of the support group, for planning and monitoring purposes, and to write an evaluative report at the end of the programme. Gains, in addition to the boy's progress, included the teacher's increased skills, the interest of other school staff in undertaking similar work, and increased involvement of the parents, as voluntary classroom helpers, in the work of the school.

Other trials included a mathematics programme with a group of four children and a language programme, involving a speech therapist as one of the support group, with a child experiencing severe speech difficulties. While the package was found to be of considerable value, some weaknesses emerged in the trials. As a result of this, some of the content was revised, for example to provide a clearer exposition of the action research approach being applied.

Essential elements

Inevitably, any assessment here of the contribution of training to the success of integration programmes must rely heavily on the Australian case studies and their literature review. The main conclusion arising from these studies was that two main factors contributed to success: a supportive school environment generally and, more specifically, a relevant professional development programme. Such a programme was seen to be needed both to enable the class teacher to develop the necessary skills and to foster positive attitudes towards integration across the school community. The following four clusters of essential elements of a comprehensive professional development programme were identified:

- comprehensiveness of package content and design: basis in theory and inclusion of awareness-raising material, informational content, practical techniques, "how to" skills and strategies for effective teaching for all students;
- the process of training: experiential, expert presenters, opportunities for practice, feedback and follow-through and time release for teacher reflection, debate and planning;
- support aspects: interactive training with other teachers, access to experts and on-going support of school visits, networking and ideas exchanges with other teachers; and
- teacher and school commitment and involvement: teacher ownership of the training, affirmation of teacher skills, whole school training together, needs analysis, basis in school needs, joint action planning and principal endorsement.

Chapter 9

Problems and Solutions

Introduction

Because of the nature of the project, focusing as it does on established integration programmes generally considered to be successful, the reports provided are bound to underestimate the extent to which problems occur in developing integration programmes more generally.

Problems which invariably prove insurmountable will not have been referred to and those occurring during the early phases, if remembered at all, may well have been recalled in relative tranquillity. Nevertheless, case study reports provided by almost all the participating countries included references to problems encountered, particularly in the earlier stages of the integration programmes studied.

Whereas some of the problems referred to would be likely to occur in the development of any innovatory programme, others are specific to integration. Some problems are likely to occur at a particular stage in an integration programme, others can occur throughout. In this chapter the sequence of presentation of problems, and of their solutions where they have been seen to exist, is in accordance with the stage at which they seem most likely to first appear.

Problems may first appear at the time a programme is being initiated, when it is first being implemented, as it is being maintained once it has been established, or as it is being evaluated. Although the section on evaluation is placed at the end of the chapter, evaluation is of course recognised as a process which should occur throughout the development of the integration programme, not just at the end.

Each of the following sections starts with large scale problems, for example those experienced at national level, and works its way down to the individual classroom. Needless to say, the larger scale problems are not necessarily either the most severe or the most resistant to change. There is also some sequencing from more general innovation problems through to those specific to integration.

Initiation

Broadly speaking, the initiation phase can be regarded as that preceding firm agreement to implement the programme. Initiation problems occurring at the national level can be exemplified conveniently by the Australian experience. Here the chosen tasks were to review relevant literature, collect training packages relevant to integration in special education, get the most promising ones sampled and evaluate the outcome.

Before this could happen, the project committee had to secure the co-operation of the Ministry of Education of each state, and that of the chief executives of the various education authorities within these states. While this was fairly effectively accomplished by letter, it took time. Furthermore, each letter sought to have a senior officer nominated as contact person, and this did not happen in all cases.

Consequently, there may have been packages in existence that were not among the 111 eventually submitted. Once the nine most promising had been selected, there were various problems in getting them tested. These included shortages of expertise or time, lack of commitment, incomplete understanding of the evaluation requirements, and logistical difficulties. As the number of potential organisers of trials considerably exceeded the number of packages to be tested in this particular project, these shortcomings did not present overwhelming problems.

One of the necessary conditions for innovation appears to be the existence of a highly motivated initiator, preferably of high status within the community but not necessarily part of the system within which innovation occurs. In Belgium, for example, while in one case study the "mover and shaker" was an inspector of special education, in another it was a doctor with a hearing-impaired child who secured paramedical services for other similarly disabled children, and in a third it was a group of parents of children with Down's syndrome.

While it is much easier for integration programmes to get started if they have active support at national, regional and district levels, there is still likely to be much convincing needed at the school level. This can take considerable time and, if the innovation has been initiated at one of the higher levels, the fact that it is operating on a "top down" basis can in itself generate some resistance. In one of the Swiss case studies, where much of the initiative had been taken at the regional level, later enquiry revealed widespread dissatisfaction at the "grass roots" level, where people thought that they should at least have been kept better informed.

The development in Canada (New Brunswick) well illustrates the time scale on which innovation at district level may have to operate. Resource rooms in the district's ordinary schools began to replace special class arrangements in the late seventies, and the special schools were closed in the early eighties.

In the mid eighties, provisional legislation shifted the onus on district authorities by obliging them to make a case for removing a child from an ordinary class, whereas hitherto the onus had been on the child to demonstrate sufficient competence to enter.

Also in the mid eighties, at district level a policy decision was made to provide for all children, with extra support as necessary, in ordinary classes in ordinary schools.

Following a period of discussion at community and school levels, this was adopted by the governing bodies of the district's schools.

At school level, in response both to general statements of intent and to specific instances of proposed integration, various kinds of expression of resistance among class teachers were referred to in case study reports. In addition to fears of being overloaded with work and lacking the skills necessary to deal with anticipated problems, there were fears of erosion of privacy and of extra accountability. Some teachers had difficulty in getting away from their perception of special educators as working with small groups in segregated settings rather than in ordinary classrooms.

If the schools did not have declared pro-integration policies actively promoted by heads and the schools' governing bodies, there could be concern as to whether this was the ''right'' thing to do. Some teachers and parents expressed fear that less able children would lower standards among the more able and that the presence of children with physical or sensory disabilities would be upsetting, or at least distracting, for the rest. Not expressed, but presumably underlying some statements, were questions as to whether these children had a right to mix with the majority.

Some resistance among special educators was reported. Some preferred one-to-one or small group work in segregated settings, and were not sure that they would have the skills necessary to work in ordinary classes or to act as advisers. For them too, work in integrated settings could involve loss of privacy and increase in public accountability. In some cases, their prestige would be associated with special schooling and could be felt to be at risk.

Furthermore, it must be recognised that the children most likely to transfer from special schools to ordinary schools as integration proceeds are the very children who are likely to stand out as assets to a special school, being among the more academically able, physically skilled and socially competent.

Reports referred to the use of various strategies to overcome some of these problems. Special educators can make preliminary visits to ordinary schools and invite ordinary school teachers to visit special schools. Sharing in tasks, in playground duty for example, can help generate mutual confidence and a mood of co-operation. One of the Swiss case study reports made particular mention of the value of having special educators take the lead in initiating integration, as they can be thought of as being likely to be the main losers in the process, and therefore unlikely to have a vested interest in advocating it.

Support teachers can explain their work in ordinary schools at meetings including parents of ordinary children. Meetings of this kind may help parents and teachers, not only to see what is involved but also to develop realistic rather than magical expectations concerning disabled children's progress, perhaps coming to see the process as being one of maximising their capabilities rather than as one of ensuring that they catch up with the rest. The Swedish report referred to three levels of in-service training for ordinary school staff at this stage: information about disabilities, awareness training to help staff understand what it is like to be disabled, and information about teaching methods.

Other strategies referred to in reports included starting with willing teachers and more capable children, starting in smaller schools, offering temporary placement with early review, placing the child in ordinary school but keeping the child on the register of the special school, preparing the child through information about the ordinary school's customs and rules, and starting integration in practical rather than academic subjects. The Danish report acknowledged the fact that anxious teachers may be over-demanding of teacher help and material resources initially; one way of showing that these are not needed is to supply them for a time.

All the professionals, parents and young people who were asked during the course of the four French case studies agreed that the process of integration should be well planned (and not disorganised or sudden), negotiated with all of the parties concerned and should take account of short, medium and long term considerations.

Implementation

The Australian project illustrated various implementation problems that can arise at national and regional levels. Some of those referred to as initiation problems arose again, not necessarily in the same places, during implementation: lack of expertise, time, motivation or material resources.

Some problems arose because of change of staff, with new staff lacking the background or the briefing of their predecessors. Others occurred as a result of bureaucratic protocol. Some packages were thought to lack relevance to the particular settings in which they were being placed. Copyright problems emerged in some instances. Despite these difficulties, the project sustained its national character, as all the major regions of the country were represented either in the production of packages or in their testing.

Implementation problems were reported in the majority of the countries undertaking case studies. In Austria, the experiment was suffering because not enough time had been allowed for associated teacher training. In Belgium, children with visual impairment had to attend a special school for a period because the ordinary schools could not mount training in Braille. In another Belgian case study involving temporary placement in special school, there were difficulties in sustaining the commitment of the ordinary school during this period.

In one of the Greek studies, integration on a part-time basis resulted in some distortion of the curriculum, with some of the children missing out on creative and performing activities. In an Irish study, assessment reports were not made available to the teachers taking on children. In this same study, opportunities for integration were limited by the fact that many classes already had 35 or more children in them. In the Netherlands, bureaucratic problems caused delays in the supply of equipment and teaching materials needed.

Some problems of stigmatisation were reported. In a Greek study, the stigma of a special classroom for children being transferred from a special school was overcome by making the room serve also as the school library and resource base for shared technical equipment, with the special class thus having particularly good access to these facilities.

In a United Kingdom school, the potential stigmatisation of a child with special needs requiring individual support in the ordinary classroom was offset by the support teacher's spending more time in that room and helping the children more generally.

As far as children with the more extensively delayed intellectual development were concerned, there was the dilemma as to whether to place them with children of the same chronological age or the same developmental age. While some compromises were made, the solution generally lay with the former, particularly if the students had reached adolescence and the teachers and parents were wary of having them with children of primary age.

The problem of using the more capable special school teachers to service integration and leaving the rest to look after an increasingly problematic clientele has already been mentioned in Chapter 6 (Part II). It was referred to in the Netherlands report but no doubt occurs elsewhere too. There is no easy solution to this problem, but it does point to the need to maintain a careful balance in deploying staff.

One of the Swiss studies reported teachers as being overloaded at the beginning of the project, when there was a great deal to do and they were not as yet fully familiar with the tasks they were undertaking. This factor must have occurred in other projects too, and should be taken into account when allocating resources.

One could expect some of the initial problems identified here to clear by themselves as integration programmes commence. In one of the Spanish studies, for example, the class teacher's misgivings about having a support teacher in the class were allayed as the support continued, and as the advantages of the opportunities to see someone else at work and to collaborate in solving problems began to emerge.

Maintenance

The main hazards of maintaining integration programmes once they are established appear to be those common to most forms of innovation: a tailing off of interest from outside and perhaps some withdrawal of resources still needed. Another hazard, pointed out in one of the Belgian case study reports, is that if the innovation was pushed through from above with neither due consultation nor time for the people undertaking it to develop "ownership", problems suppressed at the outset may well surface once the development settles.

In one of the Greek case studies, there were unmet needs for staffing to permit continuing liaison between special and ordinary schools, and for continuing access to external support services. In one of the Swiss case studies, similarly, consultative arrangements available during the main period of evaluation were withdrawn following this but were still needed. In the same study the problems inherent in the rigidity of the single curriculum prescribed for all children became more apparent as the development continued.

In another Swiss study, demarcation disputes between support service staff with different professional allegiances prevented external support services from being used optimally. In one of the Icelandic studies, the district office decision to require teaching plans from teachers claiming resources for children with special needs in their classes rekindled their resistance, perhaps to the accountability this invoked. In the same district, the fact that special schools were funded out of the national purse did little to encourage patience in dealing with tricky integration issues.

One of the Swedish studies generated reference to various means of overcoming problems of teaching children with hearing difficulties in ordinary classes. These included U-shaped seating arrangements to enable children to see each other as well as the teacher, use of supplementary pictures and texts, and replacement of note-taking by use of written handouts.

One of the Irish study reports referred to the isolation of children with special needs as a feature which emerged more strongly as their integration progressed, and it has been demonstrated in Chapter 3 (Part II) that this is a widespread phenomenon. It calls for continuing classroom monitoring of children's relationships and continuing efforts to lessen isolation should it occur.

If integration proceeds satisfactorily, many benefits for the school generally will be emerging during this stage: increased insights into the strengths as well as the weaknesses of those with special needs, perception of them as children rather than as embodiments of disability, better differentiation of teaching for all children, increased co-operation among teaching staff, greater readiness to let one's teaching be seen and critically evaluated, and so on. It should not, however, breed complacency. The United States "composite school" study points to the need for continued vigilance:

> "The school must provide an ongoing program of training and awareness for students, teachers, administrators, and parents. Student grouping for the purpose of peer tutoring should be expanded. There should be an increase in the number of structured small group activities involving students with and without disabilities. Administrators must become more sensitive to the stages of change that teachers, students and parents will experience as they expand integration efforts. The school will need to allocate additional resources to provide training, materials, equipment, and personnel (...)."

> "Although there are many obstacles to integration of students with disabilities, the composite school personnel are continually working toward achieving more optimal education for all students. As a result, we expect, in the future, an increase rather than a decrease in the success of their efforts toward integration (...)."

Evaluation

In this section reference is made to evaluations that have been undertaken as an intrinsic part of the programmes themselves, and not as a special component brought about as a result of the CERI study. These latter methodologies have been reported already in Chapter 1 (Part II), which also indicates that a lack of built-in evaluation was frequently a weakness of the integration programmes studied.

As already seen, the Australian project was exceptionally strong on evaluation. Various problems had to be faced: that holiday dates varied regionally created difficulties in collecting data; evaluation could only be sensitive to short-term change, whereas some of teachers' acquired skills would only show up in the long term; the evaluation had to be qualitative rather than quantitative. Within these limitations, however, the evaluation was detailed and rigorous. In Spain, since the launching of the integration project a system of evaluation has been in place which has a clear formative component.

Quantitative criteria were used in one of the Belgian programmes, where success was measured in terms of percentage returning to ordinary schools as well as in terms of more subjective measures of social and emotional adjustment. Similarly, in a German study involving 42 schools and children in the age range 6 to 15, the success of the integration classes was evidenced by a 50 per cent intake reduction to the special school and a 40 per cent reduction in the need for support teaching for older students in ordinary schools. In a Greek study, the device of asking ordinary school students to write about their experiences of working with the disabled was subjective but nevertheless revealing. An Italian study of an individual child made use of detailed objective records based on a systematic observation of the child's behaviour at various stages of the programme.

The Swedish programmes all made good use of evaluation techniques, including pictorial questionnaires, structured interviews, a projective test, diary writing, sociometry, video recordings and direct observation. A Swiss programme was evaluated with use of control groups over an eighteen month period and measurement of progress through sociometry, self-assessment, and tests of mathematical and linguistic ability.

To be comprehensive, evaluation of any integration programme must start at the planning stage and continue throughout, counting the programme's financial costs and assessing its effectiveness beyond the stages in which it can be buoyed by the enthusiasm and special skills of the pioneers. Internal evaluation, undertaken by programme participants, is necessary. In addition, employment of external evaluators who do not have personal commitment to the success of the programme is advisable.

Given the complexity of such an enterprise, a true experimental design involving control groups may not be feasible. Nevertheless, the evaluation should include objective measures of children's progress. Their academic achievements, their social skills and their relationship with other children and adults should all be taken into account. Progress of providers also warrants consideration, particularly as an indicator of the effectiveness of any staff development work built into the programme.

Summary assessment of progress is a necessary but insufficient aspect of evaluation. While assessments of the products may provide a scale to measure the extent of the programme's success, it is unlikely to shed much light on reasons for success or failure. For this kind of illumination, continuous assessment, albeit subjective, of the processes of integration is necessary. This enables organisers and participants to take stock of the programme as they proceed and provide whatever adjustments are necessary to overcome or compensate for emerging weaknesses.

Comment

Establishing integration programmes is clearly a complex process calling for involvement of policy makers at levels beyond that of the school and requiring strong motivation, a consultative approach, special skills, time, and appreciable investment of resources. The emergence of problems of various kinds is inevitable, and their resolution requires patience as well as resourcefulness.

Right from the planning stage, care needs to be taken to build evaluation into the programme, ensuring that the necessary expertise is available. While some resources can be withdrawn once the programme is established, it is important to check that they are not being withdrawn prematurely. Continued monitoring is necessary, though this need not be inordinately costly. While there is some support for the view that established integrated special education may be less expensive than a system relying on segregation, as an economic proposition an integration programme should be regarded as a long-term investment.

Chapter 10

Good Practice

Introduction

For anyone trying to encapsulate good practice there is the temptation to bundle together all observed virtues, including those only occasionally glimpsed in real life, producing a charter which looks splendid but which no mortal could implement.

One way to avoid this temptation, in considering features of good practice in providing integrated education for children with special needs, is to start by looking at a system which would exhibit few if any of these features but which might nevertheless be quite effective in achieving its own objectives. As the school has been identified as a key unit within the educational system as a whole, it makes sense to consider a school.

The school's main objectives would be defined in terms of its products, and these would probably be expressed in the form of examination results. In order to meet its set objectives, the school would need to admit only those children capable of achieving these results, and would therefore probably admit on the basis of the results of an entrance examination.

The school curriculum would be delineated by the final examinations, and all entrants would have to follow it in full, though it could include parallel options. In each classroom, the emphasis would be on getting through the set syllabus, and children not doing this successfully would probably either have to leave or repeat a year.

Alternatively, for these children the school may decide to modify its objectives and teach them a different syllabus in a special class. While this would cater for them educationally, they and the school would know that they were subsidiary to the school's main purpose.

From the point of view of the community as a whole, the existence of such a school would only be tenable if there were other schools prepared to contribute to the community's responsibility to have all its children educated; these other schools, suffering by comparison, might then underperform.

The fundamental difference between this school and one following an integration policy would be that the main objective of the latter would be to provide the optimum education for every child on roll. Examination targets would be defined in these terms and would therefore take account of children's differing capabilities and interests. Such a school would probably, but not necessarily, be comprehensive in its intake.

Integration programmes are means of stretching the system of ordinary schooling to include a higher proportion of the total school population. In doing so, they have to manage various tensions, providing some sort of balance between conflicting imperatives.

At district level, for example, this includes allocating resources to meet differing schools' needs but not setting up a distribution system so complex as to be unmanageable. It also includes trying to meet the needs of children of all abilities without exceeding a finite budget. For support services it involves helping teachers without encouraging overdependence. At the school level it includes providing some individual programmes without making the teacher's task impossibly complex, socially isolating the children concerned or stigmatising them.

In completing its task of presenting features of good practice in established integration programmes, this chapter relies not only on the case studies undertaken in this second phase of the OECD project, but also on the information gathered in the first phase. Thus it draws the findings of the two phases together.

Educational organisation

- government, regional and district education policies state that, wherever, practicable children with special educational needs should be educated in ordinary classes in ordinary schools – school policies endorse and actively promote this principle;
- policy makers at all levels, including school level, regularly reaffirm their commitment to integration and take opportunities, for example by publicising successful examples, to promote and sustain positive attitudes, among children, among teachers and among other adults in the community, towards those with special needs;
- government, regional and district education authorities monitor, evaluate and actively review the implementation of their integration policies;
- district education authorities ensure that children with special needs have access to educational opportunities in integrated settings well before they reach statutory school age;
- a main agreed objective of the schools in a district is together to provide effective education for all the children in that district;
- within ordinary schools, children do not have to repeat a year in order to reach a certain standard before moving up into the next year group;
- schools continuously assess the progress of their children with special educational needs and periodically review their provision – assessment is of social adjustment as well as of academic achievement, and may lead to social training programmes, perhaps aimed at reducing social isolation and low self-esteem;
- where special schools are shifting from direct provision for children to the provision of advisory and training services to ordinary schools, they maintain a balance of staffing to ensure that both kinds of provision continue to be effective;
- transition of children from special schools to ordinary schools sometimes involves considerable preparation, which may include briefing special school children on

the ways of ordinary schools, providing opportunities for ordinary school and special school class teachers to see one another at work as well as to discuss the children, and running sessions with teachers, children and parents in ordinary schools to help them understand and develop positive attitudes towards children with special needs;
— when children with special educational needs require extra educational support to follow the ordinary school curriculum, this normally occurs within ordinary classrooms rather than through small group withdrawal or placement in special classes;
— time allocated to class teachers and support teachers enables them to consult, assess and plan as well as to teach; and
— schools have resource bases designed to support and enhance the provision of special education within ordinary curriculum.

Curriculum

— school accommodation is designed to ensure that children with sensor and motor disabilities have the same access to schools as do other children of the same age; this involves not only access to the different areas of the schools but also access to their learning opportunities;
— curriculum planning at school level implements a whole school policy for special needs and ensures a balanced curriculum for all;
— where schools implement a common curriculum at each age level, this is modified to meet the differing needs of children of differing abilities;
— where schools run different curriculum options for different children, they are presented as being appropriate to children's differing abilities and interests but not as hierarchies in which some are intrinsically superior to others;
— where a child with special needs is being introduced to an ordinary class from a special school or special class, integration by easy stages may be appropriate, for example, by starting with practical rather than academic subjects;
— within each class, the teacher uses a range of strategies to take account of differing abilities – for example, allowing children to complete the same work at different rates, allowing some children to complete work in simplified form, and from time to time setting different group or individual work for different children;
— for children with special needs there is a continuum of support, ranging from minimal help in ordinary classrooms through increasingly specialised learning programmes and increasing advice and support from specialist teachers and external support service staff;
— occasionally children with special needs are withdrawn from ordinary classes particular types of work, for example, for sign language training or for physiotherapy – when this happens, the class teacher ensures that this does not unduly upset the balance of their curriculum or cause them to miss out on any vital element; and

197

– class teachers and support teachers work together flexibly, exchanging roles on occasion, together ensuring that all the children in the classes, not just those with special needs, progress optimally.

Parental and community involvement

– at all stages of national developments in integration, representatives of parent organisations are involved on a consultative basis;
– as district and within-school integration programmes are developed, parents of children with special needs, along with representatives of the communities more generally, are consulted from the outset of each stage and are invited to participate;
– when parents of children with special educational needs seek to initiate or further develop integration programmes, their views are taken as seriously by decision-makers as are those of professionals;
– parents are treated as partners in assessment, decision-making and review when their children are being considered by staff of schools and external support services with a view to special educational provision;
– parents of children with special educational needs are represented on the governing bodies of schools;
– where appropriate, parents and other members of the community are encouraged to be present in classrooms and to share in the work of the schools; and
– parents of children with special needs, particularly parents of preschool children, are helped by professionals to develop the skills needed to teach their own children.

Support services

– district education authorities ensure that the progress of children with significant disabilities is monitored and that their provision is reviewed periodically;
– where formal assessment of children's special needs is undertaken, this involves consultation with parents and draws on appropriate specialisms but does not cause inordinate delay in securing appropriate provision;
– staff of external support services apply and develop their advisory and in-service training skills, particularly in relation to within-school support staff, rather than focusing largely on assessment and placement;
– staff of support services negotiate specific and finite arrangements, including learning targets, for the support they are to provide;
– staff of support services, in consultation with school staff and parents, plan and monitor the transition of students with special needs from schools to suitable post-school experience; and

- staff of external support services and outreach staff of special schools confer to ensure that their services are complementary and together meet local needs.

Training

- initial teacher training courses ensure that all trainees gain awareness of special needs, some knowledge of disabilities and some skills in teaching children of varying abilities in normal classes;
- initial teacher training courses provide options enabling trainees with particular interests and aptitudes in special education to develop further knowledge and skills;
- teacher training establishments meet the needs for training to higher degree level in all major aspects of special education, including training to apply the expertise gained in fulfilling researching, innovating, inspectorial, administrative, managerial, advisory and teacher training roles;
- staff of teacher training establishments confer regularly with external support service staff and other providers of professional development in special education, to ensure that their respective contributions within their regions are complementary and together amount to comprehensive provision;
- regional and district education authorities monitor provision of in-service training arrangements in special education, to ensure that the needs of all their schools are met effectively;
- all teachers have professional development opportunities sufficient to enable them to understand and teach the children with special needs in their classes;
- schools run induction programmes designed to ensure that newly appointed staff are aware of school policy and practice concerning children with special needs, and become familiar with any particular methods, teaching materials and equipment used;
- where appropriate, special education in-service training opportunities for teachers are also made open to other school staff and to parents;
- where needed, school and external support service staff help parents develop advocacy skills, including those of negotiation;
- ordinary school support staff concerned with special needs have access to the training required to enable them to develop the teaching, evaluation, advisory, training and problem-solving skills they need; and
- special school staff undertaking outreach work have the in-service training opportunities required to develop the range of skills needed for support work in ordinary schools.

Resourcing

- government education departments ensure that the supply of teachers and arrangements for their training are sufficient to enable national integration policies to be fully implemented;
- at national level, distribution of educational resources does not encourage regional and district authorities to place children with special needs in special schools rather than in ordinary schools;
- the distribution of resources to schools takes realistic account of the differences in expenditure required to provide appropriate education for children of differing abilities, and in doing so builds in some incentives for teachers in ordinary schools to provide for children with special needs in ordinary classes;
- resourcing of integration programmes allows for their being relatively costly at initiation and during the earlier stages of their implementation, and takes realistic account of the costs of continued monitoring once they are established – evaluation is built into the programmes from the start; and
- within schools, banks of teaching materials and associated technical equipment are developed and maintained, to enable class teachers to differentiate their work to cater for children of differing abilities and to ensure that children with sensory or motor disabilities have full access to the curriculum – some of these resources may be developed and stored on an across-schools basis.

Appendices

I. **Framework for Case Studies**

A. **Description of the functioning of the unit;**

- the objectives or goals of the unit;
- how it works – is it a resource centre or an integrated setting, in an ordinary school or special school, etc?;
- its structure;
- its management;
- duration – how long has it been in existence? Is it time limited?;
- extent of integration – total or only for certain types of disabilities?;
- relationship with other services (other than educational, *e.g.* health, social affairs) – are these services integrated or must the student go elsewhere to obtain them?;
- how quality and provision of resources are monitored;
- how is it financed;
- the process; and
- any other relevant information.

B. **Evaluation**

The following are core questions to be considered when implementing the evaluation of the unit of study. When responding to these questions please consider the following:

   a) curriculum;
   b) socialisation experiences for disabled students;
   c) integration of educational, health and social services; and
   d) supportive services.

Evaluation questions could be given to the teachers working with the students, the administrators of the school and supportive services, the pupils involved with the programme and their parents, and also the professionals who are working in the larger context. It is very important that the people who are served (*i.e.* the pupils and their parents) be permitted to have some input in this evaluation.

Core questions are:

a) how was the programme initiated? by whom?;
b) when planning the programme, what steps were taken to avoid potential problems?;
c) what difficulties were encountered when implementing the programme?;
d) what interventions were employed to solve these implementation difficulties?;
e) what was the relative success of these interventions?;
f) were there problems encountered in maintaining the programme?;
g) what interventions have been employed to deal with these problems? are they working?;
h) what has been the relative success of these interventions?;
i) what are the remaining obstacles to integration?;
j) do you have any suggestions for overcoming these obstacles?;
k) what is the acceptance and commitment to the programme?;
l) what new insights have been gained as a result of implementing this programme?;
m) has progress been made in regards to integration by placing this school/programme in a larger context of support services?;
n) how do the students feel about this programme?; and
o) any other information you may feel is relevant to the evaluation.

Example of a school and its unit of study as it should be reported in the country's case study

Study title:

Resource centre offering assistance to integrated programmes throughout the country.

A. Description:

1. resource centre would be described being sure to address all the issues outlined above under description – *e.g.* the objectives, its structure, management, range of provisions, integration of services if it exists, staff, funding, etc.; and
2. the programmes in the country would be described including their structure and range of provisions, the process of the programme, also the staff and how they interact with the resource centre.

B. Evaluation:

Evaluation based on the above stated questions would be carried out with both administrators and staff at the resource centre and administrators and staff involved with the local programme. Additionally it is hoped that an evaluation would be carried out with the pupils involved in the local programme and their parents to determine if this programme is meeting their needs.

II. Abstracts

OECD Member countries produced reports on a total of 64 case studies, more than half of them focusing on either a single school or a group of schools. In each of these studies, however, account was taken of the context of the integration programme as well as of the programme itself, insofar as context was influential. Consequently, most of the studies focusing on schools also referred to district, regional or national arrangements for special education and several made reference to relevant in-service training programmes and other types of support service. Twelve focused on work in individual classrooms, sometimes on learning programmes devised for individual children, with the school as the context. Ten, almost all from one country, focused on in-service training. In the following pages the abstracts of the case studies are presented on a country by country basis.

1. Australia

The nine case studies selected as the Australian contribution to the OECD project were undertaken during 1990 to 1992 as a Commonwealth Project of National Significance, concerned with special education and entitled *Including Students with Disabilities in Regular Classrooms.* Members of the Project Committee, themselves representatives of the state co-ordinating committees, agreed that the focus should be on professional development initiatives established to meet the needs of staff of ordinary schools who were including children with special needs in ordinary classrooms.

The members of the Project Committee were particularly concerned that this project would highlight the good practice already occurring in the education of children with disabilities in classrooms across Australia by giving greater insight into the content, documentation and location of such practice. They were also concerned to produce a document, compiling references to professional development programmes evaluated as being exemplary, with Australia wide implications and of practical assistance to those working in the field.

The Project Committee distributed guidelines to senior personnel in each state, asking them to identify and submit training packages constituting good practice. From the 111 received, nine were selected for testing and all were enthusiastically endorsed.

Of the nine, four focused on the teacher in the classroom as the person being trained: "Action research", "Teaching students with special needs in the regular classroom", "Social skills", and "Compic in the classroom". Three focused on the whole school as the client: "The training and development pack", "Working ideas for needs satisfaction", and "Inclusive schooling – integration". One, "The helping skills workshop", focused on support service consultants, and one, the "Volunteers in special education programme" was designed for people in the broader community. Two further groups of packages, one concerned with networking and the other with special schools as resource centres, were not trialled but were of particular interest.

2. Austria

The focus of the study was the integrated classroom. The Vienna School Board started its first primary school integrated class in 1986-87, and by 1990-91 there were 46 such classes in all parts of the city.

The 11th Amendment to the School Organisation Act had permitted experimental projects testing the effectiveness of co-operative education for handicapped and non-handicapped children together to be carried out nationally, up to the eighth of the nine school levels of compulsory education in ordinary schools. In any province they could be carried out for up to a fifth of the special classes in that province, and experiments could be undertaken up until and including 1992-93. Following the success of the projects undertaken, the coalition government agreed that such projects could be continued and that new ones could be started.

In the Viennese model the project was monitored by the Integration Advisory Service. This included an advisory team, to whom children were referred when decisions were to be made concerning placement. In each case the team included inspectors, members of support services, staff of the school where enrolment was proposed, and the child's parents.

The aim of the project was to teach children with special needs in the company of ordinary children of the same age, partly to help all these children learn and prepare for their later lives in an integrated society, partly to develop specialised teaching strategies of use in future work with children with special needs.

As far as possible the number of children in a class was kept down to twenty, including no more than four with special needs. Teaching was carried out by primary school and special needs teachers together, with equal roles for both teachers. Each child with special needs had an individual teaching plan, indicating the curriculum and the particular educational aims being pursued. Assessment of the children's progress was done by the teachers. In-service training amounted to only six days a year, but attempts were being made to lengthen it.

3. Belgium

Six case studies were evaluated: four focusing on groups of schools and two on external support services. The country's movement towards the education of children with disabilities in ordinary schools started after the passing of the Special Education Act in 1970, which emphasized social integration.

One study involved a special school in placing as many as possible of its visually impaired children of otherwise normal ability in ordinary schools. Special school staff developed integrated education support roles, helping the teachers in the ordinary schools and providing advice both for teachers and for parents. The development was a success, though finding time for consultation and gaining access to in-service training continued to present problems.

A similar study was based on a special school for children whose educational retardation of two years or more could not be explained adequately in terms of general developmental disability. A special school teacher and a part-time speech therapist supported reintegration into the ordinary school.

Another special school with a similar population shifted from allowing entry at about nine years to a policy of early identification, taking children aged six on for intensive work with a view to returning them to ordinary schools after a year. Over a six year period 50 per cent were so returned, with later follow-up indicating a 95 per cent success rate.

Another study was concerned with the full or partial integration of children with hearing impairment from a special school into ordinary schools, with the help of support staff based in a rehabilitation centre.

Two studies were concerned with the work of external support services: an early help service and a research, training and advisory service. Staff included psychologists, medical and social workers, and speech therapists. Some of the children concerned had severe learning difficulties, (mainly children with Down's syndrome), others had neuro-motor impairment.

4. Canada

(New Brunswick)

The purpose of this case study was to review integration in three schools (elementary, junior high, senior high) within one school district in the Province of New Brunswick. In this district there were no special schools or classes, and the children all attended their neighbourhood schools. The types and severity of disabilities varied across schools and were dependent on the distribution occurring within the community. Allocation of funds to the schools took account of variations in special need.

The district had a strong commitment to integration. The background over many years had been one of continued progress towards full integration, including closure of the district's two special schools in the early 1980s. At district level, the student services team provided support services to the schools, including in-service training, monitoring, evaluation, and technical support.

Each school within the district had its own student services team, which included one or more methods and resource teachers, whose primary duty was to assist classroom teachers in developing learning programmes for children with special needs. Other members of this team included the guidance counsellor, who helped children solve their personal problems, and teacher assistants, who supported the class teacher by working in the classroom with the more severely disabled children. All staff had time allowed for consultation, planning, evaluation and in-service training.

Each child with special needs had a special education plan and a programme designed on an individual basis. Wherever possible, children with special needs followed the province's standard curriculum. Methods and resource teachers adjusted this for individual children in accordance with children's various strengths and needs.

In all three schools a major influence on the undoubted success of the integration programme was the collaboration that existed between class teachers and methods and resource teachers. Also influential was the support provided for methods and resource teachers, through regular problem-solving meetings with district student services staff.

5. Denmark

The case study reported, a project approved by the Ministry of Education and completed in 1981, was an early attempt to educate children with severe learning difficulties within a region's ordinary schools. It marked a transition away from the concept of these children, formerly registered at the Department of Welfare for the Mentally Deficient, as patients needing care, and towards a view of them as seekers of knowledge.

As well as testing the capabilities of ordinary schools to develop special education, the project sought to study the relationships that could be fostered between disabled and non-disabled children of the same chronological age. As part of the project, Denmark's Radio produced for the Ministry of Education a 25 minute film, "Together we are able". The film depicted the school attendance of three of the children in the project and subsequently has been shown widely, accompanied by a text booklet, demonstrating the extent to which integration can be successful.

Placement of the children was undertaken following extensive psychological and educational counselling. Education followed four principles in addition to that of integration: proximity, least interference, efficiency, and motivation.

The principle of proximity held that the children's schooling should be as close as possible to their homes. In accordance with the principle of least interference they were not given more help than necessary. Efficient education was that which, with due economy, achieved the best results; teaching was powerfully supported by the school system's psychological counselling. Finally, throughout the project every effort was made to sustain positive motivation all round.

An important aspect of the success of the project was the development of positive relationships among the children concerned. For example, there was far less teasing than there had been in the special schools. Key factors influencing success included time for consultation and access to in-service training and counselling.

6. Finland

This study was of outreach work based on a residential school for the visually impaired, within the context of services for these children across the country as a whole. The school served as the national pedagogic resource centre for visually impaired children.

The duties of the school stemmed from Law 481/83, passed in 1983 and amended in 1986, and concerned with schools for the hearing impaired and visually impaired. This empowered the Ministry of Education to order the school (along with equivalent providers for the hearing impaired) to develop teaching methods and teaching materials, and to give tutoring and guidance to disabled children and students in ordinary schools and in further and higher education, to their parents, and to teachers and other school personnel.

The school also had the duty to give temporary teaching and rehabilitation to disabled children of school age. In addition, they were to provide temporary rehabilitation, education and rehabilitation planning and follow-up for children of preschool age. Moreover, they were to make equivalent provision for young people of post-school age, in order to make it possible for them to obtain further education and to be integrated into working life and society.

The school was part of a national network of providing services for the visually impaired. Within this network, maternity hospitals notified relevant agencies of children born with visual impairment, families attended training courses, educational plans were formulated as children approached school age, and their subsequent development was monitored periodically.

As part of its fulfilment of its duties the school employed eight peripatetic teachers who visited ordinary schools, guided classroom teachers and their assistants, met with parents and consulted with staff of local authorities. As well as providing an advisory service, for example on special aids and equipment, the peripatetic teachers taught on support courses provided for children, parents and teachers at the school. The school also maintained a centre for the development, display and loan of teaching and learning materials.

7. France

The study was of four integration projects, each being the product of a local initiative, but all falling within the national framework for integration projects established by the July 1989 Education Act. The projects were developed in different regions of the country and focused on children with particular kinds of disability: young children with visual impairment, secondary age pupils with physical disabilities, autistic children, children with hearing impairment.

As each project was ongoing, the study consisted of snapshots of continuously evolving events. Two of the projects had been in existence for more than a decade, and the progress of some of the disabled children had been followed through into adulthood. The projects were evaluated both from an internal perspective, in terms of their own objectives and the progress of the children concerned, and from an external perspective, in terms of their national context and their historical evolution. Children's progress was evaluated according to four complementary criteria: academic achievements, vocational skills, personal (physical, material and psychological) independence, and social skills and communication. In addition, account was taken of the extent to which attitudes of children and teachers generally in the schools concerned had become more favourable to integration.

Key features of successful integration included careful planning, full involvement of parents and representatives of voluntary bodies concerned with the children's particular disabilities, the availability of specialist teaching help, the active participation of inspectors for special education and others influential in the implementation of educational policy in the region, and some support and adaptation on the part of all staff and pupils in the school, not just of the disabled children and those closely concerned with them.

The projects were also thought to be potentially of value in the context of movements towards decentralisation in French education, with individual project reports serving as proposals for local variations in the implementation of national regulations and providing contractual bases for programmes individually tailored to the needs of schools.

8. Germany

Of the eight units submitted, all working successfully, five were concerned with individual schools, two with groups of schools and one with the co-ordination of support services.

One of the studies set within a school was concerned with the transition of ordinary and disabled children, together, from their kindergartens to the primary school. Another was of a primary school's integration classes, each run by a class teacher and a special education teacher together. Another involved targeted support in integrated classes for 32 children with moderate to severe disabilities in a secondary school with 1 300 students and 130 teachers overall. The programme was an upward extension, backed strongly by the parents and teachers concerned, of an integration scheme started at kindergarten level. A further study illustrated the value for integration of out of school leisure courses, and another involved vocational training.

One of the studies involving groups of schools was concerned with integrative classes in a city's primary schools. The basic model consisted of a class of about twenty children, up to three of them handicapped, and a team of three staff: class teacher, part-time special school teacher, and teaching assistant. In-service training was built into the scheme: two hours per week in the first year; one hour per week in the third. In a study involving 42 schools and children in the age range 6 to 15, with a graded system of up to six lessons per disabled child per week of extra help from teachers from special schools, the success of the integration classes was evidenced by a 50 per cent reduction in intake to the special school and a 40 per cent reduction in the need for support teaching for the older students in the ordinary schools.

The study of support services was in relation to young children and their parents. The programmes of multidisciplinary support, organised on a regional basis, were founded on the premise that early support is essential, preferably before the children reach the age of three. Support staff included medical practitioners, psychologists, social workers and teachers, co-ordinated and trained by university staff.

9. Greece

The four case studies were concerned with moves towards integration in two special schools and two special classes. These moves were in line with Law 1566 of 1985, which described special educational provision as a system aimed at fostering the educational and social integration of children with special needs. The case studies provided examples of two initiatives taken to implement the country's integration policy: the establishment of locationally integrated special schools and the opening of part-time withdrawal classes in ordinary schools.

The first of the special schools was opened in 1986, served a city and surrounding rural area, and was locationally integrated with an ordinary school. Most of the special school's 29 primary and secondary age children had specific, mild or moderate learning difficulties, six were emotionally disturbed and four had sensor-motor impairment. The school had a pupil-teacher ratio of below 4:1 and also employed a psychologist, a social worker and other support staff. Integration activities included sharing playground, canteen, festive activities and an environmental studies programme with the adjacent ordinary school.

The second special school was similarly staffed and provided for 22 children with similar disabilities but with ages ranging up to 20. Since 1990 it had been situated in a single-storey purpose-converted block of a building also housing a nursery school, an elementary school and a lower level secondary school; next door were an upper level secondary school and a vocational training centre. Special school and ordinary school children mixed at mealtimes, on open days, and for some athletic activities. A few children with special needs were integrated for subjects such as carpentry, history and music.

The two special classes, operating in separate schools, each took children from across the school, though both special class teachers expressed a preference for early intervention. Special class attendance was usually part-time, though occasionally a child would attend for a whole day. Most of the work was small group tuition in language development or mathematics. There were some problems in ensuring that the children followed a balanced curriculum overall.

10.   Iceland

Each of the three case studies was of an ordinary school for children in the age range 6 to 16 years. All three schools provided an integrated education for children with special educational needs. One was an urban school with 490 children on roll, another provided for 105 children from the surrounding rural agricultural area and the third, with 49 children attending, was located in a small coastal village. Together, these three schools provided a reasonable representation of the types of ordinary schooling available to children of this age range nationally.

In 1989 the Ministry of Culture and Education published a revised version of the National Curriculum for children in this age range, stating that this curriculum would serve all children, including those with special educational needs. The 1991 Law on Comprehensive School, covering this same age range, underlined the right of every child to receive appropriate education on the ordinary school nearest to that child's home, while continuing to give parents the choice to apply for special schooling should the ordinary school fail to provide suitable education.

Several common themes emerged. All three schools were able to integrate children with significant educational and social disabilities into ordinary classrooms. In all three schools, however, children with severe learning difficulties and those with physical or multiple disabilities were conspicuous by their absence. In the rural school, this occurred despite the fact that the school included a special education unit serving the whole district.

Some of the school buildings would need adapting in order to be accessible for wheelchairs. In all the schools there were instances of behaviourally challenging children who had been expelled either temporarily or permanently from part or all of the schools' activities.

Teachers varied in their attitudes towards integration. Each school had at least one teacher who was fervently committed to providing for all children in the ordinary school, who was able to provide a good example and was a source of strength in the school.

11. Ireland

Two case studies were conducted, each examining provision for children with special needs in a group of ordinary schools.

In the first study, which took place in the midland region of the country, children in four elementary schools and one secondary school were grouped according to disability in special classes. The evaluation revealed positive outcomes for the children in special classes as well as for other children in the school.

Evaluation also showed that, while progress had been made in both curricular and social integration, consideration should be given to the following strategies aimed at improving services for children in special classes in ordinary schools and for teachers who worked with them: the extension of provision to local secondary schools; the provision of a structured health service in schools; the adoption in schools of a broader more flexible definition and understanding of integration; the provision of classroom assistants and the establishment of a network of professional support for teachers.

The second case study was of the integration of children with physical and/or communication disabilities in ordinary classes as a consequence of introducing grant-aided computers to 50 elementary schools. Findings revealed the valuable contribution of computers in facilitating integration. They pointed to an association between successful integration and positive attitudes of staff, children and parents on the one hand, and an association between unsuccessful integration and human resource limitations on the other.

In view of the trend in the educational system towards integration, the study high-lighted the need to ensure the following: that children with disabilities, girls in particular, have sufficient access to a computer; that children with disabilities benefit as much as possible from co-operation between teachers who have specialist qualifications and ordinary teachers who increasingly find themselves in charge of such children; that services, particularly in the area of health, are structured in such a way that schools become less isolated in their efforts to integrate children with special needs.

12. Italy

One of the case studies was of educational arrangements for an individual child, and the other was an analysis of reports of work in a number of ordinary classes in which children with disabilities were being educated. In accordance with Regional Law 77/80, integration has proceeded rapidly throughout the country during the past decade and virtually all partially or seriously disabled children of statutory school age now attend ordinary schools.

The individual case study concerned a boy who, on arrival at his elementary school, presented behaviour characteristic of autism, including solitariness, inability to establish relationships with people or objects, stereotyped actions, absence of normal signs of emotion, and absence of meaningful speech. Carefully targeted programmes were established, to enable him to follow the work of the class at times and sometimes work individually with a teacher. Eventually he was watching the teacher, approaching other children, taking part in simple games and making functional use of about 30 words.

The second case study, an analysis of reports of integration work in a number of ordinary school classes, was undertaken through meetings of a project group of specialists and the activities of a working party of teachers, including heads of schools as well as class teachers. Some basic procedures for achieving integration were found to be common to all the classes studied, though there were various differences in detail.

Some difficulties were encountered. For example, the teachers reporting their activities did not always explain their objectives, and when they did they tended to do so in a personal style which did not lend itself to the aggregation of data. Furthermore, the classes themselves were all different to the extent that it was difficult to make comparisons. One result of this work was the formulation of a questionnaire, detailing the essential stages of the integration process, and therefore useful in future comparative studies of ordinary school classes implementing integration programmes.

13.   Netherlands

One of the case studies was of a co-operating network of elementary schools, and the other was of a special school running an outreach service for children with visual impairment.

The network consisted of 28 schools, each being relatively small with only about 100 children on roll, in a rural region of the country. Staff of each school included a teacher designated for periodic work with children with special needs and a support teacher, whose responsibilities included organising flexible groupings of children across the school and arranging the teachers' in-service training programmes.

A key feature of the network was its co-ordination by the region's education advice centre, which organised regular meetings of staff of the schools, ran in-service training for key staff, developed working parties involving staff of different schools, and negotiated changes of school for children experiencing difficulties and needing a fresh start. While the network arrangement was successful, there were some problems: the government funding system did not altogether support integration, and there was a tendency for special needs to be met through withdrawal rather than on an in-class basis.

Among the staff of the school for children with visual impairment were 19 peripatetic teachers, mostly full-time, who supported placement of more than 300 children with visual impairment, mostly in ordinary schools, occasionally in special schools designed primarily for children with other disabilities.

The peripatetic teachers provided class teachers with information about special teaching methods and materials, offered direct teaching support, and advised and supported parents. They also contributed to training courses run at the special school for children, parents and teachers. While the system functioned successfully, there were some problems: the residual special school population was increasingly challenging, regulations governing the availability of peripatetic teachers to schools lacked flexibility, and there were some difficulties in gaining access to specialised learning materials.

14. Norway

There were two case studies, one concerned with integration arrangements in two elementary schools, and the other with a special school providing a national support service for children with visual impairment in ordinary schools.

Provision in the two elementary schools changed as a result of the country's Primary Schools Education Act, of 1975, which made local authorities responsible for the education of all their communities' children of primary age. In this particular authority, the two special schools were closed and, in accordance with parents' wishes, the children were placed in just three local elementary schools rather than being dispersed more widely, with most of the former special school teachers transferring to these same schools. The case study focused on social integration in two of these schools.

The children's social integration was generally satisfactory and appeared to be enhanced when responsibility for them was considered to be that of the whole school rather than that of just a few teachers. The fact that the proportion of disabled children was relatively high for ordinary schools probably helped too. In addition, the fact that almost all the disabled children in these two schools attended both ordinary classes and groups with other disabled children may also have been conducive to their social integration.

The National Centre for Children with Visual Impairment had residential facilities for parents, children and others attending courses. Staffing included researchers as well as teachers and teacher trainers. The centre did not employ its own team of peripatetic teachers, relying instead on special education support services run by local authorities. The centre developed and distributed specialised teaching and learning materials, for example translating books into Braille, and housed special equipment needed by those with visual impairment. At regional level it also provided some services for disabled adults.

While the centre performed a valuable function at national level, there were some problems: weaknesses in local authority support services, and delays in getting learning materials to those needing them.

15. Spain

Two of the case studies treated the support provided within schools for individual children, one with mild learning difficulties and the other with hearing impairment. Both were working within the context of national guidelines issued by the Ministry of Education, though there was no legislation prescribing their form of organisation, and consequently there were many variations across the country. The thrird case study was of a district's multidisciplinary support service, external to the schools, for children with special needs. It was carried out in the Basque Country under its own autonomous regulations in the educational domain.

The boy with mild learning difficulties was in an ordinary class in an ordinary school, and received in-class support for just over a third of the time, during some of the language, science and mathematics lessons. The support teacher also supplied the class teachers with special teaching materials or adapted teaching programmes. Teaching support for the boy with hearing impairment was similar, and in addition both received some speech therapy, outside the class. The classmates of the boy with hearing impairment were taught how to communicate with him and work was also done, by the support teacher, with his parents.

The subject of the third case study was a district's special education support team, which functioned within a more general pedagogic orientation centre. Each member of the team had an assignment of schools and a schedule for visiting each, mainly to conduct diagnostic and advisory work, collaborating with support teachers and class teachers to prepare action programmes for particular children.

On the basis of these three studies the report concluded that various conditions were necessary to the effective working of internal and external support services of the kinds illustrated. They included a relevant school policy and curriculum, active involvement of the whole teaching team, flexible criteria for organising support, clarity of procedures, credibility among school staff, and sufficient resources, particularly in terms of staffing. Other relevant factors included positive attitudes towards integration, inter-professional collaboration, continuous assessment, efficient management, in-service training, team continuity and administrative support.

16. Sweden

Each of the four case studies dealt with a number of children, representing both primary and secondary phases of education, all with the same kind of disability, being integrated into various classes in ordinary schools. All four studies included some consideration of children's relationships.

The first study was of 16 children with learning difficulties in eight ordinary schools in the same district. The class teachers interviewed considered that most of the children were at ease with their schooling and that they had friends in their classes. Special education support teachers were less confident that this was the case, but still viewed the situation positively. The children, however, tended to report that they lacked friends, that they had to suffer teasing, and that they found school boring.

The second case study was of 21 children, again with learning difficulties, in ordinary schools in three regions of the country. Although they were usually in ordinary classrooms, for some subjects it was often the case that such a child would still be segregated, by being looked after individually by a support teacher or other classroom assistant and being given work differing from that of the rest of the class. Even work in a small group tended to be a rarity. This kind of within-class segregation occurred particularly in Swedish, English, mathematics and science.

In the third study, seven physically disabled children, all requiring wheelchairs, were attending various ordinary schools in the same region. Here too they spent much of their classroom time with adults rather than with other children. They also tended to spend little time with other children after school, often because they were too tired.

The fourth study was of 215 children with hearing impairment in ordinary schools in two regions of the country. Whereas younger children were often chosen as friends, the older students in ordinary classes felt that they were outsiders. Several, particularly those needing hearing aids, had hardly any friends at school, and were isolated at home too.

17. Switzerland

One of the three case studies was concerned with support at the level of the classroom, one with a whole school approach to special needs, and one with a support service external to the schools.

The first case study, which occurred within one region of the country, included a direct comparison, undertaken over an 18 month period, of the education of children with special needs in ordinary classes and in special classes. Children with special needs in ordinary classes were not very popular, though it seemed that they would not have been more popular in special classes. Their perception of their own abilities was also lower than that of children in special classes, though in fact their progress, particularly in mathematics, was far greater. Their presence in ordinary classes did not appear to hinder the progress of able children. Overall costs of supporting these children in ordinary classes and in special classes were about the same.

The second case study, undertaken in a different region, demonstrated a team approach to educating children with special educational needs in an elementary school. Teachers worked in teams of four, each team consisting of three class teachers and a special needs specialist. For most of the time the children with special needs remained in ordinary classes, sometimes helped there by the special teacher, though they were withdrawn occasionally. For one afternoon a week, the four teachers took parallel groups of children for fine arts and music. Team meetings, some involving parents and some the school's educational psychologist, aided planning and provided support where necessary.

The third study, again from a different region, was of a peripatetic support service in a sparsely populated area. The service was illustrated through reference to the help it provided for children with visual impairment and for children with brain damage. Work with both groups involved liaison with medical and other specialists outside the region, finding ordinary school placements, advising on the teaching support needed there, and counselling parents. Some of the work with children with brain damage involved preparation for return to school following road accidents and subsequent operations.

18. United Kingdom

There were seven case studies, each focusing on an individual school. Five were ordinary schools, together providing for children throughout the period of statutory schooling, and two were special schools with outreach arrangements. The seven schools were selected as representing interesting and fairly well-developed integration practice, and as covering as wide a range of special needs as possible. They were diversely situated geographically, providing a sampling from each of the major regions of the country. Much of the legislation governing the country's integration practices was present in the Education Act of 1981, which required children with special educational needs to be educated in ordinary schools unless there were particular grounds for their being placed in special schools.

The report began by describing how integration was inaugurated in the various case study schools, the way in which it was encouraged in the early stages and longer-term developments flowing from it. Curricular aspects of integration were then discussed: the national framework of the curriculum; reasons for, and extent of, withdrawal teaching for children with special educational needs in the case study schools; staffing factors, including the pupil-teacher ratio, the use of support teachers and the part played by non-teaching assistants; and the effect of school organisation on curriculum delivery.

The second main theme of the report was the role of the special school. Integration arrangements operating in each of the two special schools were discussed. The third theme was resourcing, and here the report considered levels of staffing and facilities in each of the case study schools, looking at the ways in which they were financed.

Finally, factors which seemed to facilitate integrative practice were set out. These included legislation promoting integration, supportive local authority strategies, school policies for integration, time for teachers to consult and plan programmes, curriculum materials adapted to suit different ability levels, in-service training for all staff, flexibility of staffing to enhance sharing of skills and exchange of roles, careful siting of any segregated provision to avoid isolation, and chances to plan children's transition from one year to the next.

19. United States

A composite case study was completed to represent the status of integration in the United States. A description of a composite school, representative of a typical United States school, was developed by a panel of experts with a wide range of experience in collecting integration data. The resulting report reflected the consensus of the panel.

The composite school was typical of many schools in the United States. School personnel were experiencing difficulties in co-ordinating ordinary and special education goals and were trying to balance the monies available with the most effective progress for children.

The building complied with legislation in that it was accessible to individuals with disabilities, with teaching areas at one level only, ramps, expanded doorways, and specially designed restrooms. For the 400 children in the age range 5 to 12 on roll, including 48 with special needs, staffing included the head and 18 teachers, four of whom specialised in special education. In addition, there were three teacher aides and several part-time visiting teaching and support staff.

The amount of integration varied by the severity of disability. Children with mild disabilities received the majority of their academic and social content within ordinary classes. Children with moderate and severe disabilities received some social or academic instruction within ordinary classes, but received the majority of their education within special classes. These children also received some community-based instruction to enhance skills related to activities of daily living. All education programmes were assessed individually, and modifications were made as needed.

There were both benefits and obstacles to integration. For the obstacles to be overcome, there needed to be additional concentration on training and awareness programmes as well as additional allocation of resources. The staff of the composite school were working towards achieving optimal educational opportunities for ordinary and special education children.

MAIN SALES OUTLETS OF OECD PUBLICATIONS
PRINCIPAUX POINTS DE VENTE DES PUBLICATIONS DE L'OCDE

ARGENTINA – ARGENTINE
Carlos Hirsch S.R.L.
Galería Güemes, Florida 165, 4° Piso
1333 Buenos Aires   Tel. (1) 331.1787 y 331.2391
Telefax: (1) 331.1787

AUSTRALIA – AUSTRALIE
D.A. Information Services
648 Whitehorse Road, P.O.B 163
Mitcham, Victoria 3132   Tel. (03) 873.4411
Telefax: (03) 873.5679

AUSTRIA – AUTRICHE
Gerold & Co.
Graben 31
Wien I   Tel. (0222) 533.50.14

BELGIUM – BELGIQUE
Jean De Lannoy
Avenue du Roi 202
B-1060 Bruxelles   Tel. (02) 538.51.69/538.08.41
Telefax: (02) 538.08.41

CANADA
Renouf Publishing Company Ltd.
1294 Algoma Road
Ottawa, ON K1B 3W8   Tel. (613) 741.4333
Telefax: (613) 741.5439
Stores:
61 Sparks Street
Ottawa, ON K1P 5R1   Tel. (613) 238.8985
211 Yonge Street
Toronto, ON M5B 1M4   Tel. (416) 363.3171
Telefax: (416)363.59.63
Les Éditions La Liberté Inc.
3020 Chemin Sainte-Foy
Sainte-Foy, PQ G1X 3V6   Tel. (418) 658.3763
Telefax: (418) 658.3763

Federal Publications Inc.
165 University Avenue, Suite 701
Toronto, ON M5H 3B8   Tel. (416) 860.1611
Telefax: (416) 860.1608
Les Publications Fédérales
1185 Université
Montréal, QC H3B 3A7   Tel. (514) 954.1633
Telefax : (514) 954.1635

CHINA – CHINE
China National Publications Import
Export Corporation (CNPIEC)
16 Gongti E. Road, Chaoyang District
P.O. Box 88 or 50
Beijing 100704 PR   Tel. (01) 506.6688
Telefax: (01) 506.3101

CZECH REPUBLIC – RÉPUBLIQUE TCHÈQUE
Artia Pegas Press Ltd.
Narodni Trida 25
POB 825
111 21 Praha 1   Tel. 26.65.68
Telefax: 26.20.81

DENMARK – DANEMARK
Munksgaard Book and Subscription Service
35, Nørre Søgade, P.O. Box 2148
DK-1016 København K   Tel. (33) 12.85.70
Telefax: (33) 12.93.87

EGYPT – ÉGYPTE
Middle East Observer
41 Sherif Street
Cairo   Tel. 392.6919
Telefax: 360-6804

FINLAND – FINLANDE
Akateeminen Kirjakauppa
Keskuskatu 1, P.O. Box 128
00100 Helsinki
Subscription Services/Agence d'abonnements :
P.O. Box 23
00371 Helsinki   Tel. (358 0) 12141
Telefax: (358 0) 121.4450

FRANCE
OECD/OCDE
Mail Orders/Commandes par correspondance:
2, rue André-Pascal
75775 Paris Cedex 16   Tel. (33-1) 45.24.82.00
Telefax: (33-1) 49.10.42.76
Telex: 640048 OCDE
Orders via Minitel, France only/
Commandes par Minitel, France exclusivement :
36 15 OCDE

OECD Bookshop/Librairie de l'OCDE :
33, rue Octave-Feuillet
75016 Paris   Tel. (33-1) 45.24.81.67
(33-1) 45.24.81.81
Documentation Française
29, quai Voltaire
75007 Paris   Tel. 40.15.70.00
Gibert Jeune (Droit-Économie)
6, place Saint-Michel
75006 Paris   Tel. 43.25.91.19
Librairie du Commerce International
10, avenue d'Iéna
75016 Paris   Tel. 40.73.34.60
Librairie Dunod
Université Paris-Dauphine
Place du Maréchal de Lattre de Tassigny
75016 Paris   Tel. (1) 44.05.40.13
Librairie Lavoisier
11, rue Lavoisier
75008 Paris   Tel. 42.65.39.95
Librairie L.G.D.J. - Montchrestien
20, rue Soufflot
75005 Paris   Tel. 46.33.89.85
Librairie des Sciences Politiques
30, rue Saint-Guillaume
75007 Paris   Tel. 45.48.36.02
P.U.F.
49, boulevard Saint-Michel
75005 Paris   Tel. 43.25.83.40
Librairie de l'Université
12a, rue Nazareth
13100 Aix-en-Provence   Tel. (16) 42.26.18.08
Documentation Française
165, rue Garibaldi
69003 Lyon   Tel. (16) 78.63.32.23
Librairie Decitre
29, place Bellecour
69002 Lyon   Tel. (16) 72.40.54.54

GERMANY – ALLEMAGNE
OECD Publications and Information Centre
August-Bebel-Allee 6
D-53175 Bonn   Tel. (0228) 959.120
Telefax: (0228) 959.12.17

GREECE – GRÈCE
Librairie Kauffmann
Mavrokordatou 9
106 78 Athens   Tel. (01) 32.55.321
Telefax: (01) 36.33.967

HONG-KONG
Swindon Book Co. Ltd.
13–15 Lock Road
Kowloon, Hong Kong   Tel. 2376.2062
Telefax: 2376.0685

HUNGARY – HONGRIE
Euro Info Service
Margitsziget, Európa Ház
1138 Budapest   Tel. (1) 111.62.16
Telefax : (1) 111.60.61

ICELAND – ISLANDE
Mál Mog Menning
Laugavegi 18, Pósthólf 392
121 Reykjavik   Tel. 162.35.23

INDIA – INDE
Oxford Book and Stationery Co.
Scindia House
New Delhi 110001   Tel.(11) 331.5896/5308
Telefax: (11) 332.5993
17 Park Street
Calcutta 700016   Tel. 240832

INDONESIA – INDONÉSIE
Pdii-Lipi
P.O. Box 4298
Jakarta 12042   Tel. (21) 573.34.67
Telefax: (21) 573.34.67

IRELAND – IRLANDE
Government Supplies Agency
Publications Section
4/5 Harcourt Road
Dublin 2   Tel. 661.31.11
Telefax: 478.06.45

ISRAEL
Praedicta
5 Shatner Street
P.O. Box 34030
Jerusalem 91430   Tel. (2) 52.84.90/1/2
Telefax: (2) 52.84.93
R.O.Y.
P.O. Box 13056
Tel Aviv 61130   Tél. (3) 49.61.08
Telefax (3) 544.60.39

ITALY – ITALIE
Libreria Commissionaria Sansoni
Via Duca di Calabria 1/1
50125 Firenze   Tel. (055) 64.54.15
Telefax: (055) 64.12.57
Via Bartolini 29
20155 Milano   Tel. (02) 36.50.83
Editrice e Libreria Herder
Piazza Montecitorio 120
00186 Roma   Tel. 679.46.28
Telefax: 678.47.51
Libreria Hoepli
Via Hoepli 5
20121 Milano   Tel. (02) 86.54.46
Telefax: (02) 805.28.86
Libreria Scientifica
Dott. Lucio de Biasio 'Aeiou'
Via Coronelli, 6
20146 Milano   Tel. (02) 48.95.45.52
Telefax: (02) 48.95.45.48

JAPAN – JAPON
OECD Publications and Information Centre
Landic Akasaka Building
2-3-4 Akasaka, Minato-ku
Tokyo 107   Tel. (81.3) 3586.2016
Telefax: (81.3) 3584.7929

KOREA – CORÉE
Kyobo Book Centre Co. Ltd.
P.O. Box 1658, Kwang Hwa Moon
Seoul   Tel. 730.78.91
Telefax: 735.00.30

MALAYSIA – MALAISIE
University of Malaya Bookshop
University of Malaya
P.O. Box 1127, Jalan Pantai Baru
59700 Kuala Lumpur
Malaysia   Tel. 756.5000/756.5425
Telefax: 756.3246

MEXICO – MEXIQUE
Revistas y Periodicos Internacionales S.A. de C.V.
Florencia 57 - 1004
Mexico, D.F. 06600   Tel. 207.81.00
Telefax : 208.39.79

NETHERLANDS – PAYS-BAS
SDU Uitgeverij Plantijnstraat
Externe Fondsen
Postbus 20014
2500 EA's-Gravenhage   Tel. (070) 37.89.880
Voor bestellingen: Telefax: (070) 34.75.778

NEW ZEALAND
NOUVELLE-ZÉLANDE
Legislation Services
P.O. Box 12418
Thorndon, Wellington   Tel. (04) 496.5652
                Telefax: (04) 496.5698

NORWAY – NORVÈGE
Narvesen Info Center – NIC
Bertrand Narvesens vei 2
P.O. Box 6125 Etterstad
0602 Oslo 6   Tel. (022) 57.33.00
                Telefax: (022) 68.19.01

PAKISTAN
Mirza Book Agency
65 Shahrah Quaid-E-Azam
Lahore 54000   Tel. (42) 353.601
                Telefax: (42) 231.730

PHILIPPINE – PHILIPPINES
International Book Center
5th Floor, Filipinas Life Bldg.
Ayala Avenue
Metro Manila   Tel. 81.96.76
                Telex 23312 RHP PH

PORTUGAL
Livraria Portugal
Rua do Carmo 70-74
Apart. 2681
1200 Lisboa   Tel.: (01) 347.49.82/5
                Telefax: (01) 347.02.64

SINGAPORE – SINGAPOUR
Gower Asia Pacific Pte Ltd.
Golden Wheel Building
41, Kallang Pudding Road, No. 04-03
Singapore 1334   Tel. 741.5166
                Telefax: 742.9356

SPAIN – ESPAGNE
Mundi-Prensa Libros S.A.
Castelló 37, Apartado 1223
Madrid 28001   Tel. (91) 431.33.99
                Telefax: (91) 575.39.98

Libreria Internacional AEDOS
Consejo de Ciento 391
08009 – Barcelona   Tel. (93) 488.30.09
                Telefax: (93) 487.76.59
Llibreria de la Generalitat
Palau Moja
Rambla dels Estudis, 118
08002 – Barcelona
                (Subscripcions) Tel. (93) 318.80.12
                (Publicacions) Tel. (93) 302.67.23
                Telefax: (93) 412.18.54

SRI LANKA
Centre for Policy Research
c/o Colombo Agencies Ltd.
No. 300-304, Galle Road
Colombo 3   Tel. (1) 574240, 573551-2
                Telefax: (1) 575394, 510711

SWEDEN – SUÈDE
Fritzes Information Center
Box 16356
Regeringsgatan 12
106 47 Stockholm   Tel. (08) 690.90.90
                Telefax: (08) 20.50.21

Subscription Agency/Agence d'abonnements :
Wennergren-Williams Info AB
P.O. Box 1305
171 25 Solna   Tel. (08) 705.97.50
                Téléfax : (08) 27.00.71

SWITZERLAND – SUISSE
Maditec S.A. (Books and Periodicals - Livres
et périodiques)
Chemin des Palettes 4
Case postale 266
1020 Renens VD 1   Tel. (021) 635.08.65
                Telefax: (021) 635.07.80

Librairie Payot S.A.
4, place Pépinet
CP 3212
1002 Lausanne   Tel. (021) 341.33.47
                Telefax: (021) 341.33.45

Librairie Unilivres
6, rue de Candolle
1205 Genève   Tel. (022) 320.26.23
                Telefax: (022) 329.73.18

Subscription Agency/Agence d'abonnements :
Dynapresse Marketing S.A.
38 avenue Vibert
1227 Carouge   Tel.: (022) 308.07.89
                Telefax : (022) 308.07.99

See also – Voir aussi :
OECD Publications and Information Centre
August-Bebel-Allee 6
D-53175 Bonn (Germany)   Tel. (0228) 959.120
                Telefax: (0228) 959.12.17

TAIWAN – FORMOSE
Good Faith Worldwide Int'l. Co. Ltd.
9th Floor, No. 118, Sec. 2
Chung Hsiao E. Road
Taipei   Tel. (02) 391.7396/391.7397
                Telefax: (02) 394.9176

THAILAND – THAÏLANDE
Suksit Siam Co. Ltd.
113, 115 Fuang Nakhon Rd.
Opp. Wat Rajbopith
Bangkok 10200   Tel. (662) 225.9531/2
                Telefax: (662) 222.5188

TURKEY – TURQUIE
Kültür Yayinlari Is-Türk Ltd. Sti.
Atatürk Bulvari No. 191/Kat 13
Kavaklidere/Ankara   Tel. 428.11.40 Ext. 2458
Dolmabahce Cad. No. 29
Besiktas/Istanbul   Tel. 260.71.88
                Telex: 43482B

UNITED KINGDOM – ROYAUME-UNI
HMSO
Gen. enquiries   Tel. (071) 873 0011
Postal orders only:
P.O. Box 276, London SW8 5DT
Personal Callers HMSO Bookshop
49 High Holborn, London WC1V 6HB
                Telefax: (071) 873 8200
Branches at: Belfast, Birmingham, Bristol, Edin-
burgh, Manchester

UNITED STATES – ÉTATS-UNIS
OECD Publications and Information Centre
2001 L Street N.W., Suite 700
Washington, D.C. 20036-4910 Tel. (202) 785.6323
                Telefax: (202) 785.0350

VENEZUELA
Libreria del Este
Avda F. Miranda 52, Aptdo. 60337
Edificio Galipán
Caracas 106   Tel. 951.1705/951.2307/951.1297
                Telegram: Libreste Caracas

Subscription to OECD periodicals may also be
placed through main subscription agencies.

Les abonnements aux publications périodiques de
l'OCDE peuvent être souscrits auprès des
principales agences d'abonnement.

Orders and inquiries from countries where Distribu-
tors have not yet been appointed should be sent to:
OECD Publications Service, 2 rue André-Pascal,
75775 Paris Cedex 16, France.

Les commandes provenant de pays où l'OCDE n'a
pas encore désigné de distributeur peuvent être
adressées à : OCDE, Service des Publications,
2, rue André-Pascal, 75775 Paris Cedex 16, France.

1-1995

OECD PUBLICATIONS, 2 rue André-Pascal, 75775 PARIS CEDEX 16
PRINTED IN FRANCE
(96 95 01 1) ISBN 92-64-14399-8 - No. 47789 1995